FORMAL ASPECTS IN SECURITY AND TRUST

T0138025

IFIP – The International Federation for Information Processing

IFIP was founded in 1960 under the auspices of UNESCO, following the First World Computer Congress held in Paris the previous year. An umbrella organization for societies working in information processing, IFIP's aim is two-fold: to support information processing within its member countries and to encourage technology transfer to developing nations. As its mission statement clearly states,

> IFIP's mission is to be the leading, truly international, apolitical organization which encourages and assists in the development, exploitation and application of information technology for the benefit of all people.

IFIP is a non-profitmaking organization, run almost solely by 2500 volunteers. It operates through a number of technical committees, which organize events and publications. IFIP's events range from an international congress to local seminars, but the most important are:

• The IFIP World Computer Congress, held every second year;
• Open conferences;
• Working conferences.

The flagship event is the IFIP World Computer Congress, at which both invited and contributed papers are presented. Contributed papers are rigorously refereed and the rejection rate is high.

As with the Congress, participation in the open conferences is open to all and papers may be invited or submitted. Again, submitted papers are stringently refereed.

The working conferences are structured differently. They are usually run by a working group and attendance is small and by invitation only. Their purpose is to create an atmosphere conducive to innovation and development. Refereeing is less rigorous and papers are subjected to extensive group discussion.

Publications arising from IFIP events vary. The papers presented at the IFIP World Computer Congress and at open conferences are published as conference proceedings, while the results of the working conferences are often published as collections of selected and edited papers.

Any national society whose primary activity is in information may apply to become a full member of IFIP, although full membership is restricted to one society per country. Full members are entitled to vote at the annual General Assembly, National societies preferring a less committed involvement may apply for associate or corresponding membership. Associate members enjoy the same benefits as full members, but without voting rights. Corresponding members are not represented in IFIP bodies. Affiliated membership is open to non-national societies, and individual and honorary membership schemes are also offered.

FORMAL ASPECTS IN SECURITY AND TRUST

IFIP TC1 WG1.7 Workshop on Formal Aspects in Security and Trust (FAST), World Computer Congress, August 22-27, 2004, Toulouse, France

Edited by

Theo Dimitrakos
BITD-CCLRC
United Kingdom

Fabio Martinelli
IIT-CNR
Italy

Library of Congress Cataloging-in-Publication Data

A C.I.P. Catalogue record for this book is available from the Library of Congress.

Formal Aspects in Security and Trust/ Edited by Theo Dimitrakos, Fabio Martinelli

p.cm. (The International Federation for Information Processing)

ISBN 978-1-4419-3685-1   e-ISBN 978-0-387-24098-5   Printed on acid-free paper.

Printed in the United States of America.

9 8 7 6 5 4 3 2 1
springeronline.com

Preface

The present volume contains the post-proceedings of the second international *Workshop on Formal Aspects in Security and Trust* (FAST2004), held in Toulouse, 26-27 August 2004. FAST is an event of the 18th IFIP World Computer Congress (WCC2004) and is under the auspices of IFIP WG 1.7. on "Foundations of Security Analysis and Design".

The second international Workshop on Formal Aspects in Security and Trust (FAST2004) aims at continuing the successful effort of FAST2003 for fostering the cooperation among researchers in the areas of security and trust. The new challenges offered by the so-called ambient intelligence space, as a future paradigm in the information society, demand for a coherent and rigorous framework of concepts, tools and methodologies to provide user's trust & confidence on the underlying communication/interaction infrastructure. It is necessary to address issues relating to both guaranteeing security of the infrastructure and the perception of the infrastructure being secure. In addition, user confidence on what is happening must be enhanced by developing trust models effective but also easily comprehensible and manageable by users.

FAST sought for original papers focusing of formal aspects in: security and trust policy models; security protocol design and analysis; formal models of trust and reputation; logics for security and trust; distributed trust management systems; trust-based reasoning; digital assets protection; data protection; privacy and ID issues; information flow analysis; language-based security; security and trust aspects in ubiquitous computing; validation/analysis tools; web service security/trust/privacy; GRID security; security risk assessment; case studies . . . .

FAST2004 program consists of: two invited speakers; 16 paper presentations selected out of 33 submissions (2 withdrawn) and two panels (jointly managed with CSES workshop) on *Examining trust management models from different perspectives* and *Major trust and security challenges for business centric virtual organizations*. A few selected papers will be invited for possible publication on a special issue on the *International Journal of Information Security (IJIS)*.

We wish to thank the invited speakers, Roberto Gorrieri (University of Bologna) and Christos Nikolaou (University of Crete), and the panelists for contributing to set up a very interesting program, the PC members for their valuable efforts in properly evaluating the submissions, and the WCC2004 organizers for accepting FAST as an affiliated event and for providing a perfect environment for running the workshop.

Thanks are also due to BITD-CCLRC and IIT-CNR for the organizational and financial support for FAST2004. We also wish to thank the iTrust thematic network (http://www.itrust.uoc.gr) and the TrustCoM integrated project (www.eu-trustcom.com) under the IST framework programme of the European Commission for the sponsorship of this event.

We also wish to thank Alessandro Falleni, Beatrice Lami and Adriana Lazzaroni for a perfect local organization.

Theo Dimitrakos and Fabio Martinelli
FAST 2004 co-Chairs

Program Committee

Table of Contents

SECURITY ISSUES IN THE TUPLE-SPACE COORDINATION MODEL

Mario Bravetti Nadia Busi Roberto Gorrieri
Roberto Lucchi Gianluigi Zavattaro
Dipartimento di Scienze dell'Informazione, Università degli Studi di Bologna,
Mura Anteo Zamboni 7, I-40127 Bologna, Italy.
{bravetti,busi,gorrieri,lucchi,zavattar}@cs.unibo.it

Abstract   We present some security issues that emerge when the tuple-space coordination model is used in open systems. Then we describe SecSpaces, a tuple-space based language, which supports secure coordination in untrusted environments. Finally, we will discuss some real examples of applications interacting via tuple spaces by showing how to support some of the main security features with SecSpaces.

1.   Introduction

New networking technologies are moving to support applications for *open systems* (e.g., peer-to-peer, ad-hoc networks, Web services), in which the entities that will be involved in the application are unknown at design time. Further, the connectivity is exploding: a growing number of devices need to communicate with each other and the new challenge is how to design and to program the communication among devices.

Coordination models and languages, which advocate a distinct separation between the internal behaviour of the entities and their interaction, represent a promising approach for the development of this class of applications. The interaction is programmed by means of a coordination infrastructure that abstracts away from the exact name/location of the components and the underlying network.

One of the most prominent coordination languages is Linda [Computing Associates, 1995] in which a shared space, containing tuples of data, is used by agents to collaborate. Agents can insert new tuples into the space, consume or read tuples from the space thus implementing the so-called generative communication, in which tuples are independent of their producers.

We present some security issues that emerge when Linda is used in open systems, where any agent can access the tuple space. In this scenario, where the presence of malicious agents may compromise the behaviour of the system, designers have to deal with security. Unfortunately, Linda is not expressive enough to provide security solutions, because any agent can read, remove and reproduce any tuple available in the shared space.

We present the SecSpaces [Busi et al., 2002, Bravetti et al., 2003] coordination language, based on the tuple-space coordination model introduced by Linda, that supports security in untrusted environments by providing some access control mechanisms on tuples with a granularity at the level of single tuples. The proposed solution follows a data-driven approach: the access to a tuple is subordinated to the proof of knowledge of certain data stored into the tuple. In a few words, to access a tuple it is necessary to provide special data, that we call control fields, that must match the ones stored inside the tuple. We also describe how such control fields can be implemented and, finally, how to define the matching rule. The proposed solution has also been developed [Lucchi and Zavattaro, 2004] in the context of Web Services technology, which represents the emerging networking technology for programming Internet applications.

In order to show how the SecSpaces mechanisms can be exploited for supporting some security features (e.g., secrecy, entity authentication) we consider real examples of applications where the interaction is programmed via tuple spaces.

The paper is structured as follows. Section 2 describes the Linda coordination primitives and SecSpaces with particular care to the security mechanisms obtained by decorating tuples with control fields. Section 3 describes some real examples where the SecSpaces model is used to support some forms of secure interaction. Finally Section 4 reports the main related works and concludes the paper.

2.   SecSpaces

The SecSpaces language is an extension of Linda supporting security. In order to introduce SecSpaces we first present the Linda primitives. The Linda language provides coordination primitives that allow processes to insert new tuples into the tuple space (TS for short) or to access the tuples already stored in the shared tuple space. More precisely, a tuple is a sequence of typed values [Computing Associates, 1995] and a TS is a multiset of tuples.

Processes can exchange tuples through introducing them into the TS. The primitive $out(e)$ permits to add a new occurrence of the tuple e to the TS.

The data-retrieval primitives permit processes, by specifying a template t, to access tuples available in the TS that match the template. More precisely, a template is a sequence of fields that can be either actual or formal: a field is actual if it specifies the type and a value, while it is formal if the type only is given. Two typed values match if they have the same value, while a typed value matches a formal fields if it has the type specified in the latter. A tuple e matches the template t if t and e have the same arity and each field of e matches the corresponding field of t.

The $in(t)$ is the blocking input primitive: when a tuple e matching the template t is available in the TS, an occurrence of e is removed from the TS and the primitive returns e. The $rd(t)$ primitive is the blocking read primitive: differently from the $in(t)$, when a tuple e matching the template t is in the TS, it returns e without removing it from the TS.

Linda also provides the non-blocking version of the data-retrieval primitives: the inp and the rdp are the non-blocking version of the in and the rd, respectively. If the tuple e is in the TS, their behavior is the same as for the blocking operations, otherwise they return a special value indicating the absence of e in the TS.

Recent distributed applications such as Web services, applications for Mobile Ad Hoc Networks (MANETs), Peer to Peer Applications (P2P) are inherently open to processes, agents, components that are not known at design time. When the Linda coordination model is exploited to program the coordination inside this class of applications (see e.g. Lime [Murphy et al., 2001] in the context of MANETs and PeerSpaces [Busi et al., 2003] for P2P applications) new critical aspects come into play such as the need to deal with a hostile environment which may comprise also untrusted components.

The main issues are related with the fact that, in such a context, any entity is allowed to perform insertion, read and removal of tuples to and from the tuple space. In particular this means that any process can maliciously insert an unbounded number of tuples; in such a way, since the manager of the space has to handle any *out* operation, a process can generate a denial of service attack.

Another denial of service attack is due to the fact that any process can maliciously read/remove any tuples from the space, thus compromising the applications interacting via tuple-space. Indeed any entity can, by using the wildcard, generate a template that matches with any tuple having th same arity. Therefore, for example, a template having two wildcard fields can be used to read or remove any tuple containing two data fields. Moreover, since any entity can read/remove/reproduce any tuple from and into the space in such a model, we cannot authenticate neither the producer, nor the receiver of tuples. The threat of such lacks, that SecSpaces aims to cover, will be highlighted in the following section, but it should be rather clear that such state is to be avoided in open systems, where the applications interact by using the same tuple space and the availability of the tuples they produce is necessary to guarantee their correct behavior.

SecSpaces introduces an access control to the tuple-space coordination model which follows the data-driven mechanism. More in detail, Linda tuples are decorated with two kind of control fields: the *partition key* and the *asymmetric key*. Each tuple contains, for each possible operation the process can perform on the tuple (i.e. read and removal), a pair of control fields composed of a partition and an asymmetric key. Control fields are evaluated in the matching rule which is responsible for controlling the access to the tuple: the access to a tuple is allowed only to the entities which provide control fields matching those of the tuple associated with the operation the entity is performing. Two partition keys match if they are equal, while two asymmetric keys match if one is the co-key of the other one.

Formally, let $Mess$, ranged over by m, n, ..., be an infinite set of messages, $Partition \subseteq Mess$, ranged over by c, c_t, ..., be the set of partition keys and $AKey \subseteq Mess$, ranged over by k, k', k_t, ..., be the set of asymmetric keys. We also assume that $Partition$ (resp. $AKey$) contains a special default value, say $\#$ (resp. ?), used to allow any entity to access the space. Let $\overline{} : AKey \rightarrow AKey$ be a function such that $\overline{?} = ?$ and if $\overline{k} = k'$ then $\overline{k'} = k$. Informally, such function maps asymmetric keys to the corresponding co-keys. Moreover, as in the public-key mechanism, we assume that given an asymmetric key it is not possible to guess its co-key. In the following, we use $\vec{d}$ to denote a finite sequence of data fields.

The tuple structure in SecSpaces is defined as follows:

$$e = < \vec{d} >^{[c]_{rd}[c']_{in}}_{[k]_{rd}[k']_{in}}$$

where $\vec{d}$ is a finite sequence of data fields whose values range over $Mess$, $c, c' \in Partition$ and $k, k' \in AKey$. The sequence of data fields in $\vec{d}$ represents the content of standard Linda tuples, while c and k (resp. c' and k') are the control fields used when such tuple is accessed by a read (resp. removal) operation. In the following we use the function $key(e, op)$ (resp. $akey(e, op)$) as the one that given $op \in \{rd, in\}$ and a tuple e returns the partition key (resp. asymmetric key) of e associated to op.

Templates are decorated with one occurrence of control fields, that will be associated to the operation the process is performing:

$$t = < \vec{dt} >^{[c_t]}_{[k_t]}$$

where $\vec{dt}$ is a finite sequence of data fields, $c_t \in Partition$ is the partition key and $k_t \in AKey$ is the asymmetric key associated to t. Differently from tuples, data fields contained in $\vec{dt}$ can also be set to the wildcard value denoted with *null*: the wildcard is used to match with all field values.

DEFINITION 1 (MATCHING RULE) *Let* $e = < d_1; d_2; \ldots; d_n >^{[c]_{rd}[c']_{in}}_{[k]_{rd}[k']_{in}}$ *be a tuple,* $t = < dt_1; dt_2; \ldots; dt_m >^{[c_t]}_{[k_t]}$ *be a template and* $op \in \{rd, in\}$ *be an operation. We say that e matches t (denoted with $e \triangleright_{op} t$) if the following conditions hold:*

 1 $m = n$

 2 $dt_i = d_i$ *or* $dt_i = null, 1 \le i \le n$

 3 $key(e, op) = c_t$

 4 $\overline{akey(e, op)} = k_t$.

Condition 1. and 2. rephrase the classical Linda matching rule, that is test if e and t have the same arity and if each data field of e is equal to the corresponding field of t or if this latter one is set to wildcard. Condition 3. tests that the partition key of the tuple associated to the operation op is equal to that of the template. Condition 4. checks that the asymmetric key of the template corresponds to the co-key of the asymmetric key of the tuple associated to the operation op.

Essentially partition keys are a special kind of data field that do not accept wildcard in the matching evaluation. In this way, such keys logically partition the space and the access to a partition is restricted to those processes that know the associated key. Indeed, in order to perform an operation on the partition containing all the tuples with a certain partition key, processes must know the key which identifies that partition.

Differently from partition keys, the asymmetric keys make it possible to discriminate the permission of write, read and remove of a tuple. For instance, to read a tuple with asymmetric key k the process must provide a template with asymmetric key set to $\overline{k}$. It is worth noting that by using such keys the knowledge used to produce a tuple (k) is different from the one used for retrieving that tuple ($\overline{k}$). Therefore, by properly distributing these values we can assign processes the permission to perform a subset of the possible operations on that tuple, thus discriminating among the processes that can produce, read or remove that tuple.

EXAMPLE 2 *Some matching example follow (e $\not\triangleright$ t means that e does not match with t):*

$$< d >^{[c]_{rd}[c']_{in}}_{[k]_{rd}[k']_{in}} \triangleright_{rd} < null >^{[c]}_{[\overline{k}]}$$

$$< d >^{[c]_{rd}[c']_{in}}_{[k]_{rd}[k']_{in}} \not\triangleright_{rd} < null >^{[c]}_{[\overline{k'}]}$$

$$< d >^{[c]_{rd}[c']_{in}}_{[k]_{rd}[k']_{in}} \not\triangleright_{in} < d' >^{[c']}_{[\overline{k'}]}$$

DEFINITION 3 (RETURN VALUE) *The* rd *(resp.* in*) primitive with template*
t terminates when a tuple e such that e $\triangleright_{rd}$ *t (resp.e* $\triangleright_{in}$ *t) is available in the*
tuple space and the return value is composed of the data fields contained in
e, while control fields are not returned. For example, if the matching tuple is
$< d >_{[k]_{rd}[k']_{in}}^{[c]_{rd}[c']_{in}}$ *the return value is* $< d >$.

By such definition it follows that dynamic privileges acquisition can happen
only when control fields values are stored inside the sequence of data fields.

SecSpaces **implementation**

The study of all the issues related with a secure implementation of the
SecSpaces model has been investigated in [Lucchi and Zavattaro, 2004]. Here
we just report the way we use to implement control fields.

The implementation of partition keys is rather easy and similar to symmetric cryptography; the only assumption is that a process should not be able to
guess an unknown partition key used by other processes. Similarly to symmetric encryption keys (see e.g. [Schneier, 1996]), we need to implement the set
Partition so that to guess one of its values has low probability. Such feature
can be realized, e.g., by encoding partition keys with data composed by a large
number of bits (say 512 bits).

The main problem we have to tackle when we implement asymmetric keys
is how to satisfy the function $\overline{}$. Such function must guarantee that: i)it is
possible to check whether two keys k and k' match (i.e. to verify if $k' = \overline{k}$),
and ii)it is not possible for a process to guess $\overline{k}$ starting from the knowledge
of k. To implement such keys we exploit the public-key cryptographic mechanism. Formally, let $PlainText$, ranged over by $p, p', \ldots$, be the set of plaintexts, Key, ranged over by $PrivK, PubK, \ldots$, be the set of encryption keys
containing private and public keys. In the following, when we refer to pairs
of private and public keys $(PrivK, PubK)$, we assume that a plaintext encrypted with $PubK$ (resp. $PrivK$) can be decrypted only by using $PrivK$
(resp. $PubK$). Let $Ciphertext$, ranged over by $s, s_t, \ldots$, be the set of ciphertexts obtained by encrypting plaintexts with encryption keys (we denote with
$\{p\}_k$ the encryption of p with key k).

We encode any asymmetric keys, except the default value ? encoded with
?', with a triple $(p, PubK, s)$. The following implementation of $\overline{}$ satisfies the
requirements of asymmetric keys:

- given ?', we have that $\overline{?'} = ?'$;

- given the triple $(p, PubK, s)$, we have that $\overline{(p, PubK, s)} = (p', PubK', s')$
  if $s = \{p'\}_{PrivK'}$ and $s' = \{p\}_{PrivK}$.

Obviously, the correctness of such implementation is to be subordinate to a
perfect implementation of cryptographic operations.

3.   Examples

In this section we consider some real applications and we show how to manage the interaction by using the SecSpaces model. We show how SecSpaces makes it possible to guarantee some of the main security properties like secrecy, producer/receiver authentication and data availability. In particular we present two examples that we take from the use cases of [Gigaspaces]. For each of them, we proceed as follows: i)we describe how it works, ii)we describe the security lacks if the interaction is programmed with Linda, and iii)we describe how to support security by using SecSpaces.

Distributed Session Sharing

This example shows how to exploit a tuple-space repository for implementing a service for managing user sessions, e.g., the sessions used to control business activities.

The use case we consider consist of a customer that intends to reserve a car from one agency and a flight from another one. The car and flight reservation systems are located in separate servers. Both systems need to be able to share the user session, so that from the customer's point of view it is a single transaction. Since these services are distributed, we exploit the tuple space to implement a distributed session server that makes it possible to share the user session. The solution we are going to discuss is depicted in Fig. 1. The idea is that at any customer sessions the travel agency collects user data (shopping card, user id, etc.) and invokes (without a specific order) three services: i)the car service, ii)the flight service, and iii)the billing service, by passing as parameters the user session, shopping card and the user preferences. The information the travel agency receives from such services consists of, respectively: i)the ordered car, ii)the flight, and iii)the bill of the transaction. The car and flight services supply the corresponding request and then insert a tuple containing the fee of the supplied service and the user session id that is used as key field by the billing service that consumes both tuples and then returns the bill to the travel agency.

The main security problem is that the tuples inserted in the space are available to anyone, thus someone could maliciously use that id to perform, e.g., another business activity or to alterate the service fee. Indeed, let us suppose that car and flight services produce tuples with the following structure: $< userid, fee, preferences, serviceinfo >$, and that the billing service collects such tuples by performing two in with $< userid, null, null, null >$ as template. The threat is that such tuples can be removed/manipulated by, e.g., a malicious process, that can use the user id in a different context or can change the service fee, the user preferences or the identifier of the service ($serviceinfo$) supplying the requested task.

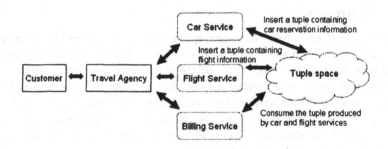

Figure 1.   Distributed user sessions managed with a tuple space

The security issues explained above can be tackled by exploiting SecSpaces. In particular, the properties that should be guaranteed are: i)secrecy of exchanged data, and ii)receiver authentication. The former is needed to guarantee that the exchanged information are not used by unauthorized users while the latter is used to guarantee that the only process which is allowed to consume the tuples $< userid, fee, preferences, serviceinfo >$ is the billing service.

Let c and c' be two partition keys and k be an asymmetric key. To support such properties, we assume that:

- c is a private partition key shared by the car and the billing service (i.e. only those services know c),

- c' is a private partition key shared by the flight and the billing service (i.e. only those services know c'), and

- k is a private data of the billing service, while $\bar{k}$ is a public data.

In this paper we do not tackle the problem of how to distribute in a secure way such values. A possible solution is to exploit classic public-key infrastructure [Schneier, 1996].

The tuples produced (and then inserted into the space by an *out*) respectively by the car and by the flight service are now the following:

$$< userid, carfee, preferences, carserviceinfo >_{[\bar{k}]_{rd}[\bar{k}]_{in}}^{[c]_{rd}[c]_{in}}$$
$$< userid, flightfee, preferences, carserviceinfo >_{[\bar{k}]_{rd}[\bar{k}]_{in}}^{[c']_{rd}[c']_{in}}$$

To access such tuples it is necessary to provide a template having c (or c') as partition key and k as asymmetric key. In particular, the billing service perform $in(< userid, null, null, null >_{[k]}^{[c]})$ and $in(< userid, null, null, null >_{[k]}^{[c']})$ to read (and remove) the tuple containing information produced by the car and by the flight service, respectively. The secrecy of the data exchanged via the tuple space is guaranteed because only the two involved services (car-billing or flight-billing) know the partition key, while the authentication of the receiver directly follows by the fact that only the billing service is able to provide k as asymmetric key.

Brokered messaging

The use case we consider here is a messaging service where the interaction between the parties is mediated by a broker. Service producers (masters) produce messages about instructions or other information such as images, files, specifying also the receiver of such messages. A special service, the broker, is responsible for analysing submitted requests such as to determine which consumer service it should be sent to. It can possibly modify or insert additional data (e.g., a timestamp) into the message and then to deliver it to the relevant service consumer.

Such interaction can be programmed by exploiting a tuple space: i)masters insert a tuple containing all the information into the space with a certain structure that the broker knows, e.g., $< broker, msg, to >$ where $broker$ is the key used to identify tuples that the broker should take into account, msg is the information represented by the message and to specifies the receiver (we assume receivers can be unequivocally identified by an id), ii)the broker reads (and removes) submitted tuples by performing an in operation with $< broker, null, null >$ as template, it analyses the information about the message and the receiver and, after having performed some controls on submitted data, inserts a the tuple $< to, msg, timestamp >$ into the space where $timestamp$ indicates when the message has been receiver by the broker, and iii)any consumers whose id is $consid$ performs an in by using $< consid, null, null >$ as template; in this way it obtains the transmitted object and its timestamp. The interaction schema of such application is described in Fig. 2.

There are several kinds of aspects that a secure implementation should take into account like the secrecy of exchanged data (in order to guarantee the confidentiality), or the authentication of the message producers and consumers that can be managed by following an approach similar to the one used in the previous example. Here we just describe how to support another aspect: the fairness between producer and consumer. Indeed, any consumer (not only the proper consumer) can consume any tuples submitted by the producer thus preventing the broker to analyse such tuple. Essentially, the problem is that we cannot guarantee non-repudiation. In such a way, for example, the consumer can take an advantage w.r.t. the producer because it can also repudiate that it has received such message.

By assuming that the broker logs the exchanged messages we can exploit asymmetric keys of SecSpaces to cover this security lack by managing the

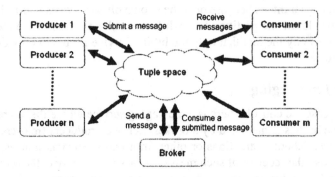

Figure 2. Brokered messaging managed with a tuple space

authentication of the receiver (the broker) for the tuples submitted by the producers. Moreover, we could manage the receiver authentication (the proper consumer) for the tuples inserted by the broker. In this way we guarantee that only the broker can consume (and then analyse) the tuples submitted by the producers and that only the receiver specified by the producer can consume the corresponding message. Technically, let k_b and k_i for $i = 1, \ldots, m$ be asymmetric keys; we make the following assumptions:

- k_b is a private information of the broker,

- k_i is a private information of the consumer i,

- $\overline{k_b}, \overline{k_i}$ for $i = 1, \ldots, m$ are public data.

The producers insert tuples with asymmetric keys (both for rd and in) set to $\overline{k_b}$, say $< broker, msg, to >_{[\overline{k_b}]_{rd}[\overline{k_b}]_{in}}$ that only the broker can access since it is the only one that knows k_b, which is needed to match the tuple. The broker consumes and analyses such tuples and by evaluating the field to selects the public key corresponding to the consumer, say k_i, and insert the tuple $< to, msg, timestamp >_{[\overline{k_i}]}$ that only the proper consumer can take since it is the only which knows k_i.

The example can be furtherly extended. Let us suppose the case where the producer can also specify that the message can be read but not removed because, e.g., it is necessary to track the execution of a complex activity or protocol. In this case the broker can set to k_i the asymmetric key of the tuple associated to the rd and to set to another value that consumers cannot match (e.g., $\overline{k_b}$) the one associated to the in. In this way consumers can only generate templates that match such tuple when it is accessed with read operations.

4. Conclusion

We have described the main security issues that emerge when Linda is used in open systems and described SecSpaces that make it possible to support some of the main security properties (e.g., secrecy, producer/receiver authentication). The adequacy of such proposal has been proved by considering some real examples of usage of tuple spaces in the interaction.

Other proposals supporting security are available in literature. The most interesting ones that deserve to be mentioned are Klaim [De Nicola et al., 1998] and SecOS [Vitek et al., 2003]. The former exploits a classic access control mechanism in which permissions describe, for each entity, which are the operations it is allowed to perform (insertion, read and removal of tuples), while the latter is based on access keys stored on tuples, which has inspired the SecSpaces language. Another approach is presented in [Handorean and Roman, 2003] where a password-based system on tuple spaces and tuples permits the access only to the authorized entities, that is those that know the password. In particular, password-based access permissions on tuples can be associated to the read and to the removal operations. Differently from SecSpaces, if an entity is allowed to remove a tuple (i.e. it knows the password associated to the removal operations), it has also the permission of reading that tuple.

We consider that the data-driven approach followed by SecOS and subsequently by SecSpaces is more suitable for open systems w.r.t. to classic one used in Klaim. In a few words, we identify the problem in the fact that to know all the possible entities that may enter in the system is a difficult task. Since in Klaim access permissions refer to entities, such task is necessary. On the other hand, the data-driven mechanism makes it possible to avoid such task since the access permissions are simply based on the proof of knowledge the entities provide when they perform coordination primitives.

The main contribution of SecSpaces is a refinement of the SecOS access permissions on tuples that make it possible to discriminate between the permissions of producing, reading and consuming a tuple. For example, in SecOS a process that can consume a tuple is also able to reproduce that tuple, thus *in* permission inherits *out* permissions. If we consider the brokered messaging example, we cannot guarantee non-repudiation of the messages received by the consumers.

References

[Bravetti et al., 2003] Bravetti, M., Gorrieri, R., and Lucchi, R. (2003). A formal approach for checking security properties in SecSpaces. In *1st International Workshop on on Security Issues in Coordination Models, Languages and Systems*, volume 85.3 of *ENTCS*.

[Busi et al., 2002] Busi, N., Gorrieri, R., Lucchi, R., and Zavattaro, G. (2002). Secspaces: a data-driven coordination model for environments open to untrusted entities. In *1st International Workshop on Foundations of Coordination Languages and Software Architectures*, volume 68.3 of *ENTCS*.

[Busi et al., 2003] Busi, N., Manfredini, C., Montresor, A., and Zavattaro, G. (2003). PeerSpaces: Data-driven Coordination in Peer-to-Peer Networks. In *Proc. of ACM Symposium on Applied Computing (SAC'03)*, pages 380–386. ACM Press.

[Computing Associates, 1995] Computing Associates, S. (1995). *Linda: User's guide and reference manual*. Scientific Computing Associates.

[De Nicola et al., 1998] De Nicola, R., Ferrari, G., and Pugliese, R. (1998). KLAIM: A Kernel Language for Agents Interaction and Mobility. *IEEE Transactions on Software Engineering*, 24(5):315–330. Special Issue: Mobility and Network Aware Computing.

[Gigaspaces] Gigaspaces. Use cases. http://www.gigaspaces.com/usecases.htm/.

[Handorean and Roman, 2003] Radu Handorean and Gruia-Catalin Roman (2003). Secure Sharing of Tuple Spaces in Ad Hoc Settings. In *1st International Workshop on on Security Issues in Coordination Models, Languages and Systems*, volume 85.3 of *ENTCS*.

[Lucchi and Zavattaro, 2004] Lucchi, R. and Zavattaro, G. (2004). WSSecSpaces: a Secure Data-Driven Coordination Service for Web Services Applications. In *Proc. of ACM Symposium on Applied Computing (SAC'04)*, pages 487–491. ACM Press.

[Murphy et al., 2001] Murphy, A., Picco, G., and Roman, G.-C. (2001). A middleware for physical and logical mobility. In *21st International Conference on Distributed Computing Systems*, pages 524–533.

[Schneier, 1996] Schneier, B. (1996). *Applied Cryptography*. Wiley.

[Vitek et al., 2003] Vitek, J., Bryce, C., and Oriol, M. (2003). Coordinating Processes with Secure Spaces. *Science of Computer Programming*, 46:163–193.

INFORMATION FLOW ANALYSIS FOR PROBABILISTIC TIMED AUTOMATA

Ruggero Lanotte[1], Andrea Maggiolo–Schettini[2] and Angelo Troina [2]

[1]*Dipartimento di Scienze della Cultura, Politiche e dell'Informazione – Università dell'Insubria*
[2]*Dipartimento di Informatica – Università di Pisa*

Abstract   In multilevel systems it is important to avoid unwanted indirect information flow from higher levels to lower levels, namely the so called *covert channels*. Initial studies of information flow analysis were performed by abstracting away from time and probability. Recently, work has been done in order to consider also aspects either of time or of probability, but not both. In this paper we propose a general framework, based on Probabilistic Timed Automata, where both *probabilistic* and *timing covert channels* can be studied. As an application, we study a system with covert channels that we are able to discover by our techniques.

1.   Introduction

In a multilevel system every agent is confined in a bounded security level; information can flow from a certain agent to another agent only if the level of the former is lower than the level of the latter. Access rules can be imposed by the system in order to control direct unwanted transmission from higher levels to lower levels; however, it could be possible to transmit information indirectly by using system side effects. Usually, this kind of indirect transmissions, called *covert channels*, do not violate the access rules imposed by the system.

The existence of covert channels has led to the more general approach of *information flow security*, which aims at controlling the way information may flow among different entities. The idea is to try to directly control the whole flow of information, rather than only the direct communication among agents. In [10] the authors introduce the notion of *non-interference*, stating, intuitively, that the low level agents should not be able to deduce anything about the activity of the high level agents. By imposing some information flow rules, it is possible to control direct and indirect leakages, as both of them give rise to unwanted information flows.

In the literature, there are many different definitions of security based on the information flow idea, and each one formulated in some system model (see, e.g., [1, 5, 7–11, 16, 19]). Most of the properties considered are based on analysis of information flow that does not take into consideration aspects of time or probability, and therefore are not useful to check the existence of probabilistic or timing covert channels. To overcome this, a significant work has been done in order to extend the study by considering either time (see, e.g., [5, 7, 9]) or probability (see, e.g., [1, 11, 19]), but, to the best of our knowledge, not both.

In this paper we propose a general framework where both probabilistic and timing covert channels can be studied. For the description of systems we choose the model of Probabilistic Timed Automata. Timed Automata have been introduced by Alur and Dill [3], extensions with probability have been proposed e.g. in [2, 6, 13, 14]. We introduce a particular class of Probabilistic Timed Automata (PTA) well-suited for the analysis of information flow security properties.

The framework of PTA allows one to specify timed systems showing a probabilistic behavior in an intuitive and succinct way. Therefore, within the framework of PTA, where time and probabilities are taken into consideration, the modeler can describe, in the same specification, different aspects of a system and analyze on a single model real-time properties, performance and reliability properties (by using classical model checking techniques) and finally information flow security properties able to detect both probabilistic and timing covert channels.

2.   Probabilistic Timed Automata

Let us assume a set X of positive real variables called *clocks*. A *valuation* over X is a mapping $v : X \rightarrow \mathbb{R}^{\geq 0}$ assigning real values to clocks. For a valuation v and a time value $t \in \mathbb{R}^{\geq 0}$, let $v + t$ denote the valuation such that $(v + t)(x) = v(x) + t$, for each clock $x \in X$.

The set of *constraints* over X, denoted $\Phi(X)$, is defined by the following grammar: $\phi ::= x \sim c \,|\, \phi \wedge \phi \,|\, \neg\phi \,|\, \phi \vee \phi \,|\, true$, where ϕ ranges over $\Phi(X)$, $x \in X$, $c \in \mathbb{Q}$ and $\sim \in \{<, \leq, =, \neq, >, \geq\}$.

We write $v \models \phi$ when *the valuation v satisfies the constraint ϕ*. Formally, $v \models x \sim c$ iff $v(x) \sim c$, $v \models \phi_1 \wedge \phi_2$ iff $v \models \phi_1$ and $v \models \phi_2$, $v \models \neg\phi$ iff $v \not\models \phi$, $v \models \phi_1 \vee \phi_2$ iff $v \models \phi_1$ or $v \models \phi_2$, and $v \models true$.

Let $B \subseteq X$; with $v[B]$ we denote the valuation resulting after resetting all clocks in B. More precisely, $v[B](x) = 0$ if $x \in B$, $v[B](x) = v(x)$, otherwise. Finally, with $\mathbf{0}$ we denote the valuation with all clocks reset to 0, namely $\mathbf{0}(x) = 0$ for all $x \in X$.

DEFINITION 1 *A Probabilistic Timed Automaton (PTA) is a sixtuple $A = (\Sigma, X, Q, q_0, \delta, \pi)$, where:*

- Σ *is a finite alphabet of actions.*

- X is a finite set of positive real variables called clocks.

- Q is a finite set of states and $q_0 \in Q$ is the initial state.

- $\delta \subseteq Q \times \Sigma \cup \{\tau\} \times \Phi(X) \times 2^X \times Q$ is a finite set of transitions. The symbol τ represents the silent or internal move. For a state q, we denote with $start(q)$ the set of transitions with q as source state, i.e. the set $\{(q_1, a, \phi, B, q_2) \in \delta \mid q_1 = q\}$.

- $\pi : \delta \rightarrow]0, 1]$ is a probability function such that $\pi(e)$ is the probability of performing the transition e. We require that $\sum_{e \in start(q)} \pi(e) = 1$.

A *configuration* of A is a pair (q, v), where $q \in Q$ is a state of A, and v is a valuation over X. The initial configuration of A is represented by $(q_0, 0)$ and the set of all the configurations of A is denoted with S_A.

There is a discrete *transition step* from a configuration $s_i = (q_i, v_i)$ to a configuration $s_j = (q_j, v_j)$ through action $a \in \Sigma \cup \{\tau\}$, written $s_i \xrightarrow{a} s_j$, if there is a transition $e = (q_i, a, \phi, B, q_j) \in \delta$ such that $v_i \models \phi$, and $v_j = v_i[B]$.

There is a continuous *timed step* from a configuration $s_i = (q_i, v_i)$ to a configuration $s_j = (q_j, v_j)$ through time $t \in \mathbb{R}^{>0}$, written $s_i \xrightarrow{t} s_j$, if $q_j = q_i$ and $v_j = (v_i + t)$.

Given a configuration $s = (q_i, v_i)$, with $Adm(s) = \{(q_i, a, \phi, B, q) \in \delta \mid v_i \models \phi\}$ we represent the set of transitions that an automaton could execute from configuration s, and we say that a transition in $Adm(s)$ is *enabled* in s. Given two configurations $s_i = (q_i, v_i)$, $s_j = (q_j, v_j)$ and given $a \in \Sigma \cup \{\tau\}$ we represent with $Adm(s_i, a, s_j) = \{(q_i, a, \phi, B, q_j) \in \delta \mid v_i \models \phi \wedge v_j = v_i[B]\}$ the set of transitions that lead from configuration s_i to configuration s_j through a transition step labeled with a. A configuration $s = (q_i, v_i)$ is called *terminal* iff $Adm(s') = \emptyset$ for all $s' = (q_i, v_i + t)$ where $t \in \mathbb{R}^{\geq 0}$; we denote with S_T the set of terminal configurations.

For configurations $s_i = (q_i, v_i)$, $s_j = (q_j, v_j)$ and $\alpha \in \Sigma \cup \{\tau\} \cup \mathbb{R}^{>0}$, we define with $P(s_i, \alpha, s_j)$ the probability of reaching configuration s_j from configuration s_i through a step $s_i \xrightarrow{\alpha} s_j$ labeled with α. Formally $P(s_i, \alpha, s_j) = \frac{\sum_{e \in Adm(s_i, \alpha, s_j)} \pi(e)}{\sum_{e \in Adm(s_i)} \pi(e)}$ if $\alpha \in \Sigma \cup \{\tau\}$ and $P(s_i, \alpha, s_j) = 1$ if $\alpha \in \mathbb{R}^{>0}$.

The probability of executing a transition step from a configuration s is chosen according to the values returned by the function π among all the transitions enabled in s, while we set to 1 the probability of executing a timed step labeled with $t \in \mathbb{R}^{>0}$. Intuitively, an automaton chooses non-deterministically whether to execute a transition step (selected probabilistically among all the transitions enabled in s) or to let time pass performing a timed step.

An *execution fragment* starting from s_0 is a finite sequence of timed and transition steps $\sigma = s_0 \xrightarrow{\alpha_1} s_1 \xrightarrow{\alpha_2} s_2 \xrightarrow{\alpha_3} \dots \xrightarrow{\alpha_k} s_k$. With *ExecFrag* we denote the set of execution fragments and with $ExecFrag(s)$ the set of execution fragments starting from s. We define $last(\sigma) = s_k$ and $|\sigma| = k$. The execution fragment σ is called *maximal* iff $last(\sigma) \in S_T$. For any $j < k$, with σ^j we define the sequence of steps $s_0 \xrightarrow{\alpha_1} s_1 \xrightarrow{\alpha_2} \ldots \xrightarrow{\alpha_j} s_j$. If $|\sigma| = 0$ we put $P(\sigma) = 1$, else, if $|\sigma| = k \geq 1$, we define $P(\sigma) = P(s_0, \alpha_1, s_1) \cdot \ldots \cdot P(s_{k-1}, \alpha_k, s_k)$.

An *execution* is either a maximal execution fragment or an infinite sequence $s_0 \xrightarrow{\alpha_1} s_1 \xrightarrow{\alpha_2} s_2 \xrightarrow{\alpha_3} \ldots$. We denote with $Exec$ the set of executions and with $Exec(s)$ the set of executions starting from s. Finally, let $\sigma \uparrow$ denote the set of executions σ' such that $\sigma \leq_{prefix} \sigma'$, where *prefix* is the usual prefix relation over sequences.

Executions and execution fragments of a PTA arise by resolving both the nondeterministic and the probabilistic choices [13]. To resolve the nondeterministic choices of a PTA, we introduce now *schedulers* of PTAs.

A *scheduler* of a PTA $A = (\Sigma, X, Q, q_0, \delta, \pi)$ is a partial function F from $Exec$ to $\mathbb{R}^{>0}$. For a scheduler F of a PTA A we define $ExecFrag^F$ (resp. $Exec^F$) as the set of execution fragments (resp. executions) $\sigma = s_0 \xrightarrow{\alpha_1} s_1 \xrightarrow{\alpha_2} s_2 \xrightarrow{\alpha_3} \ldots$ such that $\alpha_i \in \mathbb{R}^{>0}$ iff $F(\sigma^{i-1}) = \alpha_i$, for any $0 < i < |\sigma|$. We note that, if $F(\sigma)$ is not defined, then a discrete step is chosen for σ. Namely, $\alpha_i \notin \mathbb{R}^{>0}$ iff $F(\sigma^{i-1})$ undefined. A scheduler should also respect the *nonZeno* condition of divergent times. Formally we have that for any infinite sequence $\sigma = s_0 \xrightarrow{\alpha_1} s_1 \xrightarrow{\alpha_2} \ldots$ in $Exec^F$ the sum $\sum_{\alpha_i \in \mathbb{R}^{>0}} \alpha_i$ diverges.

Assuming the basic notions of probability theory (see e.g. [12]) we define the probability space on the executions starting in a given configuration $s \in S_A$ as follows. Given a scheduler F, let $Exec^F(s)$ be the set of executions starting in s, $ExecFrag^F(s)$ be the set of execution fragments starting in s, and $\Sigma^F_{Field}(s)$ be the smallest sigma field on $Exec^F(s)$ that contains the basic cylinders $\sigma \uparrow$, where $\sigma \in ExecFrag^F(s)$. The probability measure $Prob^F$ is the unique measure on $\Sigma^F_{Field}(s)$ such that $Prob^F(\sigma \uparrow) = P(\sigma)$.

In the following, A is a PTA, F is a scheduler for A, $\hat{\alpha}$ stands for α if $\alpha \in \Sigma \cup \mathbb{R}^{>0}$ and for ε (the empty string) if $\alpha = \tau$, $s \in S_A$ and $C \subseteq S_A$.

Consider now $Exec^F(\tau^* \hat{\alpha}, C)$, the set of executions that lead to a configuration in C via a sequence in $\tau^* \hat{\alpha}$. We define $Exec^F(s, \tau^* \hat{\alpha}, C) = Exec(\tau^* \hat{\alpha}, C) \cap Exec^F(s)$. Finally, given a scheduler F, we define the probability $Prob^F(s, \tau^* \hat{\alpha}, C) = Prob^F(Exec^F(s, \tau^* \hat{\alpha}, C))$ as:

$$
\begin{cases}
1 & \text{if } \alpha = \tau \wedge s \in C \\
\sum_{q \in S_A} Prob^F(s, \tau, q) \cdot Prob^F(q, \tau^*, C) & \text{if } \alpha = \tau \wedge s \notin C \\
\sum_{q \in S_A} Prob^F(s, \tau, q) \cdot Prob^F(q, \tau^* \alpha, C) + Prob(s, \alpha, C) & \text{if } \alpha \neq \tau
\end{cases}
$$

Weak bisimulation

The *bisimulation* of a system by another system is based on the idea of mutual step-by-step simulation. Intuitively, two systems A and A' are bisimilar, if whenever one of the two systems executes a certain action and reaches a configuration s, the other system is able to simulate this single step by executing the same action and reaching a configuration s' which is again bisimilar to s. A *weak bisimulation* is a bisimulation which does not take into account τ (internal) moves. Hence, whenever a system simulates an action of the other system, it can also execute some internal τ actions before and after the execution of that action. A *branching bisimulation* is, instead, a weak bisimulation where τ moves are allowed only before the execution of the action to simulate.

To abstract away from τ moves, Milner [18] introduces the notion of observable step, which consists of a single *visible* action α preceded and followed by an arbitrary number (including zero) of internal moves. Such moves are described by a *weak* transition relation $\overset{\alpha}{\Longrightarrow} = (\overset{\tau}{\longrightarrow})^* \overset{\alpha}{\longrightarrow} (\overset{\tau}{\longrightarrow})^*$, where $\longrightarrow$ is the classical strong relation, and $\overset{\tau}{\Longrightarrow} = (\overset{\tau}{\longrightarrow})^*$. It is worth noting that with such a definition a weak internal transition $\overset{\tau}{\Longrightarrow}$ is possible even without performing any internal action.

For the definition of weak bisimulation in the fully probabilistic setting, Baier and Hermanns [4] replace Milner's weak internal transitions $s \overset{\tau}{\Longrightarrow} s'$ by the probability $Prob(s, \tau^*, s')$ of reaching configuration s' from s via internal moves. Similarly, for visible actions α, Baier and Hermanns define $\overset{\alpha}{\Longrightarrow}$ by means of the probability $Prob(s, \tau^*\alpha, s')$.

DEFINITION 2 *Let $A = (\Sigma, X, Q, q_0, \delta, \pi)$ be a probabilistic timed automaton. A weak bisimulation on A is an equivalence relation $\mathcal{R}$ on S_A such that, for all $(s, s') \in \mathcal{R}$, $C \in S_A/\mathcal{R}$ and schedulers F, there exists a scheduler F' such that $Prob_A^F(s, \tau^*\alpha, C) = Prob_A^{F'}(s', \tau^*\alpha, C)$ for every $\alpha \in \Sigma \cup \{\tau\} \cup \mathbb{R}^{>0}$, and vice versa.*
Two configurations s, s' are called weakly bisimilar on A (denoted $s \approx_A s'$) iff $(s, s') \in \mathcal{R}$ for some weak bisimulation $\mathcal{R}$.

DEFINITION 3 *Two probabilistic timed automata $A = (\Sigma, X, Q, q_0, \delta, \pi)$ and $A' = (\Sigma', X', Q', q_0', \delta', \pi')$ such that $Q \cap Q' = \emptyset$ and $X \cap X' = \emptyset$ are called weak bisimilar (denoted by $A \approx A'$) if, given the probabilistic timed automaton $\hat{A} = (\Sigma \cup \Sigma', X \cup X', Q \cup Q', q_0, \delta \cup \delta', \hat{\pi})$, with $\hat{\pi}(e) = \pi(e)$ if $e \in \delta$ and $\hat{\pi}(e) = \pi'(e)$ otherwise, it holds $(q_0, \mathbf{0}) \approx_{\hat{A}} (q_0', \mathbf{0})$, where the valuation $\mathbf{0}$ is defined over all clocks of the set $X \cup X'$.*

In [15] we have given an algorithm that resorts to the theory of regions of timed automata [3] in order to decide weak bisimulation. Along the line of [15] we derive the following proposition.

PROPOSITION 4 *It is decidable to check whether two configurations or two probabilistic timed automata are weak bisimilar.*

Auxiliary Operators for Probabilistic Timed Automata

We assume two probabilistic timed automata $A_1 = (\Sigma, X_1, Q_1, r_0, \delta_1, \pi_1)$ and $A_2 = (\Sigma, X_2, Q_2, u_0, \delta_2, \pi_2)$ with $Q_1 \cap Q_2 = \emptyset$ and $X_1 \cap X_2 = \emptyset$. We also assume a set $L \subseteq \Sigma$ of synchronization actions. Finally, given a transition $e = (q, a, \phi, B, q') \in \delta_i$, with $\pi_{i_a}(e)$ we denote the normalized probability of executing transition e with respect to all other transitions starting from q and labelled with a, i.e. $\pi_{i_a}(e) = \frac{\pi_i(e)}{\sum_{e' \in start_i^a(q)} \pi_i(e')}$, where $start_i^a(q)$ denotes the set of transitions in δ_i with q as source state and a as labelling action, i.e. the set $\{(q_1, a', \phi, B, q_2) \in \delta_i \mid q_1 = q \wedge a' = a\}$.

DEFINITION 5 *The parallel composition of two PTA A_1 and A_2, with respect to the synchronization set L and the advancing speed parameter $p \in]0, 1[$, is defined as $A_1 \|_L^p A_2 = (\Sigma, X, Q, (r_0, u_0), \delta, \pi)$. The set Q of states of $A_1 \|_L^p A_2$ is given by the cartesian product $Q_1 \times Q_2$ of the states of the two automata A_1 and A_2, while the set of clocks X is given by the union $X_1 \cup X_2$. Given a state (r, u) of $A_1 \|_L^p A_2$, δ and π are obtained by the following rules:*

- *If from state r the automaton A_1 has a transition $e_1 = (r, a, \phi, B, r')$ with action $a \notin L$ and probability $\pi_1(e_1) = p'$, then $A_1 \|_L^p A_2$ has a transition $e = ((r, u), a, \phi, B, (r', u)) \in \delta$ with probability $\pi'(e) = p \cdot p'$.*

- *If from state u the automaton A_2 has a transition $e_2 = (u, a, \phi, B, u')$ with action $a \notin L$ and probability $\pi_2(e_2) = p'$, then $A_1 \|_L^p A_2$ has a transition $e = ((r, u), a, \phi, B, (r, u')) \in \delta$ with probability $\pi'(e) = (1 - p) \cdot p'$.*

- *If from state r the automaton A_1 has a transition $e_1 = (r, a, \phi_1, B_1, r')$ with action $a \in L$ and probabilities $\pi_1(e_1) = p'$ and $\pi_{1_a}(e_1) = \hat{p}'$, and from state u the automaton A_2 has a transition $e_2(u, a, \phi_2, B_2, u')$ with probabilities $\pi_2(e_2) = p''$ and $\pi_{2_a}(e_2) = \hat{p}''$, A_1 and A_2 can synchronize and therefore $A_1 \|_L^p A_2$ has a transition $e = ((r, q), \tau, \phi_1 \wedge \phi_2, B_1 \cup B_2, (r', q')) \in \delta$ with probability $\pi'(e) = p \cdot p' \cdot \hat{p}'' + (1 - p) \cdot p'' \cdot \hat{p}'$.*

- *For all $e = (q, a, \phi, B, q') \in \delta$, $\pi(e) = \frac{\pi'(e)}{\sum_{e' \in \delta \cap start(q)} \pi'(e')}$.*

Given such a definition of parallel composition, whenever A_1 and A_2 synchronize they give rise to an internal action τ. Note that, chosen a transition e_1 (e_2) with label $a \in L$ of automaton A_1 (A_2) the transition e_2 (e_1) of A_2 (A_1) that synchronizes with e_1 (e_2) is chosen according to the probability $\pi_{2_a}(e_2)$ ($\pi_{1_a}(e_1)$) normalized with respect to all the other transitions labelled with a. Besides, according to Definition 1, it holds that $\sum_{e \in start(q)} \pi(e) \in \{0, 1\}$ for each state q of $A_1 \|_L^p A_2$. This is done due to the last rule, that uses the auxiliary structure π' to compute the normalized probabilities in π.

PROPOSITION 6 *Given PTA A_1 and A_2, $A_1\|_L^p A_2$ is a PTA for all $p \in]0,1[$ and $L \subseteq \Sigma$.*

We now assume $A = (\Sigma, X, Q, q_0, \delta, \pi)$ and $L \subseteq \Sigma$.

DEFINITION 7 *The restriction of a probabilistic timed automaton A with respect to the set of actions L is given by $A \setminus L = (\Sigma, X, Q, q_0, \delta', \pi')$ where $\delta' = \delta \setminus \{(q, a, \phi, B, q') \mid a \in L\}$ and $\pi'(e) = \dfrac{\pi(e)}{\sum_{e' \in \delta' \cap start(q)} \pi(e')}$ for all $e = (q, a, \phi, B, q') \in \delta'$.*

DEFINITION 8 *The hiding of a probabilistic timed automaton A with respect to the set of actions L is given by $A/L = (\Sigma, X, Q, q_0, \delta', \pi)$ where each transition $e = (q, a, \phi, B, q')$ with $a \in L$ is replaced by the transition $e' = (q, \tau, \phi, B, q')$, where $\pi(e') = \pi(e)$.*

PROPOSITION 9 *Given a PTA A, $A \setminus L$ and A/L are PTA for all $L \subseteq \Sigma$.*

3. Security Properties

A multilevel system interacts with agents confined in different levels of clearance. In order to analyze the information flow between parties with different levels of confidentiality, the set of visible actions is partitioned into high level actions and low level actions. Formally, we assume the set of possible actions $\Sigma = \Sigma_H \cup \Sigma_L$, with $\Sigma_H \cap \Sigma_L = \emptyset$. In the following, with $l, l' \dots$ and $h, h', \dots$ we denote actions of Σ_L and Σ_H respectively. With Γ_H and Γ_L we denote the set of high level agents and low level agents. Formally, an automaton $A = (\Sigma', X, Q, q_0, \delta, \pi)$ is in Γ_H (Γ_L) if $\Sigma' \subseteq \Sigma_H$ ($\Sigma' \subseteq \Sigma_L$). For simplicity, we specify only two-level systems. More levels can by dealt with by iteratively grouping them in two clusters.

A low level agent is able to observe the execution of all the steps labelled with actions in Σ_L and all the timed steps. The basic idea of non-interference is that the high level does not interfere with the low level if the effects of high level communications are not visible by a low level agent. Finally, an important assumption when dealing with non-interference analysis is that a system is considered to be *secure* (no information flow can occur) if there is no interaction with high level agents (if high level actions are prevented).

Probabilistic Timed Non-interference

We say that a probabilistic timed automaton A satisfies the *Probabilistic Timed Non-interference* property (*PTNI*) if high level agents are not able to interfere with the observable behavior of the system from the low level point of view. Formally *PTNI* can be formulated as follows.

DEFINITION 10 *A PTA A is PTNI secure ($A \in PTNI$) $\Leftrightarrow A/\Sigma_H \approx A \setminus \Sigma_H$.*

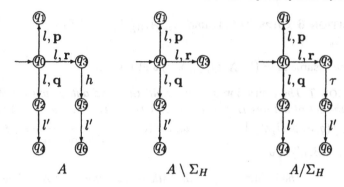

Figure 1.   A probabilistic covert channel.

$A \setminus \Sigma_H$ represents the isolated system, where all high level actions are prevented. Such a system is considered secure due to the notion of non-interference. If the observational behavior of the isolated system is equal to the behavior of A/Σ_H, representing the system which communicates with high level agents in an invisible manner for the low agents point of view, PTA A is *PTNI* secure. This property, defined in an environment where both probability and time are studied, is able to catch information flow that may occur either due to the probabilistic behavior of the system or due to the time when actions occur.

PROPOSITION 11 *It is decidable to check whether a PTA $A \in PTNI$.*

Proof. By the decidability of our weak bisimulation (see Proposition 4) and by the computable definitions of the operators of hiding and restriction.   ∎

EXAMPLE 12 *In Figure 1 we show a case of probabilistic information flow. Abstracting away from probability, the system A could be considered secure (in a purely nondeterministic setting, in both A/Σ_H and $A \setminus \Sigma_H$ a low level agent can observe the action l or the sequence ll' without further information about the execution of h). In a probabilistic framework, given $\mathbf{p} + \mathbf{r} + \mathbf{q} = 1$, action h interferes with the probability of observing either a single l or the sequence ll'. Formally, in $A \setminus \Sigma_H$, a low level agent observes either the single l with probability $\mathbf{p} + \mathbf{r}$ or the sequence ll' with probability $\mathbf{q}$. However, in A/Σ_H the event l is observed with probability $\mathbf{p}$ and the sequence ll' with probability $\mathbf{r} + \mathbf{q}$. As a consequence, $A/\Sigma_H \not\approx A \setminus \Sigma_H$, so that the PTNI property reveals the probabilistic covert channel.*

EXAMPLE 13 *In Figure 2 we show a case of timing information flow. Abstracting away from time, the system A could be considered secure (in a purely untimed nondeterministic setting, in both A/Σ_H and $A \setminus \Sigma_H$ a low level agent*

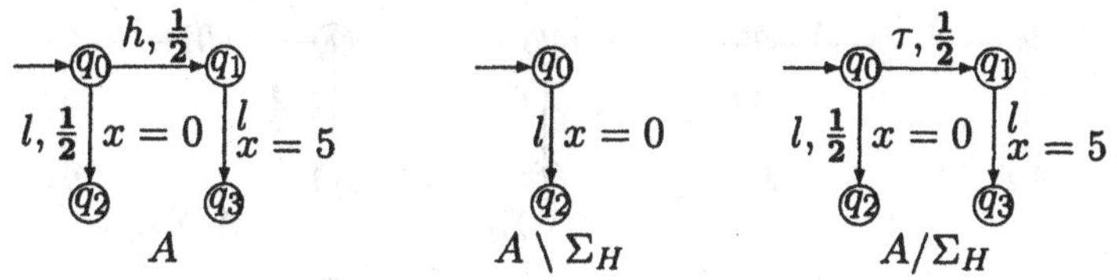

Figure 2. A timing covert channel.

can observe only the action l without further information about the execution of h). In a timed framework, given a clock $x \in \mathbb{R}^{\geq 0}$, the high action h interferes with the time of observing action l. Formally, in $A \backslash \Sigma_H$, a low level agent observes l executed immediately, while in A / Σ_H l could be either observed immediately or when the clock x reaches value 5. A low level agent, observing the event l when clock x has value 5 knows that action h has occurred. As a consequence, $A / \Sigma_H \not\approx A \backslash \Sigma_H$, so that the PTNI *property reveals the timing covert channel.*

Probabilistic Timed Non Deducibility on Composition

In [8] Focardi and Gorrieri promote the classification of a set of properties capturing the idea of information flow and non-interference. The *Non Deducibility on Composition* property (*NDC*) states that a system A in isolation has not to be altered when considering all the potential interactions of A with the high level agents of the external environment. We consider a notion of *NDC* called *Probabilistic Timed Non Deducibility on Composition (PTNDC)*.

DEFINITION 14 *A PTA A is PTNDC secure (A $\in$ PTNDC)* $\Leftrightarrow \forall \Pi \in \Gamma_H, \forall p \in]0, 1[, \forall L \subseteq \Sigma_H \quad A / \Sigma_H \approx (A ||_L^p \Pi) \backslash \Sigma_H$.

As we have seen, A / Σ_H represents the observable behavior of A from a low level agent point of view (i.e. the isolated system where all high level actions are hidden). System $(A ||_L^p \Pi) \backslash \Sigma_H$ represents, instead, system A communicating with the high agent Π and then prevented by the execution of other high level actions. If the observational behavior of the isolated system is equal to the behavior of the system communicating with any high level agent, PTA A satisfies the *PTNDC* security property.

THEOREM 15 *A $\in$ PTNDC $\Rightarrow$ A $\in$ PTNI.*

Proof. Consider $\Pi = (\emptyset, \emptyset, \{q\}, q, \emptyset, \pi) \in \Gamma_H$, i.e. an automaton representing a high level agent which does not perform any transition, and consider then the set $L = \emptyset$. If PTA A is *PTNDC*, then $\forall p \in]0, 1[, \quad A / \Sigma_H \approx (A ||_L^p \Pi) \backslash \Sigma_H$. Now, by the definition of parallel composition, $(A ||_L^p \Pi) = A$ and, therefore, $A / \Sigma_H \approx A \backslash \Sigma_H$, stating that $A \in PTNI$. ∎

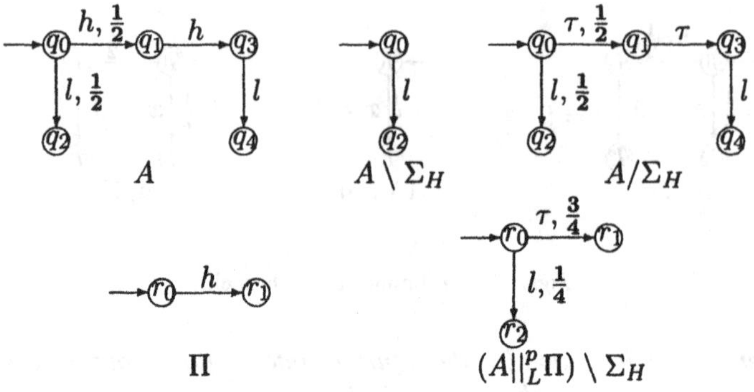

Figure 3. $A \in PTNI$, but $A \notin PTNDC$.

EXAMPLE 16 *Consider the PTA A of Figure 3. It is easy to see that A is PTNI secure, since $A/\Sigma_H \approx A \setminus \Sigma_H$. In both A/Σ_H and $A \setminus \Sigma_H$, a low level agent observes the single event l taken with probability 1. If we consider, instead, the high level agent Π of Figure 3, the set $L = \{h\}$ and $p = \frac{1}{2}$, we observe that $A/\Sigma_H \not\approx (A\|_L^p \Pi) \setminus \Sigma_H$. In fact, A/Σ_H always performs action l with probability 1, while $(A\|_L^p \Pi) \setminus \Sigma_H$ reaches a deadlock state r_1 and does not perform any visible action with probability $\frac{3}{4}$ (as it turns out after the parallel composition of A and Π). As a consequence, automaton A is not PTNDC secure.*

Theorem 15 and Example 16 show that the *PTNI* property is not able to detect some potential deadlock due to high level activities, exactly as put in evidence in [8]. For this reason we resort to the *PTNDC* property, which implies *PTNI*, in order to capture these finer undesirable behaviors.

It is worth noticing that, as it happens for the analogous properties defined in [1, 8, 9], the above definition of the *PTNDC* property is difficult to use in practice because of the universal quantification on the high level agents. Decidability of *PTNDC* depends, in fact, on the possibility of reducing all the high level automata in Γ_H to a finite case suitable for the particular automaton A we would like to study.

4.   An Application

As an application we consider a network device, also studied in [9] in a timed framework, that manages, following a mutual exclusion policy, the access to a shared buffer. Assuming that the agents on the network are classified as low and high level agents, the device implements the *no-write-down no-read-up* policy [10]. Intuitively, the policy states that high level users can only read the buffer, while low level users can only write on it. Such a policy avoids direct information flow from high level to low level, however malicious agents can exploit some covert channel in order to transmit information indirectly. For example, a low level user could get information about the high level activity by observing the amount of time the device is locked (non accessible by the low level) when high agents are reading, or by observing the frequencies with which high level agents make access on it. We would like to check whether some covert channel can be exploited by giving a specification of the network device, and then by checking the *PTNDC* property.

In the following we consider only a low level user and a high level user communicating with the network device. We assume that the low level user is always ready to write in the buffer, so we consider an agent that infinitely waits for a grant from the device and then writes in the buffer. In this manner we are considering a low level user that continuously monitors the activity of the device. We also assume that the entire procedure of receiving a grant in the network and writing in the buffer is executed in a time n. In Figure 4, we model the specification of a simple device (see the PTA B). Actions req_H, $read_H$, $grant_L$ and $write_L$ model respectively high level read requests, high level reads, low level write grants and low level writes. The set Σ_H of high level actions is $\{req_H, read_H\}$. The device B is always ready to accept an access request from the high level agent with probability $\frac{1}{2}$ and to grant a write access to the low level user with the same probability. Obviously, we always consider the device composed with a high level agent according to $\|_L^p$ (we assume $p = \frac{1}{2}$ and $L = \{req_H, read_H\}$). On the one hand, when the device is composed with a high level agent that performs action req_H with probability 1, it synchronizes with the high agent accepting his request with probability $\frac{3}{4}$. On the other hand, if the high level agent does not perform req_H, the composed system performs action $grant_L$ with probability 1. As a consequence we can find out the following covert channels. Consider the high agent Π_1 of Figure 4, which executes a read request without performing the reading afterwards. System $(B\|_L^p\Pi_1) \setminus \Sigma_H$ reaches a deadlock state that is not reached by B/Σ_H. In this way, the high level agent could transmit the bit 0 or 1 by alternatively blocking or not the device. Such a covert channel can be detected by the *PTNDC* property, in fact we have that $B/\Sigma_H \not\approx (B\|_L^p\Pi_1) \setminus \Sigma_H$ so that $B \notin PTNDC$. Another interesting covert channel arises if one considers Π_2, which locks the buffer and executes a reading only after a time k. A low level user observing the behavior of $(B\|_L^p\Pi_2) \setminus \Sigma_H$ does not receive any grant access for a time k when a req_H action is performed. In this way the high level agent could indirectly transmit value k to the low level user. We obviously have again that $B/\Sigma_H \not\approx (B\|_L^p\Pi_2) \setminus \Sigma_H$.

The two covert channels introduced above could be avoided by introducing a timeout mechanism which releases the device if $read_H$ is not performed and by always releasing the device after a fixed amount of time has passed. In Fig-

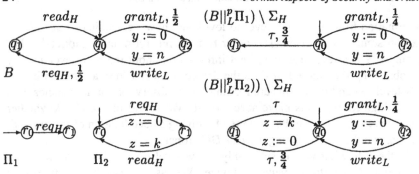

Figure 4.   Device specification with timing covert channels.

ure 5 we show a device B' that accepts a high level request, and uses a clock x as timer and t as timeout. When it executes action req_H the timer is set to 0, action $read_H$ could be performed only when $x < t$, and when x reaches value t the device unlocks the buffer going back to q_0. When transitions starting from a given state have disjoint conditions we omit probabilities since their execution depends on the time configuration, rather than on the effective probability. The timing covert channels shown in the previous case could not be exploited anymore, however device B' is still insecure. In fact the device is unavailable for the fixed amount of time when a high level access is performed, and this is clearly observable by the low level user that has to wait the termination of the high level request before obtaining access to the buffer. This represents a typical situation where the unavailability of a shared resource can be encoded as 0 or 1 in order to transmit data. Such a situation is captured by the *PTNDC* property by considering again the automaton Π_2 and assuming $k < t$. In fact we have again that $B'/\Sigma_H \not\approx (B'||_L^p \Pi_2) \setminus \Sigma_H$.

The capacity of such a covert channel could be reduced, but not totally avoided, by considering a buffer that probabilistically locks himself without any high level request. In this manner the low level user could not be sure whether the buffer is really locked by the high user or not. In Figure 5, B'' represents a device that behaves in such a manner, locking himself with a probability r. As we have said, this does not avoid entirely the covert channel, but the knowledge the low level user acquires is affected by some uncertainty. In fact, if the device is locked, the low level user could deduce that the high user locked the device with a certain probability while with probability r the device has locked himself for masking the higher user's activity.

We can completely hide the high level activity to the low level user by partitioning into two sessions the time in which users can access the buffer. During a *low session*, lasting a fixed amount of time n, only the low level user can access the buffer, then the device goes to the *high session*, where access is reserved,

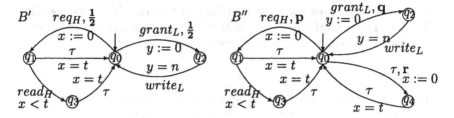

Figure 5. Improved device specifications.

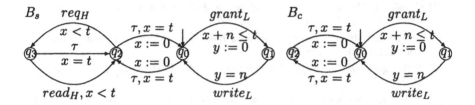

Figure 6. Secure Device.

for the same amount of time, to the high level user. This makes impossible for the low level user to discover something about the high level activity, since the same fixed amount of time is reserved to the high session even if the high user does nothing. In Figure 6 we specify a buffer B_s that behaves in such a manner: the buffer is reserved for a time t to the low level user and to the high level user alternatively. Automaton B_s is *PTNDC*, in fact, for every possible high level user Π, $(B_s||_L^p \Pi) \setminus \Sigma_H \approx B_c \approx B_s/\Sigma_H$. Intuitively, automaton B_c of Figure 6 represents the automaton resulting after the parallel composition between B_s and any high level user Π, and, therefore, B_c is weak bisimilar to B_s composed with any possible high level user Π. Finally, it easy to see that $B_c \approx B_s/\Sigma_H$.

5. Conclusions

The classical theory of non-interference must be extended to cope with real systems which may exhibit probabilistic and timing covert channels that are not captured by standard security models. In this paper we have developed a general framework where both probability and time are taken into account. By defining some information flow security property, we have shown how to detect with our model both probabilistic and timing covert channels.

We could easily give a definition of bisimulation requiring only that the difference of the probabilities in Definition 2 is less than a certain value and use it to give a measure of the security level of a system.

References

[1] A. Aldini, M. Bravetti, R. Gorrieri: *A Process-algebraic Approach for the Analysis of Probabilistic Non-interference*. Journal of Computer Security, to appear.

[2] R. Alur, C. Courcoubetis, D. L. Dill: *Verifying Automata Specifications of Probabilistic Real-Time Systems*. Real-Time: Theory in Practice, Springer LNCS 600, 28–44, 1992.

[3] R. Alur, D. L. Dill: *A Theory of Timed Automata*. Theoretical Computer Science 126:183–235, 1994.

[4] C. Baier, H. Hermanns: *Weak Bisimulation for Fully Probabilistic Processes*. Proc. of CAV'97, Springer LNCS 1254, 119–130, 1997.

[5] R. Barbuti, L. Tesei: *A Decidable Notion of Timed Non-interference*. Fundamenta Informaticae, 54(2–3):137–150, 2003.

[6] D. Beauquier: *On Probabilistic Timed Automata*. Theoretical Computer Science, 292:65–84, 2003.

[7] N. Evans, S. Schneider: *Analysing Time Dependent Security Properties in CSP Using PVS*. Proc. of Symp. on Research in Computer Security, Springer LNCS 1895, 222–237, 2000.

[8] R. Focardi, R. Gorrieri: *A Classification of Security Properties*. Journal of Computer Security, 3(1):5–33, 1995.

[9] R. Focardi, R. Gorrieri, F. Martinelli: *Information Flow Analysis in a Discrete-Time Process Algebra*. Proc. of 13th CSFW, IEEE CS Press, 170–184, 2000.

[10] J. A. Goguen, J. Meseguer: *Security Policy and Security Models*. Proc. of Symp. on Research in Security and Privacy, IEEE CS Press, 11–20, 1982.

[11] J. W. Gray III. *Toward a Mathematical Foundation for Information Flow Security*. Journal of Computer Security, 1:255–294, 1992.

[12] P. R. Halmos: *Measure Theory*. Springer-Verlag, 1950.

[13] M. Kwiatkowska, G. Norman, R. Segala, J. Sproston: *Automatic Verification of Real-time Systems with Discrete Probability Distribution*. Theoretical Computer Science, 282:101–150, 2002.

[14] M. Kwiatkowska, R. Norman, J. Sproston: *Symbolic Model Checking of Probabilistic Timed Automata Using Backwards Reachability*. Tech. rep. CSR-03-10, University of Birmingham, 2003.

[15] R. Lanotte, A. Maggiolo-Schettini, A. Troina: *Weak Bisimulation for Probabilistic Timed Automata and Applications to Security*. Proc. of SEFM'03, IEEE CS Press, 34–43, 2003.

[16] D. McCullough: *Noninterference and the Composability of Security Properties*. Proc. of Symp. on Research in Security and Privacy, IEEE CS Press, 177–186, 1988.

[17] J. K. Millen: *Hookup Security for Synchronous Machines*. Proc. of 3rd CSFW, IEEE CS Press, 84–90, 1990.

[18] R. Milner: *Communication and Concurrency*. Prentice Hall, 1989.

[19] J. T. Wittbold, D. M. Johnson: *Information Flow in Nondeterministic Systems*. Proc. of Symp. on Research in Security and Privacy, IEEE CS Press, 144–161, 1990.

DYNAMIC SECURITY LABELS AND NONINTERFERENCE

(Extended Abstract)

Lantian Zheng
Computer Science Department
Cornell University
zlt@cs.cornell.edu

Andrew C. Myers
Computer Science Department
Cornell University
andru@cs.cornell.edu

Abstract   This paper presents a language in which information flow is securely controlled by a type system, yet the security class of data can vary dynamically. Information flow policies provide the means to express strong security requirements for data confidentiality and integrity. Recent work on security-typed programming languages has shown that information flow can be analyzed statically, ensuring that programs will respect the restrictions placed on data. However, real computing systems have security policies that vary dynamically and that cannot be determined at the time of program analysis. For example, a file has associated access permissions that cannot be known with certainty until it is opened. Although one security-typed programming language has included support for dynamic security labels, there has been no demonstration that a general mechanism for dynamic labels can securely control information flow. In this paper, we present an expressive language-based mechanism for reasoning about dynamic security labels. The mechanism is formally presented in a core language based on the typed lambda calculus; any well-typed program in this language is provably secure because it satisfies noninterference.

1.   Introduction

Information flow control protects information security by constraining how information is transmitted among objects and users of various security classes. These security classes are expressed as *labels* associated with the information or its containers. Denning [5] showed how to use static analysis to ensure that programs use information in accordance with its security class, and this approach has been instantiated in a number of languages in which the type system implements a similar static analysis (e.g., [23, 9, 27, 17, 2, 19]). These type systems are an attractive way to enforce security because they can be shown to enforce *noninterference* [8], a strong, end-to-end security property. For example, when applied to confidentiality, noninterference ensures that confidential information cannot be released by the program no matter how it is transformed.

However, security cannot be enforced purely statically. In general, programs interact with an external environment that cannot be predicted at compile time, so there must be a run-time mechanism that allows security-critical decisions to be taken based on dynamic observations of this environment. For example, it is important to be able to change security settings on files and database records, and these changes should affect how the information from these sources can be used. A purely static mechanism cannot enforce this.

To securely control information flow when access rights can be changed and determined dynamically, *dynamic* labels [14] are needed that can be manipulated and checked at run time. However, manipulating labels dynamically makes it more difficult to enforce a strong notion of information security for several reasons. First, changing the label of an object may convert sensitive data to public data, directly violating noninterference. Second, label changes (and changes to access rights in general) can be used to convey information covertly; some restriction has to be imposed to prevent covert channels [25, 20]. Some mandatory access control (MAC) mechanisms support dynamic labels but cannot prevent *implicit flows* arising from control flow paths not taken at run time [4, 11].

JFlow [13] and its successor, Jif [15] are the only implemented security-typed languages supporting dynamic labels. However, although the Jif type system is designed to control the new information channels that dynamic labels create, it has not been proved to enforce secure information flow. Further, the dynamic label mechanism in Jif has limitations that impair expressiveness and efficiency.

In this paper, we propose an expressive language-based mechanism for securely manipulating information with dynamic security labels. The mechanism is formalized in a core language (based on the typed lambda calculus) with first-class label values, dependent security types and run-time label tests. Further, we prove that any well-typed program of the core language is secure because it satisfies noninterference. This is the first noninterference proof for a security-typed language in which general security labels can be manipulated and tested dynamically, though a noninterference result has been obtained for a simpler language supporting the related notion of dynamic *principals* [22].

Some previous MAC systems have supported dynamic security classes as part of a downgrading mechanism [21]; in this work the two mechanisms are considered orthogonal. While downgrading is important, it is useful to treat it as a separate mechanism so that dynamic manipulation of labels does not necessarily destroy noninterference.

The remainder of this paper is organized as follows. Section 2 presents some background on lattice label models and security type systems. Section 3 introduces the core language λ_{DSec} and uses sample λ_{DSec} programs to show some important applications of dynamic labels. Section 4 describes the type system of λ_{DSec} and the noninterference result. Section 5 covers related work, and Section 6 concludes.

2.   Background

Static information flow analysis can be formalized as a security type system, in which security levels of data are represented by security type annotations, and information flow control is performed through type checking.

2.1   Security classes

We assume that security requirements for confidentiality or integrity are defined by associating *security classes* with users and with the resources that programs access. These security classes form a lattice $\mathcal{L}$. We write $k \sqsubseteq k'$ to indicate that security class k' is at least as restrictive as another security class k. In this case it is safe to move information from security class k to k', because restrictions on the use of the data are preserved. To control data derived from sources with classes k and k', the least restrictive security class that is at least as restrictive as both k and k' is assigned. This is the least upper bound, or join, written $k \sqcup k'$.

2.2   Labels

Type systems for confidentiality or integrity are concerned with tracking information flows in programs. Types are extended with security *labels* that denote security classes. A label ℓ appearing in a program may be simply a constant security class k, or a more complex expression that denotes a security class. The notation $\ell_1 \sqsubseteq \ell_2$ means that ℓ_2 denotes a security class that is at least as restrictive as that denoted by ℓ_1.

Because a given security class may be denoted by different labels, the relation $\sqsubseteq$ generates a lattice of *equivalence classes* of labels with $\sqcup$ as the *join* (least upper bound) operator. Two labels ℓ_1 and ℓ_2 are equivalent, written $\ell_1 \approx \ell_2$, if $\ell_1 \sqsubseteq \ell_2$ and $\ell_2 \sqsubseteq \ell_1$. The join of two labels, $\ell_1 \sqcup \ell_2$, denotes the security class that is the join of the security classes that ℓ_1 and ℓ_2 denote. For example, if x has label ℓ_x and y has label ℓ_y, then the sum x+y is given the label $\ell_x \sqcup \ell_y$.

2.3   Security type systems for information flow

Security type systems can be used to enforce security information flows statically. Information flows in programs may be explicit flows such as assignments, or *implicit flows* [5] arising from the control flow of the program. Consider an assignment statement x=y, which contains an information flow from y to x. Then the typing rule for the assignment statement requires that $\ell_y \sqsubseteq \ell_x$, which means the security level of y is lower than the security level of x, guaranteeing the information flow from y to x is secure.

One advantage of static analysis is more precise control of implicit flows. Consider a simple conditional:

$$\text{if b then } x = \text{true else } x = \text{false}$$

Although there is no direct assignment from b to x, this expression has an implicit flow from b into x. A standard technique for controlling implicit flows is to introduce a *program-counter label* [4], written *pc*, which indicates the security level of the information that can be learned by knowing the control flow path taken thus far. In this example, the branch taken depends on b, so the *pc* in the then and else clauses will be joined with ℓ_b, the label of b. The type system ensures that any effect of expression *e* has a label at least as restrictive as its *pc*. In other words, an expression *e* cannot generate any effects observable to users who should not know the current program counter. In this example, the assignments to x will be permitted only if $pc \sqsubseteq \ell_x$, which ensures $\ell_b \sqsubseteq \ell_x$.

3.   The λ_{DSec} language

The core language λ_{DSec} is a security-typed lambda calculus that supports first-class dynamic labels. In λ_{DSec}, labels are terms that can be manipulated and checked at run time. Furthermore, label terms can be used as statically analyzed type annotations. Syntactic restrictions are imposed on label terms to increase the practicality of type checking, following the approach used by Xi and Pfenning in $\text{ML}_0^\Pi(C)$ [26].

From the computational standpoint, λ_{DSec} is fairly expressive, because it supports both first-class functions and state, which together are sufficient to encode recursive functions.

3.1   Syntax

The syntax of λ_{DSec} is given in Figure 1. We use the name k to range over a lattice of label values $\mathcal{L}$ (more precisely, a join semi-lattice with bottom element $\perp$), x, y to range over variable names $\mathcal{V}$, and m to range over a space of memory addresses $\mathcal{M}$.

Base Labels	k	$\in$	$\mathcal{L}$
Variables	x, y	$\in$	$\mathcal{V}$
Locations	m	$\in$	$\mathcal{M}$
Labels	ℓ, pc	$::=$	$k \mid x \mid \ell_1 \sqcup \ell_2$
Constraints	C	$::=$	$\ell_1 \sqsubseteq \ell_2, C \mid \epsilon$
Base Types	β	$::=$	$\text{int} \mid \text{label} \mid \text{unit} \mid (x{:}\tau_1)[C] * \tau_2 \mid \tau \, \text{ref} \mid (x{:}\tau_1) \xrightarrow{C\,;\,pc} \tau_2$
Security Types	τ	$::=$	β_ℓ
Values	v	$::=$	$x \mid n \mid m^\tau \mid \lambda(x{:}\tau)[C\,;pc].\,e \mid () \mid k \mid (x{=}v_1[C], \, v_2{:}\tau)$
Expressions	e	$::=$	$v \mid \ell_1 \sqcup \ell_2 \mid e_1\,e_2 \mid \,!e \mid e_1 := e_2 \mid \text{ref}^\tau e$
		$\mid$	$\text{if } \ell_1 \sqsubseteq \ell_2 \text{ then } e_1 \text{ else } e_2 \mid \text{let } (x,y){=}e_1 \text{ in } e_2$

Figure 1. Syntax of λ_{DSec}

To make the lattice explicit, we write $\mathcal{L} \models k_1 \sqsubseteq k_2$ to mean that k_2 is at least as restrictive as k_1 in $\mathcal{L}$, and $\mathcal{L} \models k = k_1 \sqcup k_2$ to mean k is the join of k_1 and k_2 in $\mathcal{L}$. The least and greatest elements of $\mathcal{L}$ are $\bot$ and $\top$. Any non-trivial label lattice contains at least two points L and H where $H \not\sqsubseteq L$. Intuitively, the label L describes what information is observable by *low-security users* who are to be prevented from seeing confidential information. Thus, *low-security* data has a label bounded above by L; *high-security* data has a label (such as H) not bounded by L.

In λ_{DSec}, a label can be either a label value k, a variable x, or the join of two other labels $\ell_1 \sqcup \ell_2$. For example, L, x, and $L \sqcup x$ are all valid labels, and $L \sqcup x$ can be interpreted as a security policy that is as restrictive as both L and x. The security type $\tau = \beta_\ell$ is the base type β annotated with label ℓ. The base types include integers, unit, labels, functions, references and products.

The function type $(x{:}\tau_1) \xrightarrow{C\,;\,pc} \tau_2$ is a dependent type since τ_1, τ_2, C and pc may mention x. The component C is a set of *label constraints* each with the form $\ell_1 \sqsubseteq \ell_2$; they must be satisfied when the function is invoked. The pc component is a lower bound on the memory effects of the function, and an upper bound on the pc label of the caller. Consequently, a function is not able to leak information about where it is called. Without the annotations C and pc, this kind of type is sometimes written as $\Pi x{:}\tau_1.\tau_2$ [12].

The product type $(x{:}\tau_1)[C] * \tau_2$ is also a dependent type in the sense that occurrences of x can appear in τ_1, τ_2 and C. The component C is a set of label constraints that any value of the product type must satisfy. If τ_2 does not contain x and C is empty, the type may be written as the more familiar $\tau_1 * \tau_2$. Without the annotation C, this kind of type is sometimes written $\Sigma x{:}\tau_1.\tau_2$ [12].

In λ_{DSec}, values include integers n, typed memory locations m^τ, functions $\lambda(x{:}\tau)[C\,;pc].\,e$, the unit value $()$, constant labels k, and pairs $(x{=}v_1[C], \, v_2{:}\tau)$. A function $\lambda(x : \tau)[C\,;pc].\,e$ has one argument x with type τ, and the components C and pc have the same meanings as those in function types. The empty constraint set C or the top pc can be omitted. A pair $(x = v_1[C], v_2 : \tau)$ contains two values v_1 and v_2. The second element v_2 has type τ and may mention the first element v_1 by the name x. The component C is a set of label constraints that the first element of the pair must satisfy.

Expressions include values v, variables x, the join of two labels $\ell_1 \sqcup \ell_2$, applications $e_1\ e_2$, dereferences $!e$, assignments $e_1 := e_2$, references $\mathtt{ref}^\tau e$, label-test expressions if $\ell_1 \sqsubseteq \ell_2$ then e_1 else e_2, and product destructors $\mathtt{let}\ (x, y) = v\ \mathtt{in}\ e_2$.

The label-test expression if $\ell_1 \sqsubseteq \ell_2$ then e_1 else e_2 is used to examine labels. At run time, if the value of ℓ_2 is a constant label at least as restrictive as the value of ℓ_1, then e_1 is evaluated; otherwise, e_2 is evaluated. Consequently, the constraint $\ell_1 \sqsubseteq \ell_2$ can be assumed when type-checking e_1.

The product destructor $\mathtt{let}\ (x, y) = e_1\ \mathtt{in}\ e_2$ unpacks the result of e_1, which is a pair, assigns the first element to x and the second to y, and evaluates e_2.

3.2   Operational Semantics

The small-step operational semantics of λ_{DSec} is given in Figure 2. Let M represent a memory that is a finite map from typed locations to closed values, and let $\langle e, M \rangle$ be a machine configuration. Then a small evaluation step is a transition from $\langle e, M \rangle$ to another configuration $\langle e', M' \rangle$, written $\langle e, M \rangle \longmapsto \langle e', M' \rangle$.

It is necessary to restrict the form of $\langle e, M \rangle$ to avoid using undefined memory locations. Let $loc(e)$ represent the set of memory locations appearing in e. A memory M is well-formed if every address m appears at most once in $dom(M)$, and for any m^τ in $dom(M)$, $loc(M(m^\tau)) \subseteq dom(M)$. By induction we can prove that evaluation preserves memory well-formedness.

The notation $e[v/x]$ indicates capture-avoiding substitution of value v for variable x in expression e. Unlike in the typed lambda calculus, $e[v/x]$ may generate a syntactically ill-formed expression if x appears in type annotations inside e, and v is not a label. However, this is not a problem because the type system of λ_{DSec} guarantees that a well-typed expression can only be evaluated to another well-typed and thus well-formed expression.

The notation $M(m^\tau)$ denotes the value of location m^τ in M, and the notation $M[m^\tau \mapsto v]$ denotes the memory obtained by assigning v to m^τ in M.

The evaluation rules are standard. In rule (E3), notation *address-space*(M) represents the set of location names in M, that is, $\{m \mid \exists \tau\ s.t.\ m^\tau \in dom(M)\}$. In rule (E8), v_2 may mention x, so substituting v_2 for y in e is performed before substituting v_1 for x. The variable name in the product value matches x so that no variable substitution is needed when assigning v_1 and v_2 to x and y. In rule

$$[E1] \quad \frac{\mathcal{L} \models k = k_1 \sqcup k_2}{\langle k_1 \sqcup k_2, M \rangle \longmapsto \langle k, M \rangle} \qquad [E3] \quad \frac{m \notin \text{address-space}(M)}{\langle \text{ref}^\tau v, M \rangle \longmapsto \langle m^\tau, M[m^\tau \mapsto v] \rangle}$$

$$[E2] \quad \langle !m^\tau, M \rangle \longmapsto \langle M(m^\tau), M \rangle \qquad [E4] \quad \langle m^\tau := v, M \rangle \longmapsto \langle (), M[m^\tau \mapsto v] \rangle$$

$$[E5] \quad \langle (\lambda(x{:}\tau)[C\,;pc].\,e)\,v,\, M \rangle \longmapsto \langle e[v/x],\, M \rangle$$

$$[E6] \quad \frac{\mathcal{L} \models k_1 \sqsubseteq k_2}{\langle \text{if } k_1 \sqsubseteq k_2 \text{ then } e_1 \text{ else } e_2,\, M \rangle \longmapsto \langle e_1,\, M \rangle}$$

$$[E7] \quad \frac{\mathcal{L} \models k_1 \not\sqsubseteq k_2}{\langle \text{if } k_1 \sqsubseteq k_2 \text{ then } e_1 \text{ else } e_2,\, M \rangle \longmapsto \langle e_2,\, M \rangle}$$

$$[E8] \quad \langle \text{let } (x,y) = (x = v_1[C],\, v_2{:}\tau) \text{ in } e,\, M \rangle \longmapsto \langle e[v_2/y][v_1/x],\, M \rangle$$

$$[E9] \quad \frac{\langle e, M \rangle \longmapsto \langle e', M' \rangle}{\langle E[e], M \rangle \longmapsto \langle E[e'], M' \rangle}$$

$$
\begin{aligned}
E[\cdot] \quad ::= \quad & [\cdot]\, e \mid v\, [\cdot] \mid [\cdot] := e \mid v := [\cdot] \mid \,![\cdot] \mid \text{ref}^\tau\, [\cdot] \mid [\cdot] \sqcup \ell_2 \mid k_1 \sqcup [\cdot] \\
& \mid \; \text{if } [\cdot] \sqsubseteq \ell_2 \text{ then } e_1 \text{ else } e_2 \mid \text{if } k_1 \sqsubseteq [\cdot] \text{ then } e_1 \text{ else } e_2 \\
& \mid \; \text{let } (x,y) = [\cdot] \text{ in } e
\end{aligned}
$$

Figure 2. Small-step operational semantics of λ_{DSec}

(E9), E represents an evaluation context, a term with a single hole in redex position, and the syntax of E specifies the evaluation order.

3.3 Example: multilevel I/O channels

As discussed in Section 1, dynamic labels are vital for precisely controlling information flows between security-typed programs and the external environment. When information is exported outside a program through an I/O channel, the receiver might want to know the exact label of the information, which calls for *multilevel communication channels* [6] unambiguously pairing the information sent or received with its corresponding security label. Supporting multilevel channels is one of the basic requirements for a MAC system [6].

In λ_{DSec}, a multilevel channel can be encoded by a memory reference of type $((x{:}\text{label}_x) * \text{int}_x)_\perp$ ref, which stores a pair composed of an integer value and its label. The confidentiality of the integer component is protected by the label component, since extracting the integer from such a pair requires testing the label component:

$$\lambda z{:}((x{:}\text{label}_x) * \text{int}_x)_\perp.\, \text{let } (x,y) = z \text{ in if } x \sqsubseteq L \text{ then } m^{\text{int}_L} := y \text{ else } ()$$

In the above code, the constraint $x \sqsubseteq L$ must be satisfied in order to store the integer component in m^{int_L}. Since the readability of the integer depends on the value of x, letting x recursively label itself ensures that all the authorized readers of the integer component can test x and retrieve the integer.

$$[C1] \quad \frac{\mathcal{L} \models k_1 \sqsubseteq k_2}{C \vdash k_1 \sqsubseteq k_2} \qquad\qquad [C2] \quad \frac{\ell_1 \sqsubseteq \ell_2 \in C}{C \vdash \ell_1 \sqsubseteq \ell_2}$$

$$[C3] \quad C \vdash \ell \sqsubseteq \top \qquad [C4] \quad C \vdash \bot \sqsubseteq \ell \qquad [C5] \quad C \vdash \ell \sqsubseteq \ell \sqcup \ell'$$

$$[C6] \quad \frac{C \vdash \ell_1 \sqsubseteq \ell_2 \quad C \vdash \ell_2 \sqsubseteq \ell_3}{C \vdash \ell_1 \sqsubseteq \ell_3} \qquad\qquad [C7] \quad \frac{C \vdash \ell_1 \sqsubseteq \ell_3 \quad C \vdash \ell_2 \sqsubseteq \ell_3}{C \vdash \ell_1 \sqcup \ell_2 \sqsubseteq \ell_3}$$

Figure 3.   Relabeling rules

Sending an integer through a multilevel channel is encoded by pairing the integer and its label and storing the pair in the reference representing the channel:

$$\lambda z : (((x : \mathtt{label}_x)) * \mathtt{int}_x)_\bot \ \mathtt{ref})_\bot . \lambda w : \mathtt{label}_w . \lambda(y : \mathtt{int}_w)[\bot] . z := (x = w, \ y : \mathtt{int}_x)$$

Like other I/O channels, a multilevel channel may have a label that is an upper bound of the security levels of the information that can be sent through the channel. Product label constraints can be used to specify the label of a multilevel channel. For example, a bounded multilevel channel can be represented by a memory reference with type $((x : \mathtt{label}_x)[x \sqsubseteq \ell] * \mathtt{int}_x)_\bot \ \mathtt{ref}$, where ℓ is the label of the channel, and the constraint $x \sqsubseteq \ell$ guarantees any information stored in the reference has a security label at most as high as ℓ. Sending information through a bounded multilevel channel often needs a run-time check as in the following code:

$$\lambda z : (((x : \mathtt{label}_x))[x \sqsubseteq \ell] * \mathtt{int}_x)_\bot \ \mathtt{ref})_\bot . \lambda w : \mathtt{label}_w .$$
$$\lambda(y : \mathtt{int}_w)[\bot] . \ \mathtt{if} \ w \sqsubseteq \ell \ \mathtt{then} \ z := (x = w, \ y : \mathtt{int}_x) \ \mathtt{else} \ ()$$

4.   Type system and noninterference

This section describes the type system of λ_{DSec} and formalizes the noninterference result (any well-typed program has the noninterference property), whose proof is presented in the full version of this paper [29].

4.1   Subtyping

The subtyping relationship between security types plays an important role in enforcing information flow security. Given two security types $\tau_1 = \beta_{1\ell_1}$ and $\tau_2 = \beta_{2\ell_2}$, suppose τ_1 is a subtype of τ_2, written as $\tau_1 \leq \tau_2$. Then any data of type τ_1 can be treated as data of type τ_2. Thus, data with label ℓ_1 may be treated as data with label ℓ_2, which requires $\ell_1 \sqsubseteq \ell_2$.

In λ_{DSec}, label terms have a restricted syntactic form so that they can be used as type annotations, and constraints on label terms are also type-level information that the type checker can use. Indeed, label constraints introduced in

$$[S1] \quad \frac{C \vdash \tau_1 \leq \tau_2 \quad C \vdash \tau_2 \leq \tau_1}{C \vdash \tau_1 \ \mathbf{ref} \leq \tau_2 \ \mathbf{ref}}$$

$$[S2] \quad \frac{C \vdash \tau_2 \leq \tau_1 \quad C \vdash \tau_1' \leq \tau_2' \quad C \vdash pc_2 \sqsubseteq pc_1 \quad C, C_2 \vdash C_1}{C \vdash (x : \tau_1) \xrightarrow{C_1 ; pc_1} \tau_1' \leq (x : \tau_2) \xrightarrow{C_2 ; pc_2} \tau_2'}$$

$$[S3] \quad \frac{C \vdash \tau_1 \leq \tau_2 \quad C \vdash \tau_1' \leq \tau_2' \quad C, C_1 \vdash C_2}{C \vdash (x : \tau_1)[C_1] * \tau_1' \leq (x : \tau_2)[C_2] * \tau_2'}$$

$$[S4] \quad \frac{C \vdash \beta_1 \leq \beta_2 \quad C \vdash \ell_1 \sqsubseteq \ell_2}{C \vdash (\beta_1)_{\ell_1} \leq (\beta_2)_{\ell_2}}$$

Figure 4.   Subtyping rules

label-test expressions, functions and pairs are critical for precise static analysis of dynamic labels.

The type system keeps track of the set of label constraints that can be used to prove relabeling relationships between labels. Let $C \vdash \ell_1 \sqsubseteq \ell_2$ denote that $\ell_1 \sqsubseteq \ell_2$ can be inferred from the set of constraints C. The inference rules are shown in Figure 3; they are standard and consistent with the lattice properties of labels. Rule (C2) shows that all the constraints in C are assumed to be true.

Since the subtyping relationship depends on the relabeling relationship, the subtyping context also needs to include the C component. The inference rules for proving $C \vdash \tau_1 \leq \tau_2$ are the rules shown in Figure 4 plus the standard reflexivity and transitivity rules.

Rules (S1)–(S3) are about subtyping on base types. These rules demonstrate the expected covariance or contravariance. In λ_{DSec}, function types contain two additional components pc and C, both of which are contravariant because they restrict where a function can be invoked. In rules (S2) and (S3), variable x is bound in the function and product types. For simplicity, we assume that x does not appear in C, since α-conversion can always be used to rename x to another fresh variable. This assumption also applies to the typing rules.

Rule (S4) is used to determine the subtyping on security types. The premise $C \vdash \beta_1 \leq \beta_2$ is natural. The other premise $C \vdash \ell_1 \sqsubseteq \ell_2$ guarantees that coercing data from τ_1 to τ_2 does not violate information flow policies.

4.2   Typing

The type system of λ_{DSec} prevents illegal information flows and guarantees that well-typed programs have a noninterference property. The typing rules are shown in Figure 5. The notation $label(\beta_\ell) = \ell$ is used to obtain the label of a type, and the notations $\ell \sqsubseteq \tau$ and $\tau \sqsubseteq \ell$ are abbreviations for $\ell \sqsubseteq label(\tau)$ and $label(\tau) \sqsubseteq \ell$, respectively.

The typing context includes a *type assignment* Γ, a set of constraints C and the program-counter label pc. Γ is a finite *ordered* list of $x : \tau$ pairs in the order that they came into scope. For a given x, there is at most one pair $x : \tau$ in Γ.

$$[INT]\quad \Gamma;C;pc \vdash n : \mathtt{int}_\perp \qquad [UNIT]\quad \Gamma;C;pc \vdash () : \mathtt{unit}_\perp$$

$$[LABEL]\quad \Gamma;C;pc \vdash k : \mathtt{label}_\perp \qquad [LOC]\quad \frac{FV(\tau)=\emptyset}{\Gamma;C;pc \vdash m^\tau : (\tau\ \mathtt{ref})_\perp}$$

$$[VAR]\quad \frac{x{:}\tau \in \Gamma}{\Gamma;C;pc \vdash x : \tau} \qquad [JOIN]\quad \frac{\Gamma;C;pc \vdash \ell_1 : \mathtt{label}_{\ell_1'} \quad \Gamma;C;pc \vdash \ell_2 : \mathtt{label}_{\ell_2'}}{\Gamma;C;pc \vdash \ell_1 \sqcup \ell_2 : \mathtt{label}_{\ell_1' \sqcup \ell_2'}}$$

$$[REF]\quad \frac{\Gamma;C;pc \vdash e : \tau \qquad C \vdash pc \sqsubseteq \tau}{\Gamma;C;pc \vdash \mathtt{ref}^\tau e : (\tau\ \mathtt{ref})_\perp} \qquad [DEREF]\quad \frac{\Gamma;C;pc \vdash e : (\tau\ \mathtt{ref})_\ell}{\Gamma;C;pc \vdash !e : \tau \sqcup \ell}$$

$$[ABS]\quad \frac{\Gamma, x{:}\tau' ; C' ; pc' \vdash e : \tau}{\Gamma;C;pc \vdash \lambda(x{:}\tau')[C';pc'].\,e : ((x{:}\tau') \xrightarrow{C';pc'} \tau)_\perp}$$

$$[ASSIGN]\quad \frac{\Gamma;C;pc \vdash e_1 : (\tau\ \mathtt{ref})_\ell \quad \Gamma;C;pc \vdash e_2 : \tau \quad C \vdash pc \sqcup \ell \sqsubseteq \tau}{\Gamma;C;pc \vdash e_1 := e_2 : \mathtt{unit}_\perp}$$

$$[L\text{-}APP]\quad \frac{\begin{array}{c}\Gamma;C;pc \vdash e_1 : ((x{:}\mathtt{label}_{\ell'}) \xrightarrow{C';pc'} \tau)_\ell \qquad \Gamma;C;pc \vdash \ell_2 : \mathtt{label}_{\ell'[\ell_2/x]} \\ C \vdash pc \sqcup \ell \sqsubseteq pc'[\ell_2/x] \quad C \vdash C'[\ell_2/x] \quad x \in FV(\tau) \cup FV(\ell') \cup FV(C') \cup FV(pc')\end{array}}{\Gamma;C;pc \vdash e_1\ \ell_2 : \tau[\ell_2/x] \sqcup \ell}$$

theorem

$$[APP]\quad \frac{\begin{array}{c}\Gamma;C;pc \vdash e_1 : ((x{:}\tau') \xrightarrow{C';pc'} \tau)_\ell \qquad \Gamma;C;pc \vdash e_2 : \tau' \\ C \vdash pc \sqcup \ell \sqsubseteq pc' \qquad C \vdash C' \qquad x \notin FV(\tau) \cup FV(\tau') \cup FV(C') \cup FV(pc')\end{array}}{\Gamma;C;pc \vdash e_1\ e_2 : \tau \sqcup \ell}$$

$$[IF]\quad \frac{\begin{array}{c}\Gamma;C;pc \vdash \ell_i : \mathtt{label}_{\ell_i'} \quad i \in \{1,2\} \\ \Gamma;C,\ell_1 \sqsubseteq \ell_2; pc \sqcup \ell_1' \sqcup \ell_2' \vdash e_1 : \tau \qquad \Gamma;C;pc \sqcup \ell_1' \sqcup \ell_2' \vdash e_2 : \tau\end{array}}{\Gamma;C;pc \vdash \mathtt{if}\ \ell_1 \sqsubseteq \ell_2\ \mathtt{then}\ e_1\ \mathtt{else}\ e_2 : \tau \sqcup \ell_1' \sqcup \ell_2'}$$

$$[UNPACK]\quad \frac{\Gamma;C;pc \vdash e_1 : ((x{:}\tau_1)[C'] * \tau_2)_\ell \qquad \Gamma, x{:}\tau_1 \sqcup \ell, y{:}\tau_2 \sqcup \ell; C, C'; pc \vdash e_2 : \tau}{\Gamma;C;pc \vdash \mathtt{let}\ (x,y) = e_1\ \mathtt{in}\ e_2 : \tau}$$

$$[PROD]\quad \frac{\begin{array}{c}\Gamma;C;pc \vdash v_1 : \tau_1[v_1/x] \qquad \Gamma, x{:}\tau_1 \vdash \tau_2 \\ \Gamma;C;pc \vdash v_2[v_1/x] : \tau_2[v_1/x] \qquad C \vdash C'[v_1/x]\end{array}}{\Gamma;C;pc \vdash (x = v_1[C'],\ v_2{:}\tau_2) : ((x{:}\tau_1)[C'] * \tau_2)_\perp} \qquad [SUB]\quad \frac{\begin{array}{c}\Gamma;C;pc \vdash e : \tau \\ C \vdash \tau \le \tau'\end{array}}{\Gamma;C;pc \vdash e : \tau'}$$

Figure 5. Typing rules for the λ_{DSec} language

A variable appearing in a type must be a label variable. Therefore, a type τ is well-formed with respect to type assignment Γ, written $\Gamma \vdash \tau$, if Γ maps all the variables in τ to label types. The definition of well-formed labels ($\Gamma \vdash \ell$) is the same. Consider $\Gamma = x_1 : \tau_1, \ldots, x_n : \tau_n$. For any $0 \le i \le n$, the type τ_i may only mention label variables that are already in scope: x_1 through x_i. Therefore, Γ is well-formed if for any $0 \le i \le n$, τ_i is well-formed with respect to $x_1 : \tau_1, \ldots, x_i : \tau_i$. For example, "$x : \mathtt{label}_L, y : \mathtt{int}_x$" is well-formed, but "$y{:}\mathtt{int}_x, x{:}\mathtt{label}_L$" is not.

The typing assertion $\Gamma \,; C \,; pc \vdash e : \tau$ means that with the type assignment Γ, current program-counter label as pc, and the set of constraints C satisfied, expression e has type τ.

Rules (INT), (UNIT), (LABEL) and (LOC) are used to check values. Value v has type $\beta_\perp$ if v has base type β. Rule (LOC) requires typed location m^τ contain no label variables so that m^τ remains a constant during evaluation. This is enforced by the premise $FV(\tau) = \emptyset$, where $FV(\tau)$ denotes the set of free variables appearing in τ.

Rules (VAR), (JOIN), (REF), (DEREF), (ASSIGN), (ABS) and (SUB) are standard for a security type system [27, 17]. Due to the space limitation, we do not include the detailed descriptions of these rules, which can be found in the full paper [29].

Rule (L-APP) is used to check applications of dependent functions. Expression e_1 has a dependent function type $((x : \mathtt{label}_{\ell'}) \xrightarrow{C' \,; pc'} \tau)_\ell$, where x does appear in ℓ', C', pc' or τ. As a result, rule (L-APP) needs to use $\ell'[\ell_2/x]$, $C'[\ell_2/x]$, $pc'[\ell_2/x]$ and $\tau[\ell_2/x]$, which are well-formed since ℓ_2 is a label. That also explains why e_1, with its dependent function type, cannot be applied to an arbitrary expression e_2: substituting e_2 for x in ℓ', C', pc' and τ may generate ill-formed labels or types. The expressiveness of λ_{DSec} is not substantially affected by the restriction, because the function can be applied to a variable that receives the result of an arbitrary expression. Rule (APP) applies when x does not appear in C', pc' or τ. In this case, the type of e_1 is just a normal function type, so e_1 can be applied to arbitrary terms.

Rule (PROD) is used to check product values. To check v_2, the occurrences of x in v_2 and τ_2 are both replaced by v_1, since x is not in the domain of Γ. If v_1 is not a label, then x cannot appear in τ_2. Thus, $\tau_2[v_1/x]$ is always well-formed no matter whether v_1 is a label or not. Rule (UNPACK) checks product destructors straightforwardly. After unpacking the product value, those product label constraints in C' are in scope and used for checking e_2.

Rule (IF) checks label-test expressions. The constraint $\ell_1 \sqsubseteq \ell_2$ is added into the typing context when checking the first branch e_1.

This type system satisfies the subject reduction property and the progress property. The proof is standard.

4.3   Noninterference theorem

This section formalizes the noninterference result: any well-typed program in λ_{DSec} satisfies the noninterference property (see the full paper [29] for the proof). Consider an expression e in λ_{DSec}. Suppose e has one free variable x, and $x : \tau \vdash e : \mathtt{int}_L$ where $H \sqsubseteq \tau$. Thus, the value of x is a high-security input to e, and the result of e is a low-security output. Then noninterference requires that for all values v of type τ, evaluating $e[v/x]$ in the same memory must generate the same result, if the evaluation terminates. For simplicity, we only consider that results are integers because they can be compared outside the context of λ_{DSec}. Let $\longmapsto^*$ denote the transitive closure of the $\longmapsto$ relationship. The following theorem formalizes the claim that the type system of λ_{DSec} enforces noninterference:

THEOREM 1 (NONINTERFERENCE) *Suppose* $x : \tau \vdash e : \text{int}_L$, *and* $H \sqsubseteq \tau$. *Given two arbitrary values* v_1 *and* v_2 *of type* τ, *and an initial memory* M, *if* $\langle e[v_i/x], M \rangle \longmapsto^* \langle v_i', M_i' \rangle$ *for* $i \in \{1, 2\}$, *then* $v_1' = v_2'$.

The noninterference property discussed here is *termination insensitive* [19] because $e[v/x]$ is required to generate the same result only if the evaluation terminates. The type system of λ_{DSec} does not attempt to control termination and timing channels. Control of these channels is largely an orthogonal problem. Some recent work [1, 18, 28] partially addresses timing channels.

5.   Related Work

Dynamic information flow control mechanisms [24, 25] track security labels dynamically and use run-time security checks to constrain information propagation. These mechanisms are transparent to programs, but cannot prevent illegal implicit flows arising from control flow paths not taken at run time.

Various general security models [10, 21, 7] have been proposed to incorporate dynamic labeling. Unlike noninterference, these models define what it means for a system to be secure according to a certain relabeling policy, which may allow downgrading labels.

Using static program analysis to check information flow was first proposed by Denning and Denning [5]; later work phrased the analysis as type checking (e.g., [16]). Noninterference was later developed as a more semantic characterization of security [8], followed by many extensions. Volpano, Smith and Irvine [23] first showed that type systems can be used to enforce noninterference, and proved a version of noninterference theorem for a simple imperative language, starting a line of research pursuing the noninterference result for more expressive security-typed languages [9, 27, 17, 3]. A more complete survey of language-based information-flow techniques can be found in [19, 29].

The Jif language [13, 15] extends Java with a type system for analyzing information flow, and aims to be a practical language for developing secure applications. However, there is not yet a noninterference proof for the type system of Jif, because of its complexity.

Banerjee and Naumann [3] proved a noninterference result for a Java-like language with simple access control primitives. Unlike in λ_{DSec}, run-time access control in this language is separate from the static label mechanism. In their language, the label of a method result may depend in limited ways on the (implicit) security state of its caller; however, it does not seem to be possible in the language to control the flow of information from an I/O channel or file based on permissions discovered at run time.

Concurrent to our work, Tse and Zdancewic proved a noninterference result for a security-typed lambda calculus (λ_{RP}) with run-time principals [22], which can be used to construct dynamic labels. However, λ_{RP} does not support references or existential types, which makes it unable to represent dynamic security policies that may be changed at run time, such as file permissions. In addition, support for references makes λ_{DSec} more powerful than λ_{RP} computationally.

6. Conclusions

This paper formalizes computation and static checking of dynamic labels in the type system of a core language λ_{DSec} and proves a noninterference result: well-typed programs have the noninterference property. The language λ_{DSec} is the first language supporting general dynamic labels whose type system provably enforces noninterference.

Acknowledgements

The authors would like to thank Greg Morrisett, Steve Zdancewic and Amal Ahmed for their insightful suggestions. Steve Chong, Nate Nystrom, and Michael Clarkson also helped improve the presentation of this work.

References

[1] Johan Agat. Transforming out timing leaks. In *Proc. 27th ACM Symp. on Principles of Programming Languages (POPL)*, pages 40–53, Boston, MA, January 2000.

[2] Anindya Banerjee and David A. Naumann. Secure information flow and pointer confinement in a Java-like language. In *IEEE Computer Security Foundations Workshop (CSFW)*, June 2002.

[3] Anindya Banerjee and David A. Naumann. Using access control for secure information flow in a java-like language. In *Proc. 16th IEEE Computer Security Foundations Workshop*, pages 155–169, June 2003.

[4] Dorothy E. Denning. *Cryptography and Data Security*. Addison-Wesley, Reading, Massachusetts, 1982.

[5] Dorothy E. Denning and Peter J. Denning. Certification of programs for secure information flow. *Comm. of the ACM*, 20(7):504–513, July 1977.

[6] Department of Defense. *Department of Defense Trusted Computer System Evaluation Criteria*, DOD 5200.28-STD (The Orange Book) edition, December 1985.

[7] Simon Foley, Li Gong, and Xiaolei Qian. A security model of dynamic labeling providing a tiered approach to verification. In *IEEE Symposium on Security and Privacy*, pages 142–154, Oakland, CA, 1996. IEEE Computer Society Press.

[8] Joseph A. Goguen and Jose Meseguer. Security policies and security models. In *Proc. IEEE Symposium on Security and Privacy*, pages 11–20, April 1982.

[9] Nevin Heintze and Jon G. Riecke. The SLam calculus: Programming with secrecy and integrity. In *Proc. 25th ACM Symp. on Principles of Programming Languages (POPL)*, pages 365–377, San Diego, California, January 1998.

[10] John McLean. The algebra of security. In *IEEE Symposium on Security and Privacy*, pages 2–7, Oakland, California, 1988.

[11] Catherine Meadows. Policies for dynamic upgrading. In *Database Security, IV: Status and Prospects*, pages 241–250. North Holland, 1991.

[12] John C. Mitchell. *Foundations for Programming Languages*. The MIT Press, Cambridge, Massachusetts, 1996.

[13] Andrew C. Myers. JFlow: Practical mostly-static information flow control. In *Proc. 26th ACM Symp. on Principles of Programming Languages (POPL)*, pages 228–241, San Antonio, TX, January 1999.

[14] Andrew C. Myers and Barbara Liskov. A decentralized model for information flow control. In *Proc. 17th ACM Symp. on Operating System Principles (SOSP)*, pages 129–142, Saint-Malo, France, 1997.

[15] Andrew C. Myers, Lantian Zheng, Steve Zdancewic, Stephen Chong, and Nathaniel Nystrom. Jif: Java information flow. Software release. Located at http://www.cs.cornell.edu/jif, July 2001–2003.

[16] Jens Palsberg and Peter Ørbæk. Trust in the λ-calculus. In *Proc. 2nd International Symposium on Static Analysis*, number 983 in Lecture Notes in Computer Science, pages 314–329. Springer, September 1995.

[17] François Pottier and Vincent Simonet. Information flow inference for ML. In *Proc. 29th ACM Symp. on Principles of Programming Languages (POPL)*, pages 319–330, 2002.

[18] Andrei Sabelfeld and Heiko Mantel. Static confidentiality enforcement for distributed programs. In *Proceedings of the 9th International Static Analysis Symposium*, volume 2477 of *LNCS*, Madrid, Spain, September 2002. Springer-Verlag.

[19] Andrei Sabelfeld and Andrew Myers. Language-based information-flow security. *IEEE Journal on Selected Areas in Communications*, 21(1):5–19, January 2003.

[20] Ravi S. Sandhu and Sushil Jajodia. Honest databases that can keep secrets. In *Proceedings of the 14th National Computer Security Conference*, Washington, DC, 1991.

[21] Ian Sutherland, Stanley Perlo, and Rammohan Varadarajan. Deducibility security with dynamic level assignments. In *Proc. 2nd IEEE Computer Security Foundations Workshop*, Franconia, NH, June 1989.

[22] Stephen Tse and Steve Zdancewic. Run-time principals in information-flow type systems. In *IEEE Symposium on Security and Privacy*, Oakland, CA, May 2004.

[23] Dennis Volpano, Geoffrey Smith, and Cynthia Irvine. A sound type system for secure flow analysis. *Journal of Computer Security*, 4(3):167–187, 1996.

[24] Clark Weissman. Security controls in the ADEPT-50 time-sharing system. In *AFIPS Conference Proceedings*, volume 35, pages 119–133, 1969.

[25] John P. L. Woodward. Exploiting the dual nature of sensitivity labels. In *IEEE Symposium on Security and Privacy*, pages 23–30, Oakland, California, 1987.

[26] Hongwei Xi and Frank Pfenning. Dependent types in practical programming. In *Proc. 26th ACM Symp. on Principles of Programming Languages (POPL)*, pages 214–227, San Antonio, TX, January 1999.

[27] Steve Zdancewic and Andrew C. Myers. Secure information flow via linear continuations. *Higher Order and Symbolic Computation*, 15(2–3):209–234, September 2002.

[28] Steve Zdancewic and Andrew C. Myers. Observational determinism for concurrent program security. In *Proc. 16th IEEE Computer Security Foundations Workshop*, pages 29–43, Pacific Grove, California, June 2003.

[29] Lantian Zheng and Andrew C. Myers. Dynamic security labels and noninterference. Technical Report 2004–1924, Cornell University Computing and Information Science, 2004.

FORMAL ANALYSIS OF A FAIR PAYMENT PROTOCOL

Jan Cederquist and Muhammad Torabi Dashti
CWI, Postbus 94079, 1090 GB Amsterdam, The Netherlands
{Cederqui,Dashti}@cwi.nl

Abstract   We formally specify a payment protocol described in [Vogt et al., 2001].
This protocol is intended for fair exchange of time-sensitive data. Here
the μCRL language is used to formalize the protocol. Fair exchange
properties are expressed in the regular alternation-free μ-calculus. These
properties are then verified using the finite state model checker from
the CADP toolset. Proving fairness without resilient communication
channels is impossible. We use the Dolev-Yao intruder, but since the
conventional Dolev-Yao intruder violates this assumption, it is forced to
comply to the resilient communication channel assumption.

1.   Introduction

A fair exchange protocol aims at exchanging items in a *fair* manner.
Informally, fair means that all involved parties receive a desired item in
exchange for their own, or neither of them does so. It has been shown
that fair exchange is impossible without a trusted third party [Pagnia
and Gärtner, 1999]. A protocol for fair exchange of money for an item
using customer's smart card as a trusted party is described in [Vogt et al.,
2001]. This protocol considers time-sensitive items and is adapted for
wireless and mobile applications which lack a reliable communication
channel. Here a version of that protocol is considered. We describe,
in contrast to [Vogt et al., 2001], the exact contents of all messages.
The protocol is formally specified and the fairness properties are verified
using a finite-state model checker.

In comparison to other security issues, such as secrecy and authenticity, fairness has not been studied formally so intensively. There are however some notable exceptions. [Shmatikov and Mitchell, 2002] use the
finite state model checker Murφ to analyze fair exchange and contract
signing protocols. They use an external intruder, based on the Dolev-
Yao intruder, that collaborates with one of the participants to model the

malicious participant. Liveness can in general not be expressed in the Murφ language. Most fair-exchange properties can however be expressed as safety properties. But this is not the case with termination (of protocol). Termination thus relies on other arguments than a verification using Murφ. [Kremer and Raskin, 2001] use a game based approach for verifying non-repudiation and fair exchange. They use *alternating transition systems* (ATS) to model protocols and *alternating temporal logic* (ATL) to express the requirements. The method is automated using the model checker Mocha. They have no explicit intruder. Instead different versions of players are considered; honest and arbitrary. ATL then offers very neat ways of expressing all desired requirements, including liveness under fairness constraints. In ATS all players follow predetermined finite sequences of steps, including intruders (arbitrary versions of players). However, describing an intruder in such a way is not practical for large protocols. In [Schneider, 1998] a non-repudiation protocol is modeled using CSP, and proofs are generated by hand. Belief logic is used to formalize a protocol in [Zhou and Gollmann, 1998] and it is discussed what may be needed for the verification of non-repudiation protocols. In [Bella and Paulson, 2001] the theorem prover Isabelle is used to model a non-repudiation protocol by an inductive definition and to prove some desired properties.

In our work we formally specify a payment protocol in the process algebraic language μCRL [Groote and Ponse, 1995]. The idea of this protocol comes from [Vogt et al., 2001], but there are some differences (see section 6). Fairness properties for this protocol are formulated in the regular alternation-free μ-calculus [Mateescu, 2000] and verified using the model checker EVALUATOR 3.0 [Mateescu, 2000] from the CADP tool set [Fernandez et al., 1996].

Our formalization in μCRL contains a Dolev-Yao intruder [Dolev and Yao, 1983]. The intruder is not separated from malicious participants. Instead, we consider different versions of participants, honest and malicious, where a malicious participant is an intruder that has access to the participant's private key. Some fairness properties are liveness properties and to prove liveness properties resilient communication channels are needed (i.e. sent messages will eventually be delivered). Since the Dolev-Yao intruder has complete control over network, some cooperation from the intruder is needed when verifying liveness properties. This cooperation is obtained using fairness constraints on the labelled transition system generated from the protocol specification in μCRL.

The rest of the paper is organized as follows. In section 2 we give an overview of properties for fair exchange protocols. The fair exchange protocol we investigate is described in section 3. In section 4 the formal analysis is described. Here the intruder model is presented and all properties verified using the model checker are given. Included in section 4 is also a brief description of some optimization techniques used to generate the state spaces. In section 5 the protocol is used in a practical context. Some concluding remarks are given in section 6.

Due to space constraints, most of our formalization of the protocol in μCRL cannot be presented in this paper. However, the complete formalization is given in [Cederquist and Dashti, 2004].

2. Fair Exchange Protocols

We assume two parties A and B. When the protocol starts, both parties have an item and they want to exchange items.

According to [Asokan, 1998], a fair exchange protocol is a protocol satisfying *effectiveness, fairness, timeliness* and *non-repudiability*. Effectiveness means that if both parties behave according to the protocol and none of them want to abort during the protocol round, then the protocol will terminate in a state where A has B's item and vice versa. An exchange protocol is called fair if, when it has terminated, either A has received B's item and B has received A's item, or none of the parties have lost their items. Timeliness means that the protocol will terminate for all parties (that behave according to the protocol) and after the termination point the degree of achieved fairness will not change. Non-repudiability is, in general, not considered as a primary requirement for fair exchange protocols, and it is omitted here.

[Asokan, 1998] distinguishes between *strong* and *weak* fairness. Strong fairness is the fairness described above. Weak fairness means that either strong fairness is achieved, or it is possible for a participant to prove to an outside party that an unfair situation has occurred. [Pagnia et al., 2003] extend Asokan's definitions by considering the parties' willingness to cooperate and compensation for suffered disadvantage.

3. Protocol Description

Here we describe the protocol which is to be analyzed in section 4. The protocol aims at fair exchange of time-sensitive data for some amount of money, between a customer (C) and a vendor (V). The exchange uses a bank (B) as a trusted online payment system and a trusted smartcard (S) attached to C. S is a tamper-proof hardware. The identity of S is however not necessarily known by V. Moreover, C is assumed to have a secure communication channel with S. When the protocol starts, V has an item m and a description $h(m)$ of m is known publicly. C wants to buy m for the amount a. Note that the item m is assumed to be confidential and should not be revealed to untrusted parties unless they pay for it. Below we describe the intended scenarios of the protocol, when all participants are honest.

In the protocol description, $pay(C, V, a)$ means that C shall pay the amount a to V, $(m)_X$ is the notation for the message m signed by X (using X's private key), and $\{m\}_X$ is the notation for m encrypted for X (using X's public key). It is assumed that m comes along with $(m)_X$ and can be extracted by anyone. For an encrypted message $\{m\}_X$ only X can extract m. A publicly known hash function h is used for describing items and payments. T and F are two symbols. By convention we use T for positive responses and F for negative.

The main scenario (when none of the participants want to abort the protocol) is described as follows:

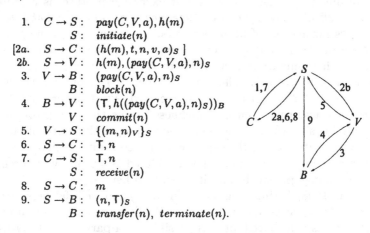

1.	$C \to S$:	$pay(C, V, a), h(m)$
	S :	$initiate(n)$
[2a.	$S \to C$:	$(h(m), t, n, v, a)_S$]
2b.	$S \to V$:	$h(m), (pay(C, V, a), n)_S$
3.	$V \to B$:	$(pay(C, V, a), n)_S$
	B :	$block(n)$
4.	$B \to V$:	$(T, h((pay(C, V, a), n)_S))_B$
	V :	$commit(n)$
5.	$V \to S$:	$\{(m, n)_V\}_S$
6.	$S \to C$:	T, n
7.	$C \to S$:	T, n
	S :	$receive(n)$
8.	$S \to C$:	m
9.	$S \to B$:	$(n, T)_S$
	B :	$transfer(n),\ terminate(n).$

(1) C sends a query to S for buying item m from V for amount a. On this request, S generates a fresh nonce n. In this way, a protocol session possesses a unique nonce. Implicitly, S also notes the time t. (2a) S sends the nonce associated to the request and time to C. Later on, in step 6, when S asks C if the item is still interesting, it just needs to send the nonce. This simplifies the formalization. The time information is signed by S to prevent C from changing it. (We abstract away from this step in the formalization.) (2b) S signs and forwards the request together with the nonce to V. Since S is trusted, this message will be sent only upon a request from C. (3) If V wants to sell m to C for price a, it forwards the request to B. B notices the signature of S, checks whether the nonce n is fresh and that C has the amount a in its account. If this is the case, the money is blocked on C's account. (4) B notifies V that a transfer of amount a from C's account to V's account is possible. After this step V knows S is trusted. (5) V informs S that C

can buy m for the amount a (n refers to a). (6) S validates the received item by comparing it with $h(m)$ and asks if C is still interested in the item. (7) If C still wants the item, it answers T. (8) S sends the item m to C. (9) S asks B to transfer the money, that was blocked on C's account, to V's account. On this request B performs the transaction.

(The "abstract" actions $initiate(n)$, $block(n)$, $receive(n)$, $transfer(n)$ and $terminate(n)$ are explained with more details in section 4.4, and so are the actions $unblock(n)$ and $cancel(n)$ below.)

There are some alternative scenarios of the protocol. When B receives a payment request, the nonce n may not be fresh or C may not have the required amount of money on its account:

$$
\begin{array}{lll}
4^1. & B \to V: & (\mathsf{F}, h((pay(C,V,a),n)_S))_B \\
5^1. & V \to S: & (n)_V \\
6^1. & S \to C: & \mathsf{F}, n \\
7^1. & S \to B: & (n, \mathsf{F})_S \\
& B: & unblock(n),\ terminate(n).
\end{array}
$$

(7^1) S asks B to unblock money at C's account. If the money was blocked earlier, with the same nonce, B unblocks it. If V does not want to sell m to C for the amount a, step 5^1 follows immediately after step $2b$.

After step 2 and before step 6 (6^1), C has the possibility to cancel the payment. This prevents V from blocking C's money without sending the item to S:

$$
\begin{array}{lll}
& C: & cancel(n) \\
6^2. & C \to S: & n \\
7^2. & S \to B: & (n, \mathsf{F})_S \\
8^2. & S \to V: & (\mathsf{F}, n)_S \\
& B: & unblock(n),\ terminate(n).
\end{array}
$$

S erases the session information after sending $unblock$ (or $transfer$) commands to B, and does not consider any message with a nonce from completed sessions.

In exchange of items whose value may change during time, the protocol provides a possibility for C to reject items in case of (intentional) delay in delivery. So, C can answer F after step 6:

$$
\begin{array}{lll}
7^3. & C \to S: & \mathsf{F}, n \\
8^3. & S \to B: & (n, \mathsf{F})_S \\
& B: & unblock(n),\ terminate(n).
\end{array}
$$

After step 2b, S can perform a *timeout*:

$$
\begin{array}{lll}
& S: & timeout \\
3^4. & S \to C: & \mathsf{F}, n \\
4^4. & S \to V: & (\mathsf{F}, n)_S \\
5^4. & S \to B: & (n, \mathsf{F})_S \\
& B: & unblock(n),\ terminate(n).
\end{array}
$$

The timeout forces a time limit on the steps 2b–7, it prevents in particular C from waiting arbitrarily before answering in step 7. Concerning timeout, our description is non-deterministic. But it can also be assumed that S reads the start time t, that was sent to C in step 2a, and that it has a limit Δt hard coded or provided by V. If the current time is greater than $t + \Delta t$, it generates a timeout.

4.   Formal Analysis

The formalization of the protocol described in section 3 is carried out in μCRL [Groote and Ponse, 1995]. The μCRL toolset includes an automatic state space (labelled transition systems) generator and symbolic state space reduction tools. The properties effectiveness, timeliness and fairness are expressed in the regular alternation-free μ-calculus [Mateescu, 2000]. The model checker EVALUATOR 3.0 [Mateescu, 2000] from the CADP tool set [Fernandez et al., 1996] is then used to verify these properties (the formulas 1 to 11, in the sections 4.4 to 4.7).

For fair exchange protocols, beside protection from external intruders, the participants need to be protected from each other. In our formal model(s), we have three cases: (i) both C and V behave according to the protocol, (ii) C is malicious (C is the attacker) and (iii) V is malicious (V is the attacker). In the cases (ii) and (iii) all messages go via the attacker, with exception of the messages between C and S, which are sent over a secure link. When verifying effectiveness, case (i) is considered. All other properties are verified for the cases (ii) and (iii).

4.1   The μCRL specification language

Here we briefly describe the symbols used in the formalization below. For a complete description of the syntax and semantics of μCRL we refer to [Groote and Ponse, 1995].

The symbols . and + are used for the sequential and alternative composition operator, respectively. The operator $\sum_{d \in D} P(d)$ behaves like $P(d_1) + P(d_2) + \cdots$. The process expression **if** b **then** p **else** q, where b is a term of sort **bool** and, p and q are processes, behaves like p if b is true, and like q if b is false. Finally, the constant δ expresses that, from now on, no action can be performed.

The notations $send(a, x, b)$ and $recv(a, x, b)$ are used for the actions "A sends message x to B" and "B receives message x from A", respectively. In our model, $send$ and $recv$ actions are synchronized, i.e. A can only perform $send(a, x, b)$ if B at the same time performs $recv(a, x, b)$ and vice versa. This synchronization point is denoted $com(a, x, b)$ (in section 3, the notation $A \rightarrow B : x$ was used for that).

4.2   Regular Alternation-free μ-calculus

The regular alternation-free μ-calculus is used here to formulate properties of (states in) labelled transition systems (see the sections 4.4–4.7). It is a fragment of μ-calculus that can be efficiently checked. Here we just briefly describe what is needed for expressing the fairness properties of the protocol we investigate. For a complete description of the syntax and semantics we refer to [Mateescu, 2000]. The regular alternation-free μ-calculus is built up from three types of formulas: *action formulas, regular formulas* and *state formulas*. We use '.', '∨' and '*' for concatenation, choice and transitive-reflexive closure, respectively, for regular formulas. $\mathcal{F}$ and $\mathcal{T}$ are used in both action formulas and state formulas. In action formulas they represent *no action* and *any action*, respectively. The meaning of $\mathcal{F}$ and $\mathcal{T}$ in state formulas are the empty set and the entire state space, respectively. The operators $\langle \cdots \rangle$ and $[\cdots]$ have their usual meaning ($\Diamond$ and $\Box$ in modal logics). Finally, μ is the minimal fixed point operator.

4.3   Intruder Models

We consider the Dolev-Yao intruder [Dolev and Yao, 1983]. It can remember all messages that have been transmitted over network. It can decrypt and sign messages, if it knows the corresponding key. It can compose new messages from its knowledge. It can also remove or delay messages in favour of others being communicated.

Below we define two intruder models in μCRL, I and I'. Both of them are equivalent to the Dolev-Yao intruder, but they behave differently under fairness constraints[1]. I is used when verifying safety properties and I' when verifying liveness properties. The reason for using both of them is that I is not suitable for liveness properties, and I' is expensive to use when generating state spaces (see section 4.8).

The intruder I acts as customer (or vendor), intruder and network. All messages (x) are sent to I explicitly. I decomposes (*decomp*) the messages and adds the pieces to its knowledge (X). I then uses its knowledge to synthesize (*synth*) new messages. How well the decomposition and the synthesis work depend on what private keys the intruder knows (abilities to sign and decrypt messages), *decomp* and *synth* are thus parameterized over users whose private keys are known. (For effi-

---

[1]We are using two notions of fairness; fairness of a protocol and fairness constraints of a labelled transition system. The second one is used to describe "fair" execution traces. In our case, a trace is fair when no possibilities are excluded forever. Then only fair execution traces are considered when proving the desired (liveness) property. To avoid confusion, we refer to these two notions as "fairness" and "fairness constraints".

ciency reasons the union $\bigcup$ also depends on known private keys.)

$$
\begin{aligned}
I(X) = (\ &\textstyle\sum_{p\in Agent, x\in Message} \\
&recv(p, x, i).I(X \textstyle\bigcup_i decomp_i(x)) + \\
&\textbf{if } synth_i(x, X) \\
&\textbf{then } send(i, x, p).I(X) \\
&\textbf{else } \delta\ ) + \\
(\ &\textstyle\sum_{m\in Item} \\
&\textbf{if } synth_i(m, X) \\
&\textbf{then } got\text{--}hold\text{--}of(m).I(X) \\
&\textbf{else } \delta\ )
\end{aligned}
$$

In order to prove liveness properties, resilient communication channels are assumed. In fact, without this assumption fair exchange is not possible, because then the attacker can simply choose to never send the item to one of the participants. In the presence of an intruder, resilient communication channels are obtained by imposing fairness constraints on the labelled transition system generated from the protocol specification. These fairness constraints are expressed directly in regular μ-calculus formulas (see property 7 in section 4.6). The use of fairness constraints makes the model checker "skip circuits" and, in particular, it eventually forces the intruder to try to synthesize and send messages whenever there is a recipient. Some amount of cooperation from the intruder is usually needed in order to prove liveness properties. But, the fact that the intruder I does not forget anything and its abilities to construct messages itself together with fairness constraints can make "too many" liveness properties true. In fact, an erroneous protocol that does not terminate without intruder, may terminate with the intruder I and fairness constraints.

The second intruder I' can also synthesize new messages from its knowledge, but it is not forced to. However, using fairness constraints, it is forced to comply to the resilient communication channel assumption. It is parameterized over a set of "resilient links" and all messages sent over these links should eventually be delivered. In our case the resilient link is the link between S and B. The corresponding messages are represented by the set Z. As I, I' gathers a set X of knowledge by intercepting all communications. But, it can explicitly forget pieces from this knowledge. The intruder uses a separate buffer Y of messages transmitted over the resilient links. When fairness constraints are used, the intruder is forced to eventually send all messages from this buffer. The resilient channel assumption will thus be preserved. Since I' can forget, it does not have to generate new messages. However, this does not restrict the intruder's power in general, as it has the choice of keeping its knowledge as well.

$$I'(X, Y) = (\sum_{p \in Agent, x \in Message}$$
$$recv(p, x, i).$$
$$\text{if } x \in Z$$
$$\text{then } I'(decomp_i(x) \bigcup_i X, insert(x, Y))$$
$$\text{else } I'(decomp_i(x) \bigcup_i X, Y)) +$$
$$(\sum_{x \in Message}$$
$$\text{if } x \in X$$
$$\text{then } I'(X \setminus \{x\}, Y)$$
$$\text{else } \delta) +$$
$$(\sum_{x \in Message, p \in Agent}$$
$$\text{if } x \in Y \vee synth_i(x, X)$$
$$\text{then } send(i, x, p).I'(X, remove(x, Y))$$
$$\text{else } \delta)$$

4.4   Abstract Actions

The CADP toolset [Fernandez et al., 1996] that we use to analyze the labelled transition system generated from a μCRL specification does not allow variables in action parameters, in regular μ-calculus formulas. So, properties containing variables should actually be checked for each instance. To avoid this, the protocol is extended with abstract actions ($initiate(n)$, $block(n)$, $receive(n)$, $transfer(n)$,...) that can be used instead of actions containing more variables. In fact, each protocol session is associated to a nonce, so abstract actions (which only contain nonces) are enough for expressing most interesting properties of the protocol. Besides, they highlight implicit steps in the protocol and render more readable properties.

For termination, the "abstract" action $terminate(n)$ in B (where n is a nonce) is used, instead of actual termination points for the users (C and V). This action is used because it is convenient to abstract away from messages to the users saying that a protocol round is terminated. This abstraction is safe since, if such messages had been used, the resilient communication channel assumption would have guaranteed their delivery. Thus $terminate(n)$ implies that the users terminate. Also note, the protocol may continue after $terminate(n)$ with another protocol round, using another (fresh) nonce.

The meaning of some of the other abstract actions need to be uniquely defined. We start with $block(n)$. Without loss of generality we can assume that $block(n)$ happens at the same time as (or immediately after) B receives $(pay(C, V, a), n)_S$. So, $block(n)$ can be defined as *the amount a is blocked* (for nonce n). The fact that a indeed is the correct amount follows from

$$[T^*.com(s, (h(m), (pay(C, V, a_1), n)_S), i).$$
$$T^*.com(i, (pay(C, V, a_2), n)_S, b)]\mathcal{F}, \tag{1}$$

where a_1 and a_2 are different amounts, and i is either c or v, depending on who is malicious. Property 1 thus says that the intruder cannot change the amount that C is willing to pay. We define *transfer*(n) and *unblock*(n) to mean that the amount, which was blocked in *block*(n), is transfered and unblocked, respectively. Now we turn to *receive*(n). It can be assumed that *receive*(n) happens at the same time as S sends an item m to C. The fact that this item is the correct item (the item C ordered) follows from

$$[T^*.com(c, (pay(C, V, a), h(m_1)), s).initiate(n).$$
$$T^*.receive(n).com(s, m_2, c)]\mathcal{F}, \tag{2}$$

where m_1 and m_2 are different items.

A malicious customer could possibly get hold of an item m by other means than from S in action *com*(s, m, c). To show that this is not the case, we verify

$$[(\neg com(s, m, c))^*.got{-}hold{-}of(m)]\mathcal{F}, \tag{3}$$

where *got–hold–of*(m) is an abstract action that occur if the malicious customer manages to synthesize the item m from gained knowledge (see definition of intruder I, section 4.3).

4.5   Effectiveness

For effectiveness all participants are assumed to be honest and none of them want to abort the protocol. First, termination is inevitable

$$[T^*.initiate(n)]\mu X(\langle T \rangle T \wedge [\neg terminate(n)]X), \tag{4}$$

for an arbitrary nonce n. Second, if S does not timeout, V does not say that C cannot buy the item, C does not answer $\mathcal{F}$ when S asks if the item is still valuable, and C does not cancel the payment, then the money will be transfered to V upon termination:

$$[(\neg(timeout \vee com(v, (n)_v, s) \vee com(c, (\mathcal{F}, n), s) \vee cancel(n) \vee$$
$$transfer(n)))^*.terminate(n)]\mathcal{F}. \tag{5}$$

Under the same conditions, the item will also be received:

$$[(\neg(timeout \vee com(v, (n)_v, s) \vee com(c, (\mathcal{F}, n), s) \vee cancel(n) \vee$$
$$receive(n)))^*.terminate(n)]\mathcal{F}. \tag{6}$$

4.6   Timeliness

First, we verify that each fair trace eventually reaches $terminate(n)$. Whenever $terminate(n)$ has not occurred, there is a path leading to $terminate(n)$:

$$[\mathcal{T}^*.initiate(n).(\neg terminate(n))^*]\langle \mathcal{T}^*.terminate(n)\rangle \mathcal{T}. \qquad (7)$$

Second, the degree of fairness does not change after termination:

$$[\mathcal{T}^*.terminate(n).\mathcal{T}^*. \\ (receive(n) \vee block(n) \vee unblock(n) \vee transfer(n))]\mathcal{F}. \qquad (8)$$

4.7   Fairness[2]

For the properties that guarantee fairness it is important that the protocol terminates, which is part of timeliness, section 4.6.

Here we split up the notion of fairness (introduced in section 2) into fairness for C and V individually. We say that the protocol is fair for C if, whenever C pays for an item, C will receive it (V potentially being malicious). Fairness for V is defined correspondingly. Fairness for C is thus formalized as

$$[(\neg receive(n))^*.transfer(n).(\neg receive(n))^*.terminate(n)]\mathcal{F}. \qquad (9)$$

From C's point of view it is also important that if money for an item is blocked and C does not receive the item, the block will be removed. The following property may thus also be considered as fairness for C:

$$[\mathcal{T}^*.block(n).(\neg(receive(n) \vee unblock(n)))^*.terminate(n)]\mathcal{F}. \qquad (10)$$

Fairness for V means that if an item (corresponding to the nonce n) is received, money will be transfered:

$$[(\neg transfer(n))^*.receive(n).(\neg transfer(n))^*.terminate(n)]\mathcal{F}. \qquad (11)$$

4.8   Model Checking Details

One of the major obstacles during this work was state space explosion. The case when the customer is malicious turned out to be most difficult to generate. Our experiments show that this is mainly due to different knowledges of the intruder, gathered during different execution traces. A

---

[2]The notion of fairness we are proving corresponds to F_5 in the hierarchy of fairness guarantees described in [Pagnia et al., 2003].

common abstraction technique in such situations is to make the knowledge of the intruder more uniform. We do that explicitly by, at the end of a protocol round, giving the intruder information about traces that were not taken. More traces will now end up in same states, with a smaller state space as result. This extra information for the intruder should be chosen carefully though to avoid "false attacks". For safety properties this technique is sound, since the intruder just becomes more powerful. This technique may however make "too many" liveness properties true. When assuming fairness constraints, an intruder with more knowledge provides more possibilities to reach a state. Instead, when generating the state space for proving liveness properties, we explicitly put a δ immediately after the action we want always to be reached. In this way, large parts of the state space will never be generated. In addition to these two methods, all actions except for the ones used in the properties are "hidden" and symbolic reduction techniques from the μCRL toolset (see [Blom et al., 2001] for a description of these techniques) are applied to reduce the state spaces.

Using the techniques described above we could generate the state spaces and prove the safety properties, with 3 nonces and 2 different items (also 1 nonce, 2 different items with 2 possible different prices), in the malicious customer and malicious vendor cases. For liveness properties (termination in case of malicious customer and vendor), it was impossible to consider concurrent sessions. The state spaces were generated for 2 items and 2 prices.

5.   Practical Considerations

It is usually not possible for a smart card to receive large chunks of data, and store or process them. This limitation can cause practical problems when the item is some large software, for instance, and the smart card should store and validate it. On the other hand, if the item validation phase is removed, it is not clear how the vendor is prevented from sending fake items. Here we suggest employing a trusted offline Item Validation Party (IVP) that guarantees correspondence between an encrypted item and the description of the item. The protocol in section 3 is modified by adding two messages at the beginning:

$$0a. \quad C \to V : \quad h(m)$$
$$0b. \quad V \to C : \quad \{m\}_{pk}, (h(m), h(\{m\}_{pk}), pk)_{IVP}.$$

In this scenario it is assumed that V generates key pairs (pk, sk) for encryption and decryption of items. There is also an IVP which validate encryptions offline. When C asks for an item with description $h(m)$, it will receive m encrypted with pk along with a certificate from IVP. In this way, C can validate the item before decrypting it. Then C buys the decryption key sk from V using the protocol (in section 3), where the public key pk replaces the description of the item $h(m)$ (in message 1) and S checks that sk and pk match.

Assuming perfect cryptography and that the key pairs (pk,sk) are used only once, makes it safe to abstract away from the two initial messages $0a$ and $0b$. Consequently, correctness of this protocol follows from correctness of the protocol described in section 3, which was treated formally.

6. Conclusion

We have formally specified a payment protocol and verified its fairness properties. The idea of the protocol comes from [Vogt et al., 2001], but there are some differences. A version of the protocol that has an online payment system (bank) is considered. We implement revocable payments using *block*, *unblock* and *transfer* (as described in section 3). To protect the vendor from the customer being passive, the smartcard can *timeout* (in fact, without *timeout* property 7 does not hold). We have also relaxed the assumptions on the communication links (eavesdropping, replay and forging of messages is possible in our model).

We have implemented an intruder that, for safety properties, is equivalent to the Dolev-Yao intruder (which is the most powerful intruder, see [Cervesato, 2001]). Our intruder is particularly suitable for verifying liveness properties, since it does not violate the resilient communication channel assumption under fairness constraints. It can be used in general purpose specification languages like μCRL.

Acknowledgments

We are grateful to the anonymous referees for their constructive and detailed comments. We would also like to thank Stefan Blom, Wan Fokkink, Jaco van de Pol and Miguel Valero for discussions and comments on earlier versions of this paper.

The first author was supported by an ERCIM Fellowship.

References

[Asokan, 1998] Asokan, N. (1998). *Fairness in electronic commerce*. PhD thesis, University of Waterloo.

[Bella and Paulson, 2001] Bella, G. and Paulson, L. C. (2001). Mechanical proofs about a non-repudiation protocol. In Boulton, R. J. and Jackson, P. B., editors, *Theorem Proving in Higher Order Logics, 14th International Conference, TPHOLs 2001*, volume 2152 of *LNCS*, pages 91–104. Springer-Verlag.

[Blom et al., 2001] Blom, S., Fokkink, W., Groote, J. F., van Langevelde, I., Lisser, B., and van de Pol, J. (2001). μCRL: A toolset for analysing algebraic specifications. In *Proceedings of the 13th International Conference on Computer Aided Verification*, volume 2102 of *LNCS*, pages 250–254. Springer-Verlag.

[Cederquist and Dashti, 2004] Cederquist, J. and Dashti, M. (2004). Formal analysis of a fair payment protocol. Technical Report SEN-R0410, Centrum voor Wiskunde en Informatica, Amsterdam, The Netherlands.

[Cervesato, 2001] Cervesato, I. (2001). The Dolev-Yao Intruder is the Most Powerful Attacker. In Halpern, J., editor, *16th Annual Symposium on Logic in Computer Science — LICS'01*, Boston, MA. IEEE Computer Society Press.

[Dolev and Yao, 1983] Dolev, D. and Yao, A. C. (1983). On the security of public key protocols. *IEEE Transactions on Information Theory*, IT-29(2):198–208.

[Fernandez et al., 1996] Fernandez, J.-C., Garavel, H., Kerbrat, A., Mateescu, R., Mounier, L., and Sighireanu, M. (1996). CADP: A protocol validation and verification toolbox. In Alur, R. and Henzinger, T. A., editors, *Proceedings of the 8th Conference on Computer-Aided Verification*, volume 1102 of *LNCS*, pages 437–440. Springer-Verlag.

[Groote and Ponse, 1995] Groote, J. and Ponse, A. (1995). The syntax and semantics of μCRL. In Ponse, A., Verhoef, C., and van Vlijmen, S. F. M., editors, *Algebra of Communicating Processes '94*, Workshops in Computing Series, pages 26–62. Springer-Verlag.

[Kremer and Raskin, 2001] Kremer, S. and Raskin, J. (2001). A game-based verification of non-repudiation and fair exchange protocols. In Larsen, K. and Nielsen, M., editors, *Proceedings of the 12th International Conference on Concurrency Theory*, volume 2154 of *LNCS*, pages 551–565. Springer-Verlag.

[Mateescu, 2000] Mateescu, R. (2000). Efficient diagnostic generation for boolean equation systems. In *Proceedings of 6th International Conference on Tools and Algorithms for the Construction and Analysis of Systems TACAS'2000*, volume 1785 of *LNCS*, pages 251–265. Springer-Verlag.

[Pagnia and Gärtner, 1999] Pagnia, H. and Gärtner, F. C. (1999). On the impossibility of fair exchange without a trused third party. Technical Report TUD-BS-1999-02, Department of Computer Science, Darmstadt University of Technology.

[Pagnia et al., 2003] Pagnia, H., Vogt, H., and Gärtner, F. C. (2003). Fair exchange. *The Computer Journal*, 46(1):55–7.

[Schneider, 1998] Schneider, S. (1998). Formal analysis of a non-repudiation protocol. In *Proceedings of The 11th Computer Security Foundations Workshop*, pages 54–65. IEEE Computer Society Press.

[Shmatikov and Mitchell, 2002] Shmatikov, V. and Mitchell, J. C. (2002). Finite-state analysis of two contract signing protocols. *Theoretical Computer Sciene*, 283(2):419–450.

[Vogt et al., 2001] Vogt, H., Pagnia, H., and Gärtner, F. C. (2001). Using smart cards for fair exchange. In *Electronic Commerce – WELCOM 2001*, volume 2232 of *LNCS*, pages 101–113. Springer-Verlag.

[Zhou and Gollmann, 1998] Zhou, J. and Gollmann, D. (1998). Towards verification of non-repudiation protocols. In *International Refinement Workshop and Formal Methods Pacific '98: Proceedings of IRW/FMP '98, Discrete Mathematics and Theoretical Computer Science Series*, pages 370–380. Springer-Verlag.

PATTERN-MATCHING SPI-CALCULUS*

Christian Haack
DePaul University

Alan Jeffrey
Bell Labs, Lucent Technologies
and DePaul University

Abstract   Cryptographic protocols often make use of nested cryptographic primitives, for example signed message digests, or encrypted signed messages. Gordon and Jeffrey's prior work on types for authenticity did not allow for such nested cryptography. In this work, we present the *pattern-matching spi-calculus*, which is an obvious extension of the spi-calculus to include pattern-matching as primitive. The novelty of the language is in the accompanying type system, which uses the same language of patterns to describe complex data dependencies which cannot be described using prior type systems. We show that any appropriately typed process is guaranteed to satisfy a strong robust safety property.

1.   Introduction

Background. Cryptographic protocols are prone to subtle errors, in spite of the fact that they are often relatively small, and so are a suitable target for formal and automated verification methods. One line of such research is the development of domain-specific languages and logics, such as BAN logic [6], strand spaces [22], CSP [20, 21] MSR [8] and the spi-calculus [3]. These languages are based on the Dolev–Yao model of cryptography [10], and often use Woo and Lam's correspondence assertions [23] to model authenticity. Techniques for proving correctness include rank functions [21, 16, 15], theorem provers [5, 19, 9], model checkers [17, 18] and type systems [1, 2, 7, 12, 13, 11].

Towards more complete and realistic cryptographic type systems.   Type systems for interesting languages are incomplete, that is they fail to type-check some safe programs. Type systems usually are tailored to a particular idiom, for example [2] treats public encryption keys but not signing keys, and [13]

*This material is based upon work supported by the National Science Foundation under Grant No. 0208459.

covers full symmetric and asymmetric cryptography but not nested uses of cryptography. In this paper, we will use the techniques developed in [12, 13, 11] to reason about protocols making use of nested cryptography and hashing.

Small core language.   While increasing the completeness of a cryptographic type system, it is also important to keep the system tractable, so that rigorous safety proofs are still feasible. For that reason, we chose to define a very small core language and obtain the full language through derived forms. The core language is extremely parsimonious: its only constructs for messages are tupling, asymmetric encryption and those for asymmetric keys. We show that symmetric encryption, hashing, and message tagging are all derived operators from this small core.

Authorization types.   The language of types is small, too. It contains key types for key pairs, encryption and decryption keys. Moreover, it contains parameterized *authorization types* of the forms $\mathsf{Public}(M)$ and $\mathsf{Secret}(M)$. Typically, the parameter M is a list of principal names. For instance, if principal B receives from an untrusted channel a ciphertext $\{\!|M|\!\}_{esA}$ encrypted with A's private signing key esA, then the plaintext M is of type $\mathsf{Public}\langle A \rangle$, because M is a public message that has been authorized *by* A.

Patterns and nested cryptography.   The process language combines the suite of separate message destructors and equality checks from previous systems [12, 13, 11] into one patten matching construct. Patterns at the process level are convenient, and are similar to the communication techniques used in other specification languages [22, 8, 4]. Notably, our system uses patterns not only in processes but also in types. This permits types for nested use of cryptographic primitives, which would otherwise not be possible. For example, previous type systems [12, 13, 11] could express data dependencies such as

$$(\exists a : \mathsf{Princ}, \exists m : \mathsf{Msg}, \exists b : \mathsf{Princ}, [!\mathsf{begun}(a,b,m)])$$

where $!\mathsf{begun}(a,b,m)$ is an *effect* ensuring that principals a and b have agreed on message m. In this paper, we extend these systems to deal with more complex data dependencies such as

$$\{\!|\#(\exists a : \mathsf{Princ}, \exists m : \mathsf{Msg}), \exists b : \mathsf{Princ}\}\!|_{dk^{-1}}[!\mathsf{begun}(a,b,m)]$$

where the effect $!\mathsf{begun}(a,b,m)$ makes use of variables a, b and m which are doubly nested in the scope of a decryption $\{\!|\cdot|\!\}_{dk^{-1}}$ and a hash function $\#(\cdot)$: such data dependencies were not previously allowed because the occurrences of a, b and m in $!\mathsf{begun}(a,b,m)$ would be considered out of scope.

Reusable long-term keys.   Another form of incompleteness is that previous systems have often been designed for verifying small (yet, subtle) protocol sketches in isolation, but not for verifying larger cryptographic systems where the same key may be used for multiple protocols. For instance, in [13] when a signing key for A is generated, its type specification fixes a finite number of message types that this key may sign. A more realistic approach for larger, possibly extensible, cryptosystems would be to generate a key for encrypting *arbitrary* data authorized by A. We show how the combination of key types, authorization types and message tagging allow keys to be generated independently of the protocols for which they will be used.

Notational conventions.. If the meta-variable x ranges over set S, then $\vec{x}$ ranges over finite sequences over S, and $\bar{x}$ ranges over finite subsets of S.

2. An Introductory Example

Before the technical exposition, we want to convey a flavor of the type system by discussing a simple example. Consider the following simple sign-then-encrypt protocol:

$$A \text{ begins! } (M,A,B)$$
$$A \rightarrow B \qquad \{\!\{sec(M,B)\}\!\}_{esA}\}_{epB}$$
$$B \text{ ends } (M,A,B)$$

The begin- and end-statements are Woo-Lam correspondence assertions [23]. They specify that Alice begins a protocol session (M,A,B), which Bob ends after message reception.

Protocol specification in pattern-matching spi.. Here are Alice's and Bob's side of this protocol expressed in pattern-matching spi calculus:

$$P_A \ \overset{\Delta}{=} \ \text{begin!}(M,A,B); \ \text{out } net \ \{\!\{sec(M,B)\}\!\}_{esA}\}_{epB}$$
$$P_B \ \overset{\Delta}{=} \ \text{inp } net \ \{\!\{sec(\exists x,B)\}\!\}_{dsA^{-1}}\}_{dpB^{-1}}; \ \text{end}(x,A,B)$$

The variable *net* represents an untrusted channel and dsA and dpB are the matching decryption keys for esA and epB. An output statement of the form (out *net N*) sends a message N out on channel *net*. A statement of the form (inp *net X;P*) inputs a message from channel *net* and then attempts to match the message against pattern X. If the pattern match succeeds then P gets executed, otherwise execution gets stuck. Existentials in patterns indicate which variables get bound as part of the pattern match. In the input pattern above, the variable x gets bound, whereas B, dsA and dpB are constants that must be matched exactly.

Type annotations.. For a type-checker to verify the protocol's correctness (and also for us to better understand and document it), it is necessary that we annotate the protocol with types. For our example, the types for the free variables are:

M : Secret	M will not be revealed to the opponent
epB : PublicCryptoEK(B)	epB is B's public encryption key
dpB : PublicCryptoDK(B)	dpB is B's matching decryption key
esA : SigningEK(A)	esA is A's private signing key
dsA : SigningDK(A)	dsA is A's matching signature verification key

No type annotations are necessary in P_A, because P_A does not have input statements. In P_B we add two type annotations. The input variable x is annotated with Secret. Moreover, we add a postcondition to the input statement that indicates that a (x,A,B)-session can safely be ended after a successful pattern match. Here is the annotated version of P_B:

$$P_B \triangleq \text{inp } net \, \{\!|\{\!|sec(\exists x : \text{Secret}, B)|\!\}_{dsA^{-1}}|\!\}_{dpB^{-1}} [!\text{begun}(x,A,B)]; \text{ end}(x,A,B)$$

These type annotations, together with our Robust Safety Theorem are enough to ensure the safety of this protocol in the presence of an arbitrary opponent.

3.   A Spi Calculus with Pattern Matching

3.1   Messages

As usual in spi calculi, messages are modeled as elements of an algebraic datatype. They may be built from atomic names and variables by pairing and asymmetric-key encryption. Moreover, there are two special symbolic operators Enc and Dec with the following meanings: if message M represents a key pair, then Enc(M) represents its encryption and Dec(M) its decryption part.

In the presentation of messages, we include asymmetric-key encryption $\{\!|M|\!\}_N$ which encrypts plaintext M with encryption key N. We also allow messages $\{\!|M|\!\}_{N^{-1}}$ which represents the encryption of plaintext M with the encryption key which matches decryption key N. This is clearly not an implementable operation: it is used in the next section when we discuss *patterns*.

Messages:

x,y,z	variables
m,n	names
$L,M,N ::=$	message
$\quad n$	name
$\quad x$	variable
$\quad ()$	empty message
$\quad (M,N)$	message pair
$\quad \{\!|M|\!\}_N$	M encrypted under encryption key N
$\quad \{\!|M|\!\}_{N^{-1}}$	M encrypted under inverse of decryption key N
$\quad \text{Enc}(M)$	encryption part of key pair M

$\mathsf{Dec}\,(M)$ decryption part of key pair M

Syntactic restriction: No subterms of the form $\{\!|M|\!\}_{(\mathsf{Dec}\,(N))^{-1}}$.
Define: A message M is *implementable* if it contains no subterms $\{\!|M|\!\}_{N^{-1}}$.

Because of the restriction that we never build messages $\{\!|M|\!\}_{(\mathsf{Dec}\,(N))^{-1}}$, we have to be careful with our definition of substitution. This is standard, except for when we substitute into a term of the form $\{\!|M|\!\}_{N^{-1}}$.

Substitution into Messages:

$$(\{\!|M|\!\}_{N^{-1}})\{\sigma\} \;\overset{\Delta}{=}\; \begin{cases} \{\!|M\{\sigma\}|\!\}_{\mathsf{Enc}\,(L)} & \text{if } N\{\sigma\} = \mathsf{Dec}\,(L) \\ \{\!|M\{\sigma\}|\!\}_{(N\{\sigma\})^{-1}} & \text{otherwise} \end{cases}$$

We will write the list $\langle M_1, \ldots, M_n \rangle$ as shorthand for $(M_1, (\ldots, (M_n, ())\ldots))$.

3.2 Patterns

Patterns are of the form $\{\vec{x}.\,M \mid \bar{A}\}$, where M is a *pattern body* and $\bar{A}$ an *assertion set*. Assertion sets are only used in type-checking, so we delay their discussion until Section 4.2. The variables $\vec{x}$ act as binders. A message N matches a pattern $\{\vec{x}.\,M \mid \bar{A}\}$ if it is of the form $N = M\{\vec{x}{\leftarrow}\vec{L}\}$, in which case variables $\vec{x}$ will be bound to messages $\vec{L}$. The pattern body M may have multiple occurrences of the same variable and it may contain variables that are not mentioned in $\vec{x}$: such variables are regarded as constants and must be matched exactly. For instance, the pattern $\{x.\,(x, \{\!|x|\!\}_y) \mid \bar{A}\}$ is matched by messages of the form $(M, \{\!|M|\!\}_y)$, but not by messages $(M, \{\!|M|\!\}_z)$ or $(M, \{\!|N|\!\}_y)$.

Patterns:

$X, Y, Z ::=$	pattern
$\{\vec{x}.\,M \mid \bar{A}\}$	pattern matching term M binding $\vec{x}$

Syntactic restrictions: $\vec{x} \subseteq \mathsf{fv}(M)$ and $\vec{x}$ distinct.
Define: A pattern $\{\vec{x}.\,M \mid \bar{A}\}$ is *implementable* if $(\mathsf{fn}(M), \mathsf{fv}(M) - \vec{x}, M \Vdash \vec{x})$.

Importantly, not all patterns are implementable. For instance, the patterns $\{x, dk.\,\{\!|x|\!\}_{dk^{-1}} \mid \bar{A}\}$ and $\{x.\,\{\!|x|\!\}_{ek} \mid \bar{A}\}$ are not implementable, because they would allow access to the plaintext without knowing the decryption key. On the other hand, $\{x.\,\{\!|x|\!\}_{dk^{-1}} \mid \bar{A}\}$ and $\{x.\,\{\!|x|\!\}_{\mathsf{Enc}\,(k)} \mid \bar{A}\}$ are implementable patterns. A syntactic restriction forbids non-implementable input patterns in processes. We formalize the notion of implementable pattern by making use of the Dolev–Yao 'derivable message' judgment $\bar{M} \Vdash \bar{N}$ meaning 'An agent which knows messages $\bar{M}$ can construct messages $\bar{N}$.'

Dolev–Yao Derivability, $\bar{M} \Vdash \bar{N}$:

(DY Id)	(DY And)	(DY Nil)	(DY Pair)
	$\dfrac{\bar{M} \Vdash N_1 \;\ldots\; \bar{M} \Vdash N_k}{\bar{M} \Vdash N_1,\ldots,N_k}$		$\dfrac{\bar{M} \Vdash N,N'}{\bar{M} \Vdash (N,N')}$
$\overline{\bar{M},N \Vdash N}$		$\overline{\bar{M} \Vdash ()}$	

(DY Id)
$$\bar{M},N \Vdash N$$

(DY And)
$$\frac{\bar{M} \Vdash N_1 \;\ldots\; \bar{M} \Vdash N_k}{\bar{M} \Vdash N_1,\ldots,N_k}$$

(DY Nil)
$$\bar{M} \Vdash ()$$

(DY Pair)
$$\frac{\bar{M} \Vdash N,N'}{\bar{M} \Vdash (N,N')}$$

(DY Split)
$$\frac{\bar{M},N,N' \Vdash L}{\bar{M},(N,N') \Vdash L}$$

(DY Key)
$$\frac{\bar{M} \Vdash N \quad k \in \{\mathsf{Enc},\mathsf{Dec}\}}{\bar{M} \Vdash k(N)}$$

(DY Encrypt)
$$\frac{\bar{M} \Vdash N,N'}{\bar{M} \Vdash \{\!|N'|\!\}_N}$$

(DY Decrypt)
$$\frac{\bar{M} \Vdash N \quad \bar{M},N' \Vdash L}{\bar{M}, \{\!|N'|\!\}_{N^{-1}} \Vdash L}$$

(DY Unencrypt)
$$\frac{\bar{M} \Vdash N \quad \bar{M},N' \Vdash L}{\bar{M}, \{\!|N'|\!\}_{\mathsf{Enc}(N)} \Vdash L}$$

We use some convenient syntactic abbreviations that treat patterns as if they were messages containing binding existentials. These 'derived forms' for patterns are defined below. For example:

$$\{\!|\, \{\!|sec(B,\exists x : \mathsf{Secret})|\!\}_{dsA^{-1}}\, |\!\}_{dpB^{-1}} [!\mathsf{begun}(x,A,B)]$$
$$\equiv\;\; \{x.\, \{\!|\, \{\!|sec(B,x)|\!\}_{dsA^{-1}}\, |\!\}_{dpB^{-1}} \mid x : \mathsf{Secret}, !\mathsf{begun}(x,A,B)\}$$

Derived Forms for Patterns:

$$M \overset{\triangle}{=} \{M \mid \}; \quad T \overset{\triangle}{=} \{x.x \mid x : T\} \text{ for fresh } x;$$
$$\exists x \overset{\triangle}{=} \{x.x \mid \}; \quad \ldots \overset{\triangle}{=} (\exists x) \text{ for fresh } x;$$
$$\{\!|X|\!\}_N \overset{\triangle}{=} \{\vec{x}.\, \{\!|M|\!\}_N \mid \bar{A}\}, \text{ if } X = \{\vec{x}.M \mid \bar{A}\};$$
$$\{\!|X|\!\}_{N^{-1}} \overset{\triangle}{=} \{\vec{x}.\, \{\!|M|\!\}_{N^{-1}} \mid \bar{A}\}, \text{ if } X = \{\vec{x}.M \mid \bar{A}\};$$
$$X[\bar{B}] \overset{\triangle}{=} \{\vec{x}.M \mid \bar{A},\bar{B}\}, \text{ if } X = \{\vec{x}.M \mid \bar{A}\};$$
$$\langle X_1,\ldots,X_n \rangle \overset{\triangle}{=} \{\vec{x}_1,\ldots,\vec{x}_n.\langle M_1,\ldots,M_n \rangle \mid \bar{A}_1,\ldots,\bar{A}_n\}, \text{ if } X_i = \{\vec{x}_i.M_i \mid \bar{A}_i\}$$

3.3   Processes

The spi-calculus with patterns is a variant of the spi-calculus, where we add pattern-matching as a primitive capability (in the spi-calculus it is derived).

Processes:

$O,P,Q,R ::=$	process
out $N\ M$	asynchronous output of M on N
inp $N\ X;P$	input from N against pattern X
new $n{:}T;P$	name generation
$P \mid Q$	parallel composition
$!P$	replication
$\mathbf{0}$	inactivity

Syntactic restrictions:
- In (out N M), both N and M are implementable messages.
- In (inp N X;P), N is an implementable message and X is an implementable pattern.

Scope:
- The scope of $\vec{x}$ in (inp N $\{\vec{x}.M \mid \overline{A}\}$;$P$) is M, $\overline{A}$ and P.
- The scope of n in new $n{:}T$;P is P.

3.4 Specifying Authenticity by Correspondence Assertions

Following [12, 13, 11], we specify authenticity properties by inserting correspondence assertions into protocol specifications.

Correspondence Assertions:

$O,P,Q,R ::=$	process
$\cdots$	as in Section 3.3
begin!(L); P	begin-many assertion
end(L); P	end assertion

A process is *safe* whenever at run-time each end(M) is preceded by a begin!(M)
(precise definitions can be found in the appendix). For example, consider process P:

$$P \triangleq P_A \mid P_B, \text{ where } P_A \triangleq (\text{begin!}(M,A,B); \text{ out } net\ (M,B))$$
$$P_B \triangleq (\text{inp } net\ (\exists x, B)[!\text{begun}(x,A,B)]; \text{ end}(x,A,B))$$

Process P is safe in isolation, but we are really interested in safety in the presence of an opponent. A process P is called *robustly safe* whenever $(O \mid P)$
is safe for all opponent processes O. The example process P is not robustly
safe, because (out net $N \mid P$) is not safe, and we ensure robust safety by adding
encryption:

$$P \triangleq \text{ new } k : \text{SigningKP}(A); \text{ (out } net\ (\text{Dec}\,(k)) \mid P_A(\text{Enc}\,(k)) \mid P_B(\text{Dec}\,(k)))$$
$$P_A(ek) \triangleq \text{ begin!}(M,A,B); \text{ out } net\ \{M,B\}_{ek}$$
$$P_B(dk) \triangleq \text{ inp } net\ \{\exists x : \text{Public}, B\}_{dk^{-1}}[!\text{begun}(x,A,B)]; \text{ end}(x,A,B)$$

The crucial property of our system is that processes that only make use of
public data are robustly safe (we will return in Section 4.3 to the definition of
a public type):

Theorem (Robust Safety) *If $\vec{T}$ are public types and $(\vec{n} : \vec{T} \vdash P)$, then P is
robustly safe.*

4. Highlights of the Type System

4.1 Environments

As is usual in most type systems, we give our judgments relative to a *typing
environment*. In our case, this typing environment is used to:

- Track the names of bound variables, for example dk and x.
- Give message types, for example $dk : \mathsf{SigningDK}(A)$ and $\{\!|x,B|\!\}_{dk^{-1}} : \mathsf{Un}$.
- List correspondences that have begun, for example $!\mathsf{begun}(x,A,B)$.

The environment containing these assertions would be:

$$dk,x; \; dk : \mathsf{SigningDK}(A), \; \{\!|x,B|\!\}_{dk^{-1}} : \mathsf{Un}, \; !\mathsf{begun}(x,A,B)$$

A significant difference to previous type systems for the spi-calculus [12, 13, 11] is that we are unifying the notions of *variable environment* and *process effect* into a common language of environments.

Environments:

$A,B,C,D ::=$	assertions
$\quad M : T$	type assertion
$\quad !\mathsf{begun}(M)$	begun-many assertion
$E,F,G ::=$	environments
$\quad \vec{x}; \vec{A}$	environment
$\mathsf{dom}(\vec{x}; \vec{A}) \stackrel{\Delta}{=} \vec{x}$	environment domain

4.2 Typed Pattern Matching

We can now explain the assertion component of a pattern $\{\vec{x}. M \mid \vec{A}\}$: it gives the precondition $\vec{A}$ which must be satisfied by any process that constructs a term matching the pattern. For example, the pattern $(\exists x : \mathsf{Public}, B)[!\mathsf{begun}(x,A,B)]$ is a derived form for $\{x. (x,B) \mid x : \mathsf{Public}, !\mathsf{begun}(x,A,B)\}$.

Typed Pattern Matching (where $X = \{\vec{x}.N \mid \vec{A}\}$):

$E \vdash M \in X \stackrel{\Delta}{=} E \vdash M : \mathsf{Top}, \vec{A}\{\vec{x}{\leftarrow}\vec{N}\}$, where $M = N\{\vec{x}{\leftarrow}\vec{N}\}$	Match
$E, M \in X \vdash \mathcal{J} \stackrel{\Delta}{=} E, M : \mathsf{Top}, \vec{A}\{\vec{x}{\leftarrow}\vec{N}\} \vdash \mathcal{J}$, where $M = N\{\vec{x}{\leftarrow}\vec{N}\}$	Unmatch

4.3 Kinds and Subkinding

A message is *publishable* if it may be sent to an untrusted target. A message is *untainted* if it has been received from a trusted source. An important part of the type system is a *kinding relation* $(T :: K)$ that assigns kinds K to types T. The type system is designed so that the following statements hold:

- If $(T :: K)$ and $\mathsf{Public} \in K$, then members of type T are publishable.
- If $(T :: K)$ and $\mathsf{Tainted} \notin K$, then members of type T are untainted.

We say that type T is *public* (respectively *tainted*) if $(T :: K \ni \mathsf{Public})$ (respectively $(T :: K \ni \mathsf{Tainted})$) for some kind K.

Kinds and Subkinding:

$$K, H, J \subseteq \{\mathsf{Public}, \mathsf{Tainted}\}$$

$$\frac{(\mathsf{Public} \in H) \Rightarrow (\mathsf{Public} \in K) \quad (\mathsf{Tainted} \in K) \Rightarrow (\mathsf{Tainted} \in H)}{K \leq H}$$

4.4 Types and Subtyping

We will now give the grammar of types, together with the definition of kinding and subtyping. We discuss each of the types in more detail below.

Types:

$T, U, V ::=$	types
$K\,\mathsf{Top}$	top type
$K\,\mathsf{Auth}(L)$	authorized type
$(K,H)\,KT(X)$	key type
$KT ::=$	key type symbols
EK	encryption key
DK	decryption key
KP	key pair

Kinding $T :: K$:

$K\,\mathsf{Top} :: K; \quad K\,\mathsf{Auth}(L) :: K;$

$(K,H)\,\mathsf{KP}(X) :: K \cap H; \quad (K,H)\,\mathsf{EK}(X) :: K; \quad (K,H)\,\mathsf{DK}(X) :: H$

Kinds are used to define subtyping. The rule (Subty Public Tainted) states that any message of public type also has any tainted type, as in [13]. The subtyping rules (Subty Top) and (Subty Auth) are new and have not been part of [13].

Subtyping, $T \leq U$:

(Subty Refl)

$$\frac{}{T \leq T}$$

(Subty Top)

$$\frac{T :: K \quad K \leq H}{T \leq H\,\mathsf{Top}}$$

(Subty Auth)

$$\frac{K \leq H}{K\,\mathsf{Auth}(L) \leq H\,\mathsf{Auth}(L)}$$

(Subty Public Tainted)

$$\frac{T :: K \cup \{\mathsf{Public}\} \quad U :: H \cup \{\mathsf{Tainted}\}}{T \leq U}$$

4.5 Top Types

Top types have the form $K\,\mathsf{Top}$ and are the most general types of kind K, by (Subty Top). Moreover, $\{\mathsf{Tainted}\}\,\mathsf{Top}$ is the greatest type of the entire type hierarchy. We define the following derived forms:

Derived Forms for Top Types:

$\text{Secret} \triangleq \emptyset\,\text{Top}; \quad \text{Public} \triangleq \{\text{Public}\}\,\text{Top}; \quad \text{Un} \triangleq \{\text{Public}, \text{Tainted}\}\,\text{Top};$

$\text{Top} \triangleq \text{Tainted} \triangleq \{\text{Tainted}\}\,\text{Top}$

4.6   Authorization Types

A novel feature of this system is *authorization types*. A message $M : K\,\text{Auth}(L)$ is a message of kind K which requires authorization by or for L.

Derived Forms for Authorization Types:

$\text{Secret}(L) \triangleq \emptyset\,\text{Auth}(L); \qquad \text{Tainted}(L) \triangleq \{\text{Tainted}\}\,\text{Auth}(L);$

$\text{Public}(L) \triangleq \{\text{Public}\}\,\text{Auth}(L); \qquad \text{Un}(L) \triangleq \{\text{Public}, \text{Tainted}\}\,\text{Auth}(L)$

In meaningful authorization types, parameter L is usually a list of principal names. For example, $\text{Public}\langle A, B, C\rangle$ is the type of public messages M that require authorizations *by* principals A, B and C. These authorizations are acquired by A, B and C digitally signing M.

4.7   Key Types

In this system, key types are extremely general: in examples, we will often use specialized derived key types for applications such as signing, as discussed in Section 5.2. The key type $(K, H)\,KT(X)$ contains a pattern X. These keys will be used to encrypt plaintext messages M to produce ciphertexts which have an authorization type $J\,\text{Auth}(L)$. In order to form the ciphertext, we require the pair (M, L) to match the pattern X. The key type $(K, H)\,KT(X)$ also contains a kind K, which is the kind of the encryption key, and a kind H, which is the kind of the decryption key. For example, in Section 5.2 we define principal A's signing key to be:

$$\text{SigningEK}(A) \triangleq (\emptyset, \{\text{Public}\})\,\text{EK}(\exists x : \text{Secret}(A, y), \exists y)$$

A key es_A of type $\text{SigningEK}(A)$ is a secret encryption key, whose matching decryption key is public. Thus, it is a signing key. It is typically used to encrypt messages M of type $\text{Public}(A, \vec{B})$ to produce ciphertexts $\{\!|M|\!\}_{es_A}$ of type $\text{Public}(\vec{B})$: thus, by signing the message, A removes her name from the list of principals required to authorize it.

4.8   Output and Input

The interesting rules for the process judgment $E \vdash P$ are for input and output.

$$\frac{E \vdash N : \text{Un}, \ M : \text{Un}}{E \vdash \text{out}\, N\, M} \qquad \frac{\vec{x} \cap \text{dom}(E) = \emptyset \qquad E \vdash N : \text{Un} \quad \vec{x}, E, M : \text{Un} \vdash \overline{A} \quad \vec{x}, E, \overline{A} \vdash P}{E \vdash \text{inp}\, N\, \{\vec{x}.\, M \mid \overline{A}\}; P}$$

In the output rule, message M has to be of type Un in order to be sent out on the untrusted channel N. Note that M may also be sent out if M's type is any other public type, because each public type is a subtype of Un.

4.9 Encryption

There are two typing rules for encryption, which only differ in the kind attributes of the types. The first rule applies to encryption with a trusted key:

$$\frac{\text{Tainted} \notin K \cup H^{-1} \quad E \vdash N : (K,H)\,\mathsf{EK}(X),\ (M,L) \in X}{E \vdash \{\!|M|\!\}_N : \mathsf{Public}(L)} \qquad \begin{aligned} \mathsf{Public}^{-1} &\triangleq \mathsf{Tainted} \\ \mathsf{Tainted}^{-1} &\triangleq \mathsf{Public} \end{aligned}$$

The condition Tainted $\notin K \cup H^{-1}$ expresses that the ciphertext is only publishable if the encryption key is untainted and the corresponding decryption key is not public. Otherwise, the following rule is used for encryption:

$$\frac{\text{Tainted} \in K \cup H^{-1} \quad J = (J' - \{\mathsf{Tainted}\}) \cup (K - \{\mathsf{Public}\})}{E \vdash \{\!|M|\!\}_N : J\,\mathsf{Auth}(L)}$$
$$E \vdash N : (K,H)\,\mathsf{EK}(X),\ (M,L) \in X,\ M : J'\,\mathsf{Top}$$

Note that here the ciphertext type $J\,\mathsf{Auth}(L)$ is only public if the plaintext type $J'\,\mathsf{Top}$ is public, and is tainted if the encryption key is tainted.

4.10 Decryption

There are two typing rules for decryption, which only differ in how they treat kinds and authorizations. The first rule applies if both the decryption key and the ciphertext are untainted, and is the inverse of the rule for encryption with a trusted key:

$$\frac{\text{Tainted} \notin H \cup J \quad E \vdash N : (K,H)\,\mathsf{DK}(X) \quad E, (M,L) \in X \vdash B}{E, \{\!|M|\!\}_{N^{-1}} : J\,\mathsf{Auth}(L) \vdash B}$$

The second decryption rule applies if we cannot trust the ciphertext; in particular we do not know who has authorized the ciphertext:

$$\frac{\text{Tainted} \in J \quad E \vdash N : (K,H)\,\mathsf{DK}(X) \quad x, E, (M,x) \in X \vdash B}{E, \{\!|M|\!\}_{N^{-1}} : J\,\mathsf{Top} \vdash B}$$
$$(\text{Tainted} \in H \cup K^{-1}) \ \Rightarrow\ (x, E, M : J\,\mathsf{Top}, x : \mathsf{Top} \vdash (M,x) \in X)$$

Note that when we apply this rule, the authorization is unknown, so we replace it by a fresh variable x, which acts as a placeholder for the 'real' authorization. If the decryption key is untrusted, then we have an additional requirement: we can only add (M,x) to the assumption list if it is derivable from $(x, E, M : J\,\mathsf{Top}, x : \mathsf{Top})$; as a result, untrusted keys can only be used when the pattern X is quite 'weak'.

5.   Derived Forms and Examples

5.1   Tagging

In previous type systems for cryptographic protocols [12, 13, 11], message tags were introduced using *tagged union types*. These types are sound, and they allow a key to be used in more than one protocol, but unfortunately they require the protocol suite to be known *before* the key is generated, since the plaintext type of the key is given as the tagged union of all the messages in the protocol suite. In this paper, we adopt a variant of *dynamic types* to allow a key to be generated with no knowledge of the protocol suite it will be used for.

In our system, we give message tags a type of the form $\ell : X \rightarrow \text{Auth}(Y)$, which can be used to tag messages M of kind $(J \cup \text{Tainted})$ to get tagged messages $\ell(M) : J\text{Auth}(L)$. For example, our previous protocol becomes:

$$P \triangleq \text{new } k : \text{SigningKP}(A); \ (\text{out } net \ (\text{Dec}(k)) \mid P_A(\text{Enc}(k)) \mid P_B(\text{Dec}(k)))$$
$$P_A(ek) \triangleq \text{begin!}(M,A,B); \ \text{out } net \ \{\!|snd(M,B)|\!\}_{ek}$$
$$P_B(dk) \triangleq \text{inp } net \ \{\!|snd(\exists x : \text{Public}, B)|\!\}_{dk^{-1}}[!\text{begun}(x,A,B)]; \ \text{end}(x,A,B)$$
$$snd : (\exists x : \text{Public}, \exists b : \text{Public}) \rightarrow \text{Auth}(\exists a : \text{Public}, \ldots)[!\text{begun}(x,a,b)]$$

Tags are not primitive in the pattern-matching spi-calculus, instead we can encode tags as public key pairs, and message tagging as encryption. We treat message tags ℓ as names with a globally agreed type.

$$\ell(M) \triangleq \{\!|M|\!\}_{\text{Enc}(\ell)}; \qquad \ell(X) \triangleq \{\!|X|\!\}_{\text{Enc}(\ell)};$$
$$(X \rightarrow \text{Auth}(Y)) \triangleq (\{\text{Public}\}, \{\text{Public}\})\text{KP}(X,Y)$$

5.2   Signing Keys

A goal of this type system is to allow principals to have just one signing key, which can be used for any protocol, rather than requiring different signing key types for different protocols. Message tags are then used to ensure the correctness of each protocol.

The type for a signing key is designed to support nested signatures, for example $\{\!|\{\!|M|\!\}_{esA}|\!\}_{esB}$ is a message M signed by A (using her signing key $esA : \text{SigningEK}(A)$) and B (using his signing key $esB : \text{SigningEK}(B)$). This message can be given type $\{\!|\{\!|M|\!\}_{esA}|\!\}_{esB} : \text{Secret}$ as long as $M : \text{Secret}\langle A,B,y\rangle$ for some y, and type $\{\!|\{\!|M|\!\}_{esA}|\!\}_{esB} : \text{Public}$ as long as $M : \text{Public}\langle A,B,y\rangle$ for some y. This form of nested signing was not supported by [12, 13, 11].

$$\text{Signing}KT(L) \triangleq (\emptyset, \{\text{Public}\})KT(\exists x : \text{Secret}(L,y), \exists y)$$

A long version of this paper [14] contains a proof that the protocol in Section 5.1 is well-typed.

5.3   Public Encryption Keys

Public encryption is dual to signing: the encryption key is public, and the decryption key is kept secret. One crucial difference is that although our type system supports nested uses of signatures, it does not support similar nested uses of public-key encryption. As a result, although we can support sign-then-encrypt, we cannot support encrypt-then-sign, due to the well-known problems with encrypt-then-sign applications (see, for instance, the analysis of the CCITT X.509 protocol in [6]).

$$\mathsf{PublicCrypto}KT(L) \overset{\Delta}{=} (\{\mathsf{Public}\},\emptyset)\,KT(\exists x : \mathsf{Secret}(L),\ldots)$$

5.4   Symmetric Keys

Symmetric cryptography is not primitive in pattern-matching spi-calculus, instead we encode it using asymmetric cryptography:

$$\{M\}_N \overset{\Delta}{=} \{\!|M|\!\}_{\mathsf{Enc}(N)}; \quad \{X\}_N \overset{\Delta}{=} \{\!|X|\!\}_{\mathsf{Enc}(N)}; \quad \mathsf{SymK}(X) \overset{\Delta}{=} (\emptyset,\emptyset)\,\mathsf{KP}(X,\ldots)$$

5.5   Hashing

We can encode hashing as encryption with a hashing key, where the matching decryption key has been discarded.

$$\#(M) \overset{\Delta}{=} hash(\{\!|M|\!\}_{ekH}) \quad \text{where } ekH : (\{\mathsf{Public}\},\emptyset)\,\mathsf{EK}(\ldots)$$
$$\text{and } hash : \{\!|\exists x : \mathsf{Secret}(y)|\!\}_{ekH} \to \mathsf{Auth}(\exists y)$$

From this point on, we assume that each environment E is implicitly extended by the above type assertions for the special global names ekH and $hash$. We can then adapt the example from Section 5.1 to allow A to sign the message digest of M rather than signing the entire message:

$$A \text{ begins! } (M,A,B)$$
$$A \to B \qquad M, \{\!|\#(snd(B,M))|\!\}_{esA}$$
$$B \text{ ends } (M,A,B)$$

This example uses the types which were introduced in previous examples, a full version is given in a long version of this paper [14].

Appendix

Structural Process Equivalence, $P \equiv Q$:

$P \equiv P$	(Struct Refl)
$P \equiv Q \Rightarrow Q \equiv P$	(Struct Symm)
$P \equiv Q, Q \equiv R \Rightarrow P \equiv R$	(Struct Trans)
$P \equiv Q \Rightarrow P \mid Q \equiv P \mid R$	(Struct Par)
$P \mid 0 \equiv P$	(Struct Par Zero)
$P \mid Q \equiv Q \mid P$	(Struct Par Comm)

$(P \mid Q) \mid R \equiv P \mid (Q \mid R)$ (Struct Par Assoc)
$!P \equiv P \mid !P$ (Struct Repl Par)

State Transition, $(\bar{A} ::: P) \to (\bar{B} ::: Q)$:

(Redn Equiv)
$$\frac{P \equiv P' \quad (\bar{A} ::: P') \to (\bar{B} ::: Q') \quad Q' \equiv Q}{(\bar{A} ::: P) \to (\bar{B} ::: Q)}$$

$n \notin \text{fn}(\bar{A}, Q) \Rightarrow (\bar{A} ::: (\text{new } n{:}T; P) \mid Q) \to (\bar{A}, n{:}T ::: P \mid Q)$ (Redn New)
$(\underline{A} ::: (\text{begin!}(M); P) \mid Q) \to (A, !\text{begun}(M) ::: P \mid Q)$ (Redn Begin)
$(\bar{A}, !\text{begun}(M) ::: (\text{end}(M); P) \mid Q) \to (\underline{A}, !\text{begun}(M) ::: P \mid Q)$ (Redn End)
$(\bar{A} ::: (\text{out } L \ M\{\vec{x} \leftarrow \vec{N}\} \mid \text{inp } L \ \{\vec{x}. M \mid A\}; P) \mid Q) \to (\bar{A} ::: P\{\vec{x} \leftarrow \vec{N}\} \mid Q)$ (Redn IO)

Good Environment, $E \vdash \diamond$:

(Good Env)
$$\frac{\text{fv}(\bar{A}) \subseteq \bar{x}}{\bar{x}; \bar{A} \vdash \diamond}$$

Right Rules, $E \vdash \bar{A}$:

(Id)   (And)   (Empty)
$$\frac{E, A \vdash \diamond}{E, A \vdash A} \qquad \frac{E \vdash A_1 \quad \cdots \quad E \vdash A_n \quad n \geq 0}{E \vdash A_1, \ldots, A_n} \qquad \frac{E \vdash \diamond}{E \vdash () : \text{Public}}$$

(Sub)   (Pair)
$$\frac{E \vdash M : T \quad T \leq U \quad \text{fv}(U) \subseteq \text{dom}(E)}{E \vdash M : U} \qquad \frac{E \vdash M : K \text{Top}, \ N : K \text{Top}}{E \vdash (M, N) : K \text{Top}}$$

(Enc Part)   (Dec Part)
$$\frac{E \vdash M : (K, H) \text{KP}(X)}{E \vdash \text{Enc}(M) : (K, H) \text{EK}(X)} \qquad \frac{E \vdash M : (K, H) \text{KP}(X)}{E \vdash \text{Dec}(M) : (K, H) \text{DK}(X)}$$

(Encrypt Trusted)
$$\frac{\text{Tainted} \notin K \cup H^{-1} \quad E \vdash N : (K, H) \text{EK}(X), \ (M, L) \in X}{E \vdash \{\!|M|\!\}_N : \text{Public}(L)}$$

(Encrypt Untrusted)
$$\frac{\text{Tainted} \in K \cup H^{-1} \quad J = (J' - \{\text{Tainted}\}) \cup (K - \{\text{Public}\}) \quad E \vdash N : (K, H) \text{EK}(X), \ (M, L) \in X, \ M : J' \text{Top}}{E \vdash \{\!|M|\!\}_N : J \text{Auth}(L)}$$

Left Rules, $E, \bar{A} \vdash B$:

(Unsub)   (Split)
$$\frac{\text{fv}(T) \subseteq \text{dom}(E) \quad E, M : U \vdash A \quad T \leq U}{E, M : T \vdash A} \qquad \frac{E, M : K \text{Top}, N : K \text{Top} \vdash A}{E, (M, N) : K \text{Top} \vdash A}$$

(Decrypt Trusted)

Tainted $\notin H \cup J$

$$\frac{E \vdash N : (K,H)\,\mathsf{DK}(X) \quad E,(M,L) \in X \vdash B}{E, decrypt(M,N) : J\,\mathsf{Auth}(L) \vdash B}$$

(Decrypt Untrusted)

$$\frac{\mathsf{Tainted} \in J \quad E \vdash N : (K,H)\,\mathsf{DK}(X) \quad x \notin \mathrm{dom}(E) \quad x,E,(M,x) \in X \vdash B}{(\mathsf{Tainted} \in H \cup K^{-1}) \;\Rightarrow\; (x,E,M:J\,\mathsf{Top},x:\mathsf{Top} \vdash (M,x) \in X)}{E, decrypt(M,N) : J\,\mathsf{Top} \vdash B}$$

where $decrypt(M,N) \;\triangleq\; \begin{cases} \{\!| M |\!\}_{\mathsf{Enc}(L)} & \text{if } N = \mathsf{Dec}(L) \\ \{\!| M |\!\}_{N^{-1}} & \text{otherwise} \end{cases}$

Well-typed Processes, $E \vdash P$:

(Proc Out)

$$\frac{E \vdash N : \mathsf{Un}, \; M : \mathsf{Un}}{E \vdash \mathsf{out}\, N\, M}$$

(Proc In)

$$\frac{\vec{x} \cap \mathrm{dom}(E) = \emptyset \qquad E \vdash N : \mathsf{Un} \quad \vec{x},E,M : \mathsf{Un} \vdash \bar{A} \quad \vec{x},E,\bar{A} \vdash P}{E \vdash \mathsf{inp}\, N\, \{\vec{x}.M \mid \bar{A}\}; P}$$

(Proc New)

$$\frac{E,n:T \vdash P \quad n \notin \mathrm{fn}(E)}{E \vdash \mathsf{new}\, n{:}T;\, P}$$

(Proc Par)

$$\frac{E \vdash P \quad E \vdash Q}{E \vdash P \mid Q}$$

(Proc Repl)

$$\frac{E \vdash P}{E \vdash\, !P}$$

(Proc Stop)

$$\frac{E \vdash \diamond}{E \vdash \mathbf{0}}$$

(Proc Begin Many)

$$\frac{E, !\mathsf{begun}(M) \vdash P}{E \vdash \mathsf{begin}!(M);\, P}$$

(Proc End)

$$\frac{E \vdash\, !\mathsf{begun}(M) \quad E \vdash P}{E \vdash \mathsf{end}(M);\, P}$$

Well-typed Computation States, $\vdash \bar{A} ::: P$:

(State)

$$\frac{\bar{A} \text{ nominal} \quad \bar{A} \vdash \bar{A}' \quad \bar{A}' \vdash P}{\vdash \bar{A} ::: P}$$

References

[1] M. Abadi. Secrecy by typing in security protocols. *Journal of the ACM*, 46(5):749–786, September 1999.

[2] M. Abadi and B. Blanchet. Secrecy types for asymmetric communication. In *Foundations of Software Science and Computation Structures*, volume 2030 of *Lecture Notes in Computer Science*, pages 25–41. Springer, 2001.

[3] M. Abadi and A.D. Gordon. A calculus for cryptographic protocols: The spi calculus. *Information and Computation*, 148:1–70, 1999.

[4] C. Bodei, M. Buchholtz, P. Degano, F. Nielson, and H. Riis Nielson. Automatic validation of protocol narration. In *Proc. CSFW03*, pages 126–140. IEEE Press, 2003.

[5] D. Bolignano. An approach to the formal verification of cryptographic protocols. In *Third ACM Conference on Computer and Communications Security*, pages 106–118, 1996.

[6] M. Burrows, M. Abadi, and R.M. Needham. A logic of authentication. *Proceedings of the Royal Society of London A*, 426:233–271, 1989.

[7] I. Cervesato. Typed MSR: Syntax and examples. In *First International Workshop on Mathematical Methods, Models and Architectures for Computer Network Security*, volume 2052 of *Lecture Notes in Computer Science*, pages 159–177. Springer, 2001.

[8] I. Cervesato, N. A. Durgin, P. D. Lincoln, J. C. Mitchell, and A. Scedrov. A meta-notation for protocol analysis. In *Proc. IEEE Computer Security Foundations Workshop*, pages 55–69, 1999.

[9] E. Cohen. TAPS: A first-order verifier for cryptographic protocols. In *13th IEEE Computer Security Foundations Workshop*, pages 144–158. IEEE Computer Society Press, 2000.

[10] D. Dolev and A.C. Yao. On the security of public key protocols. *IEEE Transactions on Information Theory*, IT–29(2):198–208, 1983.

[11] A. D. Gordon and A. S. A. Jeffrey. Typing one-to-one and one-to-many correspondences in security protocols. In *Proc. Int. Software Security Symp.*, volume 2609 of *Lecture Notes in Computer Science*, pages 263–282. Springer-Verlag, 2002.

[12] A.D. Gordon and A. Jeffrey. Authenticity by typing for security protocols. In *14th IEEE Computer Security Foundations Workshop*, pages 145–159. IEEE Computer Society Press, 2001.

[13] A.D. Gordon and A. Jeffrey. Types and effects for asymmetric cryptographic protocols. In *15th IEEE Computer Security Foundations Workshop*, pages 77–91. IEEE Computer Society Press, 2002.

[14] C. Haack and A. S. A. Jeffrey. Pattern-matching spi-calculus (longer draft). Available from http://fpl.cs.depaul.edu/ajeffrey/fast04Long.pdf, 2004.

[15] J. Heather. *'Oh! . . . Is it* really *you?' Using rank functions to verify authentication protocols*. PhD thesis, Royal Holloway, University of London, 2000.

[16] J. Heather and S. Schneider. Towards automatic verification of authentication protocols on an unbounded network. In *13th IEEE Computer Security Foundations Workshop*, pages 132–143. IEEE Computer Society Press, 2000.

[17] G. Lowe. Breaking and fixing the Needham-Schroeder public-key protocol using CSP and FDR. In *Tools and Algorithms for the Construction and Analysis of Systems*, volume 1055 of *Lecture Notes in Computer Science*, pages 147–166. Springer, 1996.

[18] W. Marrero, E.M. Clarke, and S. Jha. Model checking for security protocols. In *DIMACS Workshop on Design and Formal Verification of Security Protocols*, 1997. Preliminary version appears as Technical Report TR–CMU–CS–97–139, Carnegie Mellon University, May 1997.

[19] L.C. Paulson. The inductive approach to verifying cryptographic protocols. *Journal of Computer Security*, 6:85–128, 1998.

[20] A.W. Roscoe. Modelling and verifying key-exchange protocols using CSP and FDR. In *8th IEEE Computer Security Foundations Workshop*, pages 98–107. IEEE Computer Society Press, 1995.

[21] S.A. Schneider. Verifying authentication protocols in CSP. *IEEE Transactions on Software Engineering*, 24(9):741–758, 1998.

[22] F.J. Thayer Fábrega, J.C. Herzog, and J.D. Guttman. Strand spaces: Why is a security protocol correct? In *IEEE Computer Society Symposium on Research in Security and Privacy*, pages 160–171, 1998.

[23] T.Y.C. Woo and S.S. Lam. A semantic model for authentication protocols. In *IEEE Computer Society Symposium on Research in Security and Privacy*, pages 178–194, 1993.

DECIDABILITY OF OPACITY WITH NON-ATOMIC KEYS

Laurent Mazaré
VERIMAG
Centre Équation, 2 av de Vignates
38610 GIÈRES FRANCE
laurent.mazare@imag.fr

Abstract   The most studied property, secrecy, is not always sufficient to prove the security of a protocol. Other properties such as anonymity, privacy or opacity could be useful. Here, we use a simple definition of opacity which works by looking at the possible traces of the protocol using a new property over messages called similarity. The opacity property becomes a logical constraint involving both similarities and syntactic equalities. The main theorem proves that satisfiability of these constraints and thus opacity are decidable without having to make the hypothesis of atomic keys. Moreover, we use syntactic equalities to model some deductions an intruder could make by performing bit-to-bit comparisons (i.e. known-ciphertext attack).

Keywords: Opacity, Security, Formal Verification, Dolev-Yao Constraints, Rewriting Systems, Decidability.

The full version of this paper (including proofs) is available at
http://www-verimag.imag.fr/~lmazare/FAST04.pdf.

1.   Introduction

During the last decade, verification of security protocols has been widely investigated. The majority of the studies focussed on demonstrating secrecy properties using formal methods (see for example [Clarke et al., 1998], [Comon-Lundh and Cortier, 2003], [Comon-Lundh and Cortier, 2002] or [Goubault-Larrecq, 2000]). These methods have lead to effective algorithms and so to concrete tools for verifying secrecy such as these proposed by the EVA project [Bozga et al., 2002] or the Avispa project [Avispa, 1999]. However, checking security protocols requires studying other properties such as anonymity or opacity: hiding a piece of information from an intruder. For example, in a voting protocol, whereas the intruder is able to infer the possible values of the vote (yes or no), it should be impossible for him to guess which vote was expressed, only by observing a session of this protocol. Checking a protocol should include a way of formalizing the informations that were leaked and that the intruder can guess. In the last few years, attempts have been made to properly define opacity properties, to prove their decidability in certain cases and to propose some verification algorithms. As far as we know, other versions of opacity ([Boisseau, 2003], [Hughes and Shmatikov, 2004]) have been given in the literature but none of these criterion were implemented. Our notion of opacity is very close to the one introduced in [Hughes and Shmatikov, 2004] except that we use a formalism dedicated to protocols studies when they use a more general functional approach.

In this paper, we adopt a simple definition for opacity. The intruder C has a passive view of a protocol session involving two agents A and B. He is able to read any exchanged messages but he cannot modify, block or create a message. A property will be called *opaque* if there are two possible sessions of the protocol such that: in one of these, the property is true whereas it is not in the other, and it is impossible for the intruder to differentiate the messages from these two sessions from the messages exchanged in the original session. The starting point is the notion of similarity. This binary relation noted $\sim$ is an equivalence relation between messages. Two messages are similar if it is not feasible for the intruder to differentiate them. A typical example is two different messages encoded by a key that the intruder cannot infer. From the point of view of the intruder, these messages will be said similar. This notion is of course dependent of the knowledge of the intruder given by Dolev-Yao theory [Dolev and Yao, 1983]: if the intruder is able to infer any of the used keys, then similarity will be equivalent to syntactic equality. This notion of similarity will allow us to express opacity properties as constraints. These constraints will also include syntactic equality. Equalities are used to show that the intruder can perform bit-to-bit comparisons between some messages (this is best known in the literature as known-ciphertext attacks). Let us give a simple example that will be useful throughout this paper. A simple electronic voting protocol is given by the transmission between A (the voter) and S (the authority counting votes). Variable v is the expressed vote chosen among the possible values *yes* or *no*.

$$A \rightarrow S : \{v\}_{pub(S)}$$

If the intruder intercepts the value of $\{v\}_{pub(S)}$, then as he can compare it to $\{yes\}_{pub(S)}$ and $\{no\}_{pub(S)}$, the intruder is able to deduce the value of v. We will say that the intruder performed a bit-to-bit comparison between $\{v\}_{pub(S)}$ and $\{yes\}_{pub(S)}$ (or $\{no\}_{pub(S)}$).

The aim of this paper is to formalize opacity as two constraints involving similarities and equalities taking into account possible bit-to-bit comparisons. The main result is decidability of satisfiability for such constraints using a finite-model property.

The remainder of this paper is organized as follows. In section 2, we recall usual definition for messages and protocols. Similarity over messages is introduced in section 3 and some useful properties are given. This section also formalizes the opacity property and translates it to a constraint. Both section 2 and 3 are very close to sections appearing in [Mazaré, 2004], they give the necessary basis to formalize the following sections. Then, section 4 proves that satisfiability for such constraints is decidable. Section 5 introduces the bit-to-bit comparisons in our constraints. Eventually, section 6 shows how to use this technique on a simple example, and section 7 concludes this paper.

2. Cryptographic Protocols

Let *Atoms* and X be two infinite countable disjoint sets. *Atoms* is the set of atomic messages a, b,... Set X contains variables called "protocol variables" x, y,...

DEFINITION 1 (MESSAGE) *Let* Σ *be the signature* $Atoms \cup \{pair, encrypt\}$ *where pair and encrypt are two binary functions. The atomic messages are considered constant functions. Then a* message *is a first order term over* Σ *and the set of variables* X, *namely an element of* $T(\Sigma, X)$. *A message is said to be* closed *if it is a closed term of* $T(\Sigma, X)$, *i.e. a term of* $T(\Sigma)$.

In the rest of this paper, we will use the following notations:

$$\langle m_1, m_2 \rangle = pair(m_1, m_2) \qquad \{m_1\}_{m_2} = encrypt(m_1, m_2)$$

Height of message m can be easily defined recursively and will be noted $|m|$. Substitutions σ from X to $T(\Sigma, X)$ are defined as usual. Application of substitution σ to message m will be noted $m\sigma$. If σ is defined by $x\sigma = n$ and $y\sigma = y$ for any other variable y, then we could write $m[x\backslash n]$ instead of $m\sigma$. The domain of a substitution σ is the set $dom(\sigma)$ of variables x such that $x\sigma \neq x$.

The set of variables used in a message m is noted $var(m)$ (or $free(m)$).

DEFINITION 2 (PROTOCOL) *Let Actors be a finite set of participants called* actors. *The set of* programs *Progs is given by the following* *syntax where B is in Actors, m_1, m_2 and m are messages.*

$$G \ ::= \ \epsilon \ | \ !_B m.G$$
$$| \ ?m.G \ | \ if \ m_1 = m_2 \ then \ G \ else \ G \ fi$$

A protocol over the set of actors Actors is a function from Actors to Progs associating a program to each actor.

The intuitive semantic of programs is the usual one: signification of $!_B m$ is to send the message m to agent B, signification of $?m$ is to receive a message and using pattern matching, to replace the variables learnt from m in the rest of the program.

For the following, the set of actors is fixed to *Actors*. Let *free* be the function giving free variables of a program. It is easy to define *free* in the usual recursive way. Then, *free* can be extended over protocols. An instance of the protocol P is a protocol $P\sigma$ where σ instantiates exactly the free variables of P with closed messages. For that purpose, it is possible to rename every bound variable with a fresh variable such that bound variables are distinct and not in the free variables set. The substitution σ is called a *session* of the protocol P. When there is no risk of confusion on the protocol, its name will be omitted. Thus, we will talk about a session σ.

DEFINITION 3 (PROTOCOL SEMANTIC) *The semantic of a protocol is the transition system over protocols defined by the following rules:*

- *If m is a closed message and σ is the most general unifier of m and m' (m' is called the proto-message of m),*

$$\frac{Prog(A) = !_B m.P_A \quad Prog(B) = ?m'.P_B}{Prog \xrightarrow{m} Prog[A \to P_A; B \to P_B]\sigma}$$

Note that, if σ does not exist, the protocol can be blocked. The transition is from the protocol Prog to the protocol $Prog[A \to P_A; B \to P_B]$, i.e. the protocol linking A to program P_A, B to program P_B and other actors D to program $Prog(D)$.

- *If m_1 and m_2 are the same closed message,*

$$\frac{Prog(A) = if \ m_1 = m_2 \ then \ P_A \ else \ G \ fi}{Prog \to Prog[A \to P_A]}$$

- *If m_1 and m_2 are two distinct closed messages,*

$$\frac{Prog(A) = if \ m_1 = m_2 \ then \ G \ else \ P_A \ fi}{Prog \to Prog[A \to P_A]}$$

A protocol P *terminates* iff for any Q such that $P \to^* Q$, it is possible to reach the state ϵ: $Q \to^* \epsilon$. Note that only closed protocols could terminate. A *run* of a session σ for a protocol P is an ordered set of messages $r = r_1.r_2...r_n$ such that

$$P\sigma \xrightarrow{r_1} ... \xrightarrow{r_n} \epsilon$$

A protocol session is *deterministic* if it has exactly only one possible run. This run will be noted $run(P\sigma)$. In the following sections, protocols will always be considered deterministic, i.e. each of their sessions is deterministic.

Eventually, to simplify notations, instead of writing:

$$Prog(A) =!_S\{v\}_{pub(S)} \qquad Prog(S) =?\{v\}_{pub(S)}$$

We will shorten this to: $A \to S : \{v\}_{pub(S)}$.

This paper will make an extensive use of Dolev-Yao theory [Dolev and Yao, 1983]. Let E be a set of messages and m be a message, then we will note $E \vdash m$ if m is deducible from E using Dolev-Yao inferences.

3. Similarity and Opacity

3.1 Similarity

The intuitive definition of opacity is that an intruder is not able to distinguish a run where the property is satisfied from a run where it is not. To distinguish two messages, the intruder can decompose them, according to his knowledge but if he does not know the key k for example, he will not be able to make the difference between two different messages encoded by this key k. Two such messages will be called similar messages. This definition will be formalized using inference rules.

An *environment* is a finite set of closed messages. Usually, it will denote the set of messages known by the intruder. This definition will suppose that we only use symmetric key cryptography. However, all the following results can easily be generalized to public key cryptography.

DEFINITION 4 (SIMILAR MESSAGES) *Two closed messages m_1 and m_2 are said to be* similar *for the environment env iff $env \vdash m_1 \sim m_2$ where $\sim$ is the smallest (w.r.t set inclusion) binary relation satisfying:*

$$\frac{a \in Atoms}{a \sim a} \qquad \frac{u_1 \sim u_2 \quad v_1 \sim v_2}{\langle u_1, v_1 \rangle \sim \langle u_2, v_2 \rangle}$$

$$\frac{env \vdash k \quad u \sim v}{\{u\}_k \sim \{v\}_k} \qquad \frac{\neg env \vdash k \quad \neg env \vdash k'}{\{u\}_k \sim \{v\}_{k'}}$$

Intuitively, this means that an intruder with the knowledge *env* will not be able to distinguish two similar messages. The environment name will be omitted as soon as it is not relevant for comprehension. Our definition of $\sim$ is very closed to the $\equiv$ operator introduced by Abadi and Rogaway in [Abadi and Rogaway, 2000], except that we have an explicit environment to tell which keys are compromised instead of using directly the messages linked by the $\equiv$ operator.

Moreover, the definition of $\sim$ could easily be extended to non-closed environments and messages by adding the inference: $\frac{x \in X}{x \sim x}$. This can also be achieved by defining $m \sim n$ for non-closed messages as $m\sigma \sim n\sigma$ for each σ such that $m\sigma$ and $n\sigma$ are closed.

PROPERTY 1 *The binary relation $\sim$ is an equivalence relation: let m_1, m_2 and m_3 be three messages.*

$$m_1 \sim m_1 \quad m_1 \sim m_2 \Rightarrow m_2 \sim m_1$$

$$m_1 \sim m_2 \wedge m_2 \sim m_3 \Rightarrow m_1 \sim m_3$$

To prove that the $\sim$ relation is compatible with the context operation, we will have to suppose that only atomic keys are allowed. This hypothesis is only required for the following property.

PROPERTY 2 (CONTEXT) *Let m_1, m_2, m_3 and m_4 be four messages. If m_3 and m_4 have only one free variable x,*

$$m_1 \sim m_2 \wedge m_3 \sim m_4 \Rightarrow m_3[x \backslash m_1] \sim m_4[x \backslash m_2]$$

And in particular,

$$m_1 \sim m_2 \Rightarrow m_3[x \backslash m_1] \sim m_3[x \backslash m_2]$$

Let m and n be two messages and x a variable. Let σ be a substitution such that $x\sigma \sim n\sigma$. Then

$$m\sigma \sim m[x \backslash n]\sigma$$

When considering similarity, an important problem is: given an environment env and a closed message m, what is the set of closed message n such that

$$env \vdash n \text{ and } env \vdash m \sim n$$

Note that the main difficulty is that we do not necesseraly have $env \vdash m$.

For that purpose, the $fresh$ function will be introduced. It is inductively defined over messages by the following equalities where all the variables y have to be instantiated with different fresh variables (i.e. variables that do not appear anywhere else).

$$fresh(a) \quad = \quad a$$

$$
\begin{aligned}
fresh(x) &= x \\
fresh(\langle m, m' \rangle) &= \langle fresh(m), fresh(m') \rangle \\
fresh(\{m\}_k) &= \{fresh(m)\}_k \text{ if } env \vdash k \\
fresh(\{m\}_k) &= \{y\}_k \text{ if } env \nvdash k, \ y \text{ is a fresh variable}
\end{aligned}
$$

PROPERTY 3 *For every substitution σ, we have*

$$
m\sigma \sim fresh(m)\sigma
$$

The reciprocal of this property is that if m is similar to n, then n is an instance of $fresh(m)$, i.e. $fresh(m)$ where all free variables are instantiated by closed messages.

PROPERTY 4 *Let m and n be two closed messages. If $m \sim n$, then there exists a substitution σ that acts over the free variables of $fresh(m)$ such that $n = fresh(m)\sigma$.*

3.2 The Opacity Problem

Let us consider a protocol PR and one of its session σ. We will be interested in predicates over σ, namely properties ψ that act over variables instantiated by σ. Such properties may express the identity of an agent, or the value of a vote, for instance. The opacity problem considered here relies on several hypothesis:

- The intruder C has a passive view of protocol session σ involving two agents A and B. Passive means that the intruder can intercept and view any messages exchanged by A and B but is not able to block, modify nor to send any message.

- The intruder knows the protocol used PR.

- The intruder has an initial knowledge c_0, which is a predicate (for example, $c_0 = (k_1 = k_2)$ means that C knows that the keys that will instantiate k_1 and k_2 are the same).

If we consider the witness run $run(P\sigma) = m_1.m_2...m_n$, property ψ will be opaque if there exist two possible sessions σ_1 and σ_2 of the protocol giving messages similar to the witness messages (m_1 to m_n) where for example, $\psi\sigma_1$ is true and $\psi\sigma_2$ is false. In this case, the intruder will not be able to deduce any knowledge on $\psi\sigma$. Of course, there is no need to find both σ_1 and σ_2: if $\psi\sigma$ is true, then we could use σ instead of σ_1, as exchanged messages are the same, they are similar. But we will keep this notation with three substitutions to show the symmetry of this problem.

DEFINITION 5 (OPACITY) *A property ψ is said to be* opaque *for a protocol session σ of P iff there exist two sessions of the protocol σ_1 and σ_2 such that*

$$c_0\sigma_1 \wedge p_1 \sim m_1 \wedge ... \wedge p_n \sim m_n \wedge \psi\sigma_1$$

$$c_0\sigma_2 \wedge q_1 \sim m_1 \wedge ... \wedge q_n \sim m_n \wedge \neg\psi\sigma_2$$

Where $p_1.p_2...p_n$ is the run of the protocol P related to σ_1, $q_1.q_2...q_n$ is related to σ_2 and $m_1.m_2...m_n$ is related to σ. Note that the three runs must have the same length n.

The environment *env* used in the previous conjunctions is $\{m_1, ..., m_n, p_1, ..., p_n, q_1, ..., q_n\}$ and could be augmented with an initial knowledge of the intruder env_0.

We defined opacity for a protocol session, this can be extended to protocols by saying that a property is opaque in a protocol if it is opaque for all its session. The problem is that the number of possible sessions (and their size) is unbounded. This leads to an unbounded number of possible behaviors for a protocol. In the following, we give a method to check opacity for a given session but we lack the method to extend it to a whole protocol.

For instance, let us consider the simple electronic voting protocol. Suppose that the session observed by the intruder is $\sigma = [v\backslash yes]$. Then, the environment will be $env = \{yes, no, pub(S), \{yes\}_{pub(S)}\}$. The predicates expressing the opacity of the vote value will be:

$$\{v\}_{pub(S)} \sim \{yes\}_{pub(S)} \wedge v = yes$$

$$\{v\}_{pub(S)} \sim \{yes\}_{pub(S)} \wedge \neg v = yes$$

As both predicates are satisfiable, the vote value is opaque in this case.

Our property of opacity can also be used to check anonymity. For example, if we take a definition of anonymity closed to the one given in [Schneider and Sidiropoulos, 1996], we just have to add a "restricted view" for the intruder, i.e. the intruder only intercepts some of the exchanged messages (for example, when considering a system with both secure and insecure channels). Then, opacity for property "identity of such actor" will be similar to what is defined as anonymity.

4.   Initial Predicates and Satisfiability

In this section, the environment *env* is a finite set of closed messages. We will first define a class of predicates called *initial predicates*. Then, we will show that satisfiability for such predicates is decidable.

DEFINITION 6 (INITIAL PREDICATES) *The set IP of initial predicates is given by the following formulas:*

$$P ::= P_A | P \wedge P$$

$$P_A ::= m \sim n | m = n | \bot | \top$$

Where m and n are two messages.

THEOREM 1 *Satisfiability of initial predicates is decidable.*

PROOF 1 *Due to space limitation, the proof cannot be given here, but is available in the full version of this paper.* ∎

5. Syntactic Equality

The addition of syntactic equality in predicates will be used to model the intruder performing bit-to-bit comparison between two deducible messages. For example, if the intruder has intercepted $\{v\}_{pub(S)}$ and has a bit-to-bit value equal to $\{yes\}_{pub(S)}$, then he can deduce that the value of v is yes. Two such messages will be called *identifiable messages*. We will show in this section that the knowledge brought by identifiable messages is computable. A kind of attack close to this one has already been studied with different techniques under the name of *guessing attacks* in [Lowe, 2002], [Gong et al., 1993] or [Delaune, 2003]. But these studies do not precisely link the values to the proto-messages as will be done here. In the previous section, we used the Dolev-Yao model: the only way to obtain some information from a ciphertext was to find the right key and to decode it. Here, we use a model where the intruder has stronger deduction capacities. This hypothesis holds for some encryption schemes but most of them use random bits so that these attacks are impossible to perform.

DEFINITION 7 *Let $M = \{m_1, ..., m_n\}$ be a finite set of messages and σ be a substitution such that $M\sigma$ is closed. We define $\vdash_\sigma$ as follows.*

$$\frac{}{M \vdash_\sigma m_i}(1) \qquad \frac{M \vdash_\sigma m \quad M \vdash_\sigma n}{M \vdash_\sigma \langle m,n \rangle}(2) \qquad \frac{M \vdash_\sigma m \quad M \vdash_\sigma n}{M \vdash_\sigma \{m\}_n}(3)$$

$$\frac{M \vdash_\sigma \langle m,n \rangle}{M \vdash_\sigma m}(4) \qquad \frac{M \vdash_\sigma \langle m,n \rangle}{M \vdash_\sigma n}(5) \qquad \frac{M \vdash_\sigma \{m\}_n \quad M\sigma \vdash n\sigma}{M \vdash_\sigma m}(6)$$

The meaning of $M \vdash_\sigma m$ is that an intruder knowing M and looking at $M\sigma$ can link the prototype m to its value $m\sigma$. The intruder can add to its knowledge $m = m\sigma$ but is not allowed to discompose m and $m\sigma$ as soon as some keys could be not deducible. But, if the intruder can find two times the same message linked to two different prototypes m and n, then he will be able to deduce the syntactic equality $m = n$.

Note that $M \vdash_\sigma m$ implies $M\sigma \vdash m\sigma$. The inverse is of course false (take for example $m = x$, $M = \{y\}$ and $x\sigma = y\sigma = a$). First, we will prove a general property on our new theory: its locality.

PROPERTY 5 (LOCALITY) *The theory $\vdash_\sigma$ is local: if $M \vdash_\sigma m$, then there exists a proof of $M \vdash_\sigma m$ such that for any intermediate occurrence of $M \vdash_\sigma m'$ in the proof, m' is either a sub-message of m, or a sub-message of a message present in M.*

A direct application of this property is that if the last rule used in a minimal proof of $M \vdash_\sigma m$ is a decomposition, then m is a sub-message of a message of M.

DEFINITION 8 (IDENTIFIABLE MESSAGES) *Two messages m and n are said to be identifiable for σ and M iff*

- $m \neq n$

- $M \vdash_\sigma m$ *and* $M \vdash_\sigma n$

- $m\sigma = n\sigma$

m and n are minimal *iff there does not exist a non initial position p such that $m_{|p}$ and $n_{|p}$ are identifiable ($m_{|p}$ is the sub-term of m occuring at position p).*

If two messages m and n are identifiable, then the intruder can add $m = n$ to its knowledge. Now, we want to be able to add all the knowledge that can be inferred to the intruder's knowledge without testing any possible couple of messages. We want to show that this knowledge is computable in a finite time. For that purpose, we will state two distinct properties.

PROPERTY 6 *The set of minimal identifiable messages is computable.*

To prove this property, we will have to use the locality of our theory. This property will lead us to a decision algorithm capable of producing every possible pair of minimal identifiable messages. Let m and n be two minimal identifiable messages. Consider minimal proofs for $M \vdash_\sigma m$ and $M \vdash_\sigma n$, using the symmetry between m and n, only three combinations of final rules for $M \vdash_\sigma m$ and $M \vdash_\sigma n$ are possible.

- These rules are both 2 or 3: then either $m = \langle m_1, m_2 \rangle$ and $n = \langle n_1, n_2 \rangle$, either $m = \{m_1\}_{m_2}$ and $n = \{n_1\}_{n_2}$. Let us consider the case of pairs. As we have $m \neq n$, we have $m_1 \neq n_1$ or $m_2 \neq n_2$. To fix the idea, we will consider $m_1 \neq n_1$. We have, of course,

$m_1\sigma = n_1\sigma$ and $M \vdash_\sigma m_1$ and $M \vdash_\sigma n_1$. So m_1 and n_1 are identifiable, there is a contradiction with the minimality of the pair m, n. That is why, these rules cannot occur at the end of minimal proofs.

- If both rules are in 1, 4, 5 and 6. Then m and n are sub-messages from M. These messages are only in finite number.

- If the rule concerning m is in 1, 4, 5 and 6 and the rule concerning n is in 2 and 3. Then m is a sub-message of M. As $m\sigma = n\sigma$, we have $n\sigma$ in $SM(M\sigma)$ (sub-messages, i.e. sub-terms of $M\sigma$). So we have

$$|n\sigma| \leq max(|p|, p \in SM(M\sigma))$$

And we obtain a bound of the length of n:

$$|n| \leq max(|p|, p \in SM(M\sigma))$$

The atoms occurring in n have to occur in M and the variables occurring in n have to be instantiated by σ. So there are only a finite number of possible messages for n.

To find all the minimal similar messages, we have to test all the messages whose lengths are below $max(|p|, p \in SM(M\sigma))$. Messages from $SM(M)$ are in that set. These messages can only use atoms used in M and variables instantiated by σ. That is why the set of messages to be tested is finite. Moreover, checking that two messages are identifiable and minimal can be done in a finite time too, and so all the minimal identifiable messages can be found in a finite time.

PROPERTY 7 *If m and n are identifiable and $p_1,...,p_k$ are the positions such that $m_{|p_i}$ and $n_{|p_i}$ are identifiable and minimal, then for any model σ,*

$$\sigma \models (m = n \Leftrightarrow m_{|p_1} = n_{|p_1} \wedge ... \wedge m_{|p_k} = n_{|p_k})$$

Using properties stated in this section, we now have a method to model what an intruder can guess using bit-to-bit comparisons. Our method is easy to apply but inefficient as it tests any couple of message whose lengths are below a fixed bound. It produces constraints of the form $m = n$, they can be added to the opacity predicates. As we show in the previous section, satisfiability of the resulting predicates will remain decidable. More formally, M will be the awaited trace of the protocol in terms of proto-messages augmented with the initial knowledge of the intruder and *env* will be the set of intercepted messages as long as the initial knowledge, so we will usually take $env = M\sigma$. Then, opacity of a property P will be checked as satisfiability of to predicates $S \wedge P$ and $S \wedge \neg P$ where S contains similarities that occur in the opacity constraint. We will have to compute the set of minimal identifiable messages m_1, n_1 to m_k, n_k. This gives use another predicate E defined by:

$$E = (m_1 = n_1 \wedge ... \wedge m_k = n_k)$$

And so, we will study satisfiability of two predicates: $E \wedge S \wedge P$ and $E \wedge S \wedge \neg P$. This will be applied in the next section on two very simple electronic voting protocols.

6.   Example: A Simple Electronic Vote Protocol

6.1   Simple Does Not Mean Secure

Let us consider the most simple electronic voting protocol. A is the voter and S the authority that will count the different votes. The possible votes are *yes* and *no*. Of course, one of the objective is that the expressed vote remains opaque. In a first version, the vote will just be sent from A to S encoded using the public key of S. The protocols is written:

$$A \rightarrow S : \{v\}_{pub(S)}$$

Where v is chosen among the values *yes* and *no*. Let us suppose that the expressed vote is *yes*, so the substitution σ is defined by $\sigma = [v \backslash yes]$. Then M is the set $\{\{v\}_{pub(S)}, yes, no, pub(S)\}$. The environment *env* is the set $M\sigma$. The value of $max(|p|, p \in SM(M\sigma))$ is 2 ($pub(S)$ is considered as an atomic message). We easily obtain the set of minimal identifiable messages:

$$\{(\{v\}_{pub(S)}, \{yes\}_{pub(S)})\}$$

So $E = (\{v\}_{pub(S)} = \{yes\}_{pub(S)})$, the constraints of opacity related to the value of v are:

$$\{v\}_{pub(S)} = \{yes\}_{pub(S)} \wedge \{v\}_{pub(S)} \sim \{yes\}_{pub(S)} \wedge v = yes$$

$$\{v\}_{pub(S)} = \{yes\}_{pub(S)} \wedge \{v\}_{pub(S)} \sim \{yes\}_{pub(S)} \wedge v = no$$

By using our rewriting system on the second predicate, we have

$$v = yes \wedge \{v\}_{pub(S)} \sim \{yes\}_{pub(S)} \wedge v = no$$

And so this constraint can be rewrited to $\bot$, the second constraint is not satisfiable. The value of v is not opaque: the intruder can guess the vote. Intuitively, we already shew how the intruder could guess the vote in the introduction. Now, we want to fix this opacity flaw by modifying the protocol.

6.2   Adding Complexity

The technique used by the intruder is to guess which message can be encrypted and to compare the result with the intercepted message. As we do not want the intruder to guess which message can be encrypted, we add a nonce in the protocol:

$$A \rightarrow S : \{\langle v, n \rangle\}_{pub(S)}$$

As in the previous example, let us suppose that the expressed vote is *yes* and the nonce is instantiated by a fresh atom N, so the substitution σ is defined by $\sigma = [v \backslash yes, n \backslash N]$. Then M is the set $\{\{\langle v, n \rangle\}_{pub(S)}, yes, no, pub(S)\}$. The environment *env* is the set $M\sigma$. The value of $max(|p|, p \in SM(M\sigma))$ is 3. But now, the set of minimal identifiable messages is empty, so the constraints of opacity concerning the value of v are:

$$\{\langle v, n \rangle\}_{pub(S)} \sim \{\langle yes, N \rangle\}_{pub(S)} \wedge v = yes$$

$$\{\langle v, n \rangle\}_{pub(S)} \sim \{\langle yes, N \rangle\}_{pub(S)} \wedge v = no$$

It is easy to see that both constraints are satisfiable, so we now have that the expressed vote is opaque. This protocol can be used without fearing that an intruder can guess the value of the vote using bit-to-bit comparisons.

7.   Conclusion

In this paper, we extended the notions presented in [Mazaré, 2004]: opacity is also defined as satisfiability of two constraints, but we do not need the hypothesis that keys are atomic anymore. However, the method introduced in [Mazaré, 2004] can be applicated to real case whereas our new method to decide satisfiability of constraints is far more complex. The set of predicates which satisfiability is decidable has been extended to predicates using syntactic equalities and non-atomic keys. Moreover, we introduced a new technique to determine what an intruder can guess using bit-to-bit comparisons. Now, we have two distinct theories: on one side Dolev-Yao $\vdash$ and on the other side $\vdash_\sigma$. Even if the two theories are closely linked, an idea for future work would be to produce a single theory modeling both kind of attacks. Another interesting extension would be to make the intruder active. If C can intercept and modify the messages, could he find the right messages to alter such that the property is not opaque any more ?

Acknowledgements

The author wishes to thank the anonymous reviewers for their very helpful and constructive comments.

References

Abadi, M. and Rogaway, P. (2000). Reconciling two views of cryptography (the computational soundness of formal encryption). In *IFIP International Conference on Theoretical Computer Science (IFIP TCS2000)*, Sendai, Japan. Springer-Verlag, Berlin Germany.

Avispa (1999). The Avispa Project. http://www.avispa-project.org/.

Boisseau, A. (2003). *Abstractions pour la vérification de propriétés de sécurité de protocoles cryptographiques*. PhD thesis, Laboratoire Spécification et Vérification (LSV), ENS de Cachan.

Bozga, L., Lakhnech, Y., and Périn, M. (2002). Abstract interpretation for secrecy using patterns. Technical report, EVA : http://www-eva.imag.fr/.

Clarke, E., Jha, S., and Marrero, W. (1998). Using state space exploration and a natural deduction style message derivation engine to verify security protocols. In *IFIP Working Conference on Programming Concepts and Methods*.

Comon-Lundh., H. and Cortier, V. (2002). Security properties: Two agents are sufficient. Technical report, LSV.

Comon-Lundh, H. and Cortier, V. (2003). New decidability results for fragments of first-order logic and application to cryptographic protocols. In *14th Int. Conf. Rewriting Techniques and Applications (RTA'2003)*, volume 2706 of *LNCS*.

Delaune, S. (2003). Intruder deduction problem in presence of guessing attacks. Workshop on Security Protocols Verification (SPV'03), co-located with the 14th International Conference on Concurrency Theory (CONCUR'03).

Dolev, D. and Yao, A. C. (1983). On the security of public key protocols. *IEEE Transactions on Information Theory*, 29(2):198–208.

Gong, L., Lomas, M. A., Needham, R. M., and Saltzer, J. H. (1993). Protecting poorly chosen secrets from guessing attacks. *IEEE Journal on Selected Areas in Communications*, 11(5):648–656.

Goubault-Larrecq, J. (2000). A method for automatic cryptographic protocol verification. In *International Workshop on Formal Methods for Parallel Programming: Theory and Applications*, volume 1800 of *LNCS*.

Hughes, D. and Shmatikov, V. (2004). Information hiding, anonymity and privacy: A modular approach. *Journal of Computer Security*, 12(1):3–36.

Lowe, G. (2002). Analysing protocols subject to guessing attacks. In *Proc. of the Workshop on Issues in the Theory of Security (WITS'02)*.

Mazaré, L. (2004). Using unification for opacity properties. In *Proc. of the Workshop on Issues in the Theory of Security (WITS'04)*. To appear.

Schneider, S. and Sidiropoulos, A. (1996). CSP and anonymity. In *ESORICS*, pages 198–218.

VIRTUAL ANALYSIS AND REDUCTION OF SIDE-CHANNEL VULNERABILITIES OF SMARTCARDS

Jerry den Hartog
Department of Computer Science, Universiteit Twente
hartogji@cs.utwente.nl

Erik de Vink
Department of Mathematics and Computer Science, TU Eindhoven
Leiden Institute of Advanced Computer Science, Leiden University
evink@win.tue.nl

Abstract   This paper focuses on the usability of the PINPAS tool. The PIN-PAS tool is an instruction-level interpreter for smartcard assembler languages, augmented with facilities to study side-channel vulnerabilities. The tool can simulate side-channel leakage and has a suite of utilities to analyze this. The usage of the tool, for the analysis of a cryptographic algorithm is illustrated using the standard AES and RSA. Vulnerabilities of the implementations are identified and protective measures added. It is argued, that the tool can be instrumental for the design and realization of secure smartcard implementations in a systematic way.

Keywords: smartcard, side-channel attack, power analysis, fault analysis, DPA, simulation, countermeasures, systematic hardening

1.   Introduction

Since the ground-breaking papers of Paul Kocher Kocher, 1996; Kocher et al., 1999 a vast amount of research on power analysis and other side-channel attacks have been reported in the literature (e.g. Boneh et al., 1997; Messerges, 2000; Coron et al., 2001; Quisquater and Samyde, 2001). Taking all types of attacks into account for a concrete implementation of a cryptographic algorithm on a specific smartcard and, furthermore, investigating the feasibility of all appropriate countermeasure is a daunting task. Apart from experience and engineering principles, feedback on intermediate stages during the development —instead of after the implementation phase— is valuable to the smartcard algorithm programmer. The PINPAS tool, discussed here, can be used to provide this information. More generally, the tool aims to contribute to a better understanding of side-channel vulnerability and systematic hardening of a smartcard application.

PINPAS is an instruction-level interpreter for smartcard assembler together with facilities to collect and process side-channel information. In this paper we focus on the usability aspects of the tool when assessing the side-channel vulnerability of an implementation of a cryptographic algorithm. As running examples, we investigate the vulnerability for differential power analysis (DPA) of the AES and RSA algorithm. We show, for basic smartcard implementations, how attacks and the effectiveness of subsequent countermeasures can be analyzed.

In outline, the approach works as follows: First, a candidate algorithm is implemented in the assembler language of the targeted smartcard. Then, power traces are collected by the PINPAS tool while interpreting the implementation. Next, iteratively, the feasibility of a DPA attack is estimated and necessary countermeasures are put in place.

The PINPAS tool is still only a prototype. However, it clearly shows the advantage of software-based feedback for side-channel attacks on smartcards. The benefits of the tool include the following:

- Side-channel analysis can already start early in the development process as no physical card or laboratory setup is needed.

- Time consuming measurements and signal-analysis can largely be avoided.

- It is easy to switch platform and card type and change the attack parameters such as the side-channel, attack point, etc.

- The tool provides quick feedback on the effectiveness of introduced countermeasures.

- The simulation environment enables one to balance resource utilization, performance and security, respectively.

- The flexible setup allows for easy experimentation with new potential attack or defense techniques. Additionally, the PINPAS tool provides a setting to study hypothetical side-channel leakage.

The idea of performing timing attacks and differential power analysis on a simulator is a clear one and may not be completely new. However, the PINPAS tool is, to our best knowledge, the first tool reported in the academic literature. Moreover, the increase of computing power and maturity of object-oriented programming languages have witnessed further evolution since the advent of SPA and DPA. Today, an industrial-sized tool based on PINPAS has come in reach. In fact, the prototype has been adopted for further development.

Because of its broad applicability in early development stages, its flexibility and ease of use, while avoiding involved physical measurements, the PINPAS tool can be valuable to smartcard manufacturers, algorithm designers, evaluators as well as researchers. The PINPAS tool provides an instrument to study information leakage via side-channels in a systematic sway. With the tool, countermeasures can be evaluated for their effectiveness. This way, the prototype may serve as a stepping stone toward a general theory of generating safe code from vulnerable algorithms. An overview of the PINPAS tool was reported in den Hartog et al., 2003.

2. The PINPAS tool

The PINPAS tool is a Java program that provides a number of virtual machines for various smartcard assembler languages. On top of this, the tool facilitates various type of side-channel attacks, both first and higher-order. (The former type focuses on side-channel information from one single source; the latter seeks to combine such information retrieved from several places.) Given a particular implementation code of a cryptographic algorithm the tool provides an environment to assess the vulnerability of the implementation, in particular for timing attacks and for power analysis. Thus, the PINPAS tool consists of two main building blocks: a simulator and an analyzer.

The simulator part for a particular brand of smartcard is based on the overall architecture and the instruction set of the smartcard. If one wishes to do so, one can restrict the so-called power profile to the modeling of the CPU and storage, neglecting possible co-processors or dedicated components. Typically, a number of registers and memory space is allocated by the simulator, comprising –together with the program counter– its state. Instructions then are interpreted as state transformations. They affect the program counter, the registers and memory. For each instruction a Java method is defined in the class implementing the simulation of the smartcard. Interpretation of a program for the smartcard consists of a loop that repeatedly calls the Java method that corresponds to the card instruction to be executed. As an aside, note that system calls and native APIs need not to be represented as low level operations; Java methods that reflect the input/output behavior of such card components suffice. This way, the simulator abstracts away from aspects that are not directly related to the cryptographic algorithm itself.

The analyzer part supports the collection of abstract power traces. A physical model of the smartcard architecture and the instruction set are parameters to the tool. A rather coarse approach, very much like common practice in actual power attacks to smartcards though, only takes the Hamming weight of data into account. On the other side of the spectrum, one can generate sampling information in a format compatible to that of the oscilloscope. Although the tool-generated power traces cannot, by their nature, be exactly the same of those generated physically, experiments have shown a clear similarity between the two. While obtaining selected or randomly generated input values from file one-by-one, the tool produces, by running the algorithm on the virtual machine, as many abstract power traces as desired.

In addition, the tool provides a few built-in mechanisms for further manipulation. In particular the DPA selection criteria or brute-force byte attacks can be launched automatically. Note that, power traces are produced directly from the assembler code, thus bypassing time and effort needed to collect power traces physically from the algorithm loaded onto a smartcard. Also, post processing of power traces to eliminate noise and jitter has become a non-issue in this setting; by construction, the traces are noise-free and lined up. However, in principle, physically collected power traces can be presented to the analyzer part of the tool as well.

3.   A case study: AES and RSA

In the previous section we described the tool developed in the PINPAS project. In this section, we demonstrate the steps in the development of a secure smartcard implementation of a cryptographic algorithm. In particular, we will create, in several steps, implementations of the AES and RSA algorithms for a typical smartcard. For simplicity we have chosen a generic platform based on the Hitachi H8 RISC-processor.

3.1   AES and the PINPAS tool

The advanced encryption standard AES algorithm NIST, 2001; Daemen and Rijmen, 2002 is a block cipher which uses a number of rounds consisting of reversible linear 'confusion' and non-linear 'diffusion' transformations. The linear transformations exploit exclusive ors with key material and AES's typical shifting and moving of rows and columns.

The non-linear transformation includes a manipulation of bytes by S-boxes.

Starting point for the smartcard implementation discussed here, was a C-coded version of the AES algorithm. The C-code was optimized with the efficiency of the resulting machine code in mind. Next, the gcc compiler was run to generate Hitachi H8 code from this. In the discussion below we will concentrate on the case of an 128-bit key length.

The analysis of the smartcard implementation starts off with some standard procedures that are provided by the tool. A preliminary power analysis shows that the different rounds can be distinguished from the power signature. Also other information, such as the use of specific input bytes, can be revealed.

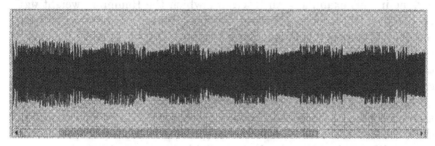

Partial power trace for AES showing 6 complete rounds

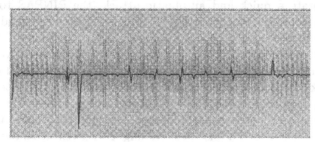

Zoomed view of the usage of second input byte and the power trace (gray)

Starting from the assumption that Hamming weights of data may leak, an attacker can focus on the first linear transformation using key material, a so-called addroundkey. The crucial instruction in this code fragment is

$$\text{data[i] XOR key[i]} \tag{1}$$

which, obviously, xors two bytes. In the first round the data value is known: It is simply the input to the algorithm. Thus, guessing the ith byte of the key will allow one to predict the outcome of the xor. Having such a criterion available a power attack can be launched.

In the tool this criterion, or trace condition, – forming two groups of traces with Hamming weights larger and smaller than 4, respectively – can be reflected by the following piece of Java code.

```
boolean select( Trace trace )
{  wgt = hammingWgt( trace.getInputByte( i ) ^ keyguess );
   if ( wgt > 4 ) return true;
   if ( wgt < 4 ) return false;
   throw new UnsortableException();
}
```

The exception `UnsortableException();` is used to discard traces, as is done in this example with traces for which the Hamming weight `wgt` equals 4. (Other, more advanced trace conditions can be used as well, but for the purpose here, the above will do.)

The tool will divide the power traces in two groups according to the trace condition. The average power consumption over these two groups is compared, resulting in a so-called difference trace. If the key byte is guessed correctly, a difference in average power consumption will occur at the position of the instruction in equation (1) and result in a peak in the difference trace. For an incorrect guess, a random partition of the traces without significant peaks in the difference trace is expected.

To facilitate a quick and automatic attack, the PINPAS tool was directed to record the power traces only for a small window including the instruction to be analyzed. Apart from speeding up the simulation, such facilities are also convenient when memory usage becomes a bottleneck.

An experiment using 250 traces discovered all but a few bits of the 128 bit round key. Because of the linearity of the attacked xor instruction, a relatively high spike in the difference trace will already occur when 6 or more bits of the key byte are guessed correctly. Therefore, there is a small probability that a false positive might be given while iteratively stepping through all possible key byte values. This probability can be reduced by using more traces. The same experiment based on 500 traces predicted all key bytes without error.

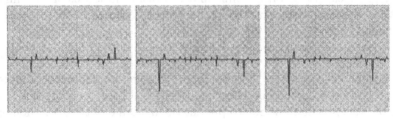

Difference trace for an incorrect, almost correct and correct guess

Several countermeasures have been proposed to protect against the power analysis attacks, including hiding of data by random masking Golić and Tymen, 2003 or distribution of critical data over different locations Chari et al., 1999; Goubin and Patarin, 1999. Other countermeasures seek to make the aligning traces and the averaging of power consumption more difficult. In particular, 'no-op' insertion introducing random waits and randomization of control flow. Of course, due to the limited resources, one needs to carefully balance the improvement of security yielded by these techniques and the resource utilization and performance of the resulting algorithm.

In order to defend the AES implementation described above, we introduce a countermeasure that randomizes the flow of control. The observation is that in the exclusive or with bytes of the key in the addroundkey section can be done in any order. The adapted code is as follows:

```
int[] order = permutation of 0..15
data[ order[i] ] = data[ order[i] ] XOR key[ order[i] ]
```

Experiments with the PINPAS tool show that the countermeasure is effective. Repeating the DPA based on 500 traces no longer revealed the key. We expected that simply more traces would suffice for a successful DPA attack. Surprisingly, using 8000 traces (with 8000 traces being 16 times 500 traces) did not prove successful either. Thus, the tool helped not only in providing experimental evidence of the strength of the countermeasure in reducing the vulnerability, but also provided feedback on our engineering intuition. Recall that in the setting of the tool the synthesized traces are noise-free; in physical experiments even more traces need to be collected. However, it should be noted that other DPA attacks are still possible, e.g. in the subbytes or shiftrows routines.

3.2   RSA and the PINPAS tool

As a second example we discuss the familiar RSA algorithm Rivest et al., 1978. Encryption in the RSA algorithm uses exponentiation modulo a large composite n. For our implementation of RSA we assume to have a co-processor available on the card. The co-processor is used for two operations: squaring and multiplication in $\mathbb{Z}/n\mathbb{Z}$. We focus on the common case of 512 bit numbers.

Using the operations provided by the co-processor, exponentiation can be implemented as follows.

```
r = 1;
for( int i = 0; i < 512; i++ )
```

```
{ r = SQR( r, n );
  if ( keybit(i) == 1 ) r = MUL( r, m, n );
}
```

An SPA attack on this code is well-known, see e.g. Kocher, 1996; Dhem et al., 1998. The multiplication MUL in the code above is done only if the current bit of the key equals 1. By inspection of the shape of the power consumption trace, one can distinguish the different rounds in the algorithm. Moreover, one can determine for a round, by examining its length, whether it consists of only a squaring or also includes a multiplication. This way, the key can directly be read from the power trace.

The standard countermeasure to remedy this vulnerability is to introduce a dummy multiplication into the code above for key bits which are zero.

```
if ( keybit(i) == 1 ) r = MUL( r, m, n );
else dummy = MUL( r, m, n );
```

As all rounds are then of equal length, one can no longer decide the value of a key byte by simply looking at the power consumption trace. Unfortunately, as a side-effect of this defense, the vulnerability to DPA attacks has been increased.

In the RSA algorithm the intermediate result for the variable r depends on part of the key only. A DPA attack can be launched attacking this value. By guessing e.g. the first byte of the key, the intermediate value after 8 rounds can be predicted for given inputs. As before, a spike in the difference trace indicates a correct guess for the key.

In contrast to the attack on the AES discussed above, the attack on RSA has a cumulative nature. In order to find a byte of the key, all more significant bytes should already have been found. If no byte value results in a significant peak it is likely that one of the previous byte values has been guessed incorrectly.

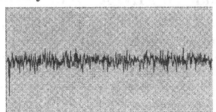

The correct key guess for the first byte of the key[1]

---

[1] The tool has been instructed to only record power consumption values at points relevant to the attack.

Experiments with the tool showed that the correct key could be obtained using 125 traces. A complication in the attack is that significant peaks are induced by a wrong guess, such as a shifted key value. However, one can eliminate these peaks by narrowing the window of analysis to the correct round, for example the 8th round for the first byte (MSB) of the key. The availability of the tool helped unraveling the occurrence of peaks at unexpected locations in the difference traces.

Due to the mathematical setting of RSA several countermeasures available for block ciphers, such as (non-multiplicative) masking and distribution, do not apply here. Perhaps they are applicable for a completely different implementation of RSA, but it is hard to see how the co-processor can then be exploited. In the same vein, although random waits can be introduced, it seems likely that in practice, the attacker can recognize and remove these from the power trace. When simulating traces in the tool this is straightforward.

Experiments with the tool indicate that hardware defenses are effective. For example, adding to the co-processor an internal buffer that does not leak for storage of the intermediate result can help reduce the DPA sensitivity. Countermeasures in hardware can be incorporated in the tool, relatively easy, by adapting the Java classes implementing the various machine instructions and adjustment of the power profile. As seen from our discussion above, this co-processor must also implement a dummy multiplication operation which yields the same power signature as a real multiplication, but does not update the internal buffer.

4. Significance of theoretical attacks

In the previous section we have demonstrated how attacks on AES and RSA can be simulated in the PINPAS tool. Here we discuss the practical relevance of the results found using the tool.

4.1 Measured vs. synthesized traces

Power traces generated by the simulation cannot, by their nature, be the same as physically measured traces. However, a reasonable approximation is possible. So, what is a reasonable approximation? From a security standpoint the amount of information leaked in the power consumption is more relevant than, for example, the absolute difference with actually measured values.

To do a correct analysis using the tool it is important that attacks possible on the physical card can also be mimicked in the tool. This means that information leakage in the power consumption trace of a physical card should also be present in the simulated power trace. On the other hand, adding countermeasures cost money, time, performance, etc. Thus, from a practical stand point, having too much information in a simulated power trace is also not too attractive as this may cause a waste of effort defending against attacks which are not really possible anyway.

The power traces synthesized by the tool contain no noise, in contrast to physically measured traces. Experiments, in which random noise has been added to the synthesized power traces, have confirmed that this does not affect the vulnerability to a DPA attack. The absence of noise has several clear advantages in the analysis. One can concentrate on the actual vulnerabilities in the code without a need for advanced signal processing to align traces and reduce noise and jitter. Also, because less traces are required for an attack, the amount of computation is limited. Note that, when testing only with traces obtained from physical measurements one may miss a vulnerability merely due to the fact that an insufficiently many traces were used.

In comparing generated traces versus power traces with noise obtained from physical measurement we observe the following: First, if no attack is found on the generated traces, there will be none on the measure power traces either. Second, if an attack was found, one will likely be able to reconstruct this for measured power traces, possibly requiring more measurements. The absence of a vulnerability for measured traces may very well be due to the signal-to-noise ratio. By using generated traces one can focus on the intrinsic lack of safety of an implementation and devote time to finding the proper countermeasures.

4.2   Hamming weight and other side-channel information

In the simulations used for the power analysis attacks in the previous section, the Hamming weight of manipulated data leaks in the power trace. Different cards may leak different information in their power consumption. The PINPAS tool is rather flexible in the power profile that is used, allowing the simulation to be adapted to the card under consideration. Experience with smartcard hardware has shown that the leakage of information in the power consumption is, in large part, due to activity on the memory bus. Depending on the implementation of the memory bus, the power consumption of the memory bus may be related to changes of the value on the bus rather than to the actual value on the bus. This means that in many cases assuming that the Hamming weight leaks in the power consumption is probably an overestimation of the amount of information that an attacker can obtain through power analysis. A power profile that captures the more restricted information leakage has also been included in the tool.

As with noiseless traces, using Hamming weight leakage is playing it safe: If no attacks are found with this strong form of leakage, it is unlikely that there will be attacks on measured traces. It does mean, however, that the practicality of attacks found in the tool needs to be considered. In other words, if an attack is found, does one need to spend considerable effort to prevent it or is it merely a theoretical attack? To answer this question, the attack can be repeated on a different power consumption profile which contains less information leakage, all the way down to the actual hardware if needed (and a card is available). Having predefined and tested the attacks and potential weak points expedites the testing process on the hardware.

The attack on the AES in the previous section relies in an essential way on leakage of Hamming weights. This means that this attack does work directly on cards with a more restricted form of information leakage. The attack may still provide useful information if the attacker can determine part of the value on the bus before the attacked instruction. Intimate knowledge of the smartcard architecture and ad-hoc analysis of the smartcard, along with heuristics, can be used to obtain the previous value on the bus. If one can safely assume, that the attacker is not able to obtain this information, using a power profile with less information leakage is appropriate. Tests in the tool using such a power profile confirmed, that the described attack no longer works in this setting. However, other attacks on AES can still be mounted. For example, by guessing one byte of the key, the value of the output of the first non-linear transformation (S-box) can be predicted. By looking at only a single bit of this predicted value the attack will still work using the adapted power profile. Note that, a defense using randomization of control flow, such as introduced in the previous section, can also be used to help to protect against this attack.

The SPA attack on RSA using timing of rounds only uses the general shape of the power graph and easily translates to an attack on physical traces. The DPA attack on the version of RSA strengthened against the timing attack also used the fact that Hamming weights leak, but not in an essential way; instead of predicting a byte of the intermediate value, a single bit could be used. This attack requires more traces, but will still work with the power profile with less information leakage.

In conclusion, one can use a liberal leakage profile for an initial analysis of an implementation. If vulnerabilities are found either countermeasures can be introduced or attacks can be re-tested with a more restrictive power profile. In this way, one can make precise which assumptions about the power consumption are essential for the safety of the particular implementation.

5.   Concluding remarks

Above we have illustrated the usability of the PINPAS tool for the case of AES and RSA. It was explained how implementations of these two algorithms can be run on the tool and side-channel vulnerabilities can be identified. Next it was discussed how the effectiveness of the countermeasures can be assessed. Finally the relevance of attacks on synthesized traces for the security of a smartcard was treated.

We have argued, that it is advantageous to have a software tool for the analysis of side-channel vulnerabilities available. The discussed attacks are relatively straightforward. However, the approach is flexible and suited to examine, e.g., higher-order strategies. For the particular case of the strengthened AES implementation discussed above, summing up the power consumption at all locations in the power trace where the particular instruction can be loaded in the randomized execution will reveal the key using the same number of traces. For RSA the results for multiple bits or bytes can be combined to strengthen the correlation and amplifying the spikes. It should be noted, that such refined attack scenarios are also necessary in order to keep up with the developments of unconventionally wired smartcard (glue logic) and associated a-typical power profile. More generally, the tool can be deployed for higher-order scenarios on implementations using masking or duplication Chari et al., 1999; Goubin and Patarin, 1999; Akkar and Goubin, 2003 to test, e.g., the increase in the number of power traces needed. Currently, the points of attack are selected manually, but it would be an interesting add-on to the tool to do this automated (most likely, through integration with other tools for security analysis, such as dependency checkers and high-level program verifiers). A long-term goal of the PINPAS project is the construction of a code optimizer that eliminates side-channel vulnerabilities automatically. For the development of a theory of secure program transformations, building on the notion of non-interference (see, e.g., Goguen and Meseguer, 1982; Ryan and Schneider, 2001; R. Focardi, 2000), the experiments performed with the tool play a crucial role.

In the previous sections we mainly focused on power analysis. However, also for other flavors of side-channel attacks the PINPAS tool can be exploited fruitfully. For example, successful timing attacks have been conducted. Also, the general idea of injecting hardware faults into the smartcards execution Boneh et al., 1997; Biham and Shamir, 1997 can easily be mimicked in the tool, much more precisely and practically as compared to a physical set-up. The virtual machine can be instructed to temporarily step outside its main interpretation cycle and perform a state transformation according to a faulty instruction (as physically could have been enforced by a power glitch, light flash, card tear or other means of card stressing). Due to the modular architecture of the tool this can be implemented straightforwardly, e.g. along the lines of Dusart et al., 2003 for AES and Boneh et al., 1997 for RSA. Thus, also for fault analysis, the clean setting of the tool helps to avoid time-consuming and labourious experiments (with, occasionally, annihilating consequences for the smartcard used) while still obtaining a clear indication of the particular vulnerabilities of the algorithm on the card.

Recent work Schramm et al., 2003; Schramm et al., 2004 reports on enhancing crypto-analytical collision attacks Dobbertin, 1998; Biham, 2002 with side-channel information resulting in successful attacks on DES and AES. The crux in this hybrid approach is that high correlation of power traces indicate that a collision has occurred. Practical experiments support the view that collision attacks constitute a powerful technique, that is insensitive to various countermeasures. It turns out that relatively few power traces are needed. However, having total control, as in the software setting of the PINPAS tool advocated in this paper, may be advantageous in collecting further experimental evidence for the reach of collision attacks.

Acknowledgments

We gratefully acknowledge the contributions of Jan Verschuren and Jaap de Vos to this research.

References

Akkar, M.-L. and Goubin, L. (2003). A generic protection against high-order differential power analysis. In Johansson, T., editor, *Proc. FSE 2003*, pages 192–205. LNCS 2887.

Biham, E. (2002). How to decrypt or even substitute DES-encrypted messages in 2^{28} steps. *Information Processing Letters*, 84:117–124.

Biham, E. and Shamir, A. (1997). Differential fault analysis of secret key cryptosystems. In Kaliski Jr., B.S., editor, *Proc. Crypto'97*, pages 513–525. LNCS 1294.

Boneh, D., DeMillo, R.A., and Lipton, R.J. (1997). On the importance of checking cryptographic protocols for faults. In Furny, W., editor, *Proc. EuroCrypt'97:*, pages 37–51. LNCS 1233.

Chari, S., Jutla, C.S., Rao, J.R., and Rohatgi, P. (1999). Towards sound approaches to counteract power-analysis attacks. In Wiener, M., editor, *Proc. Crypto'99*, pages 398–412. LNCS 1666.

Coron, J.-S., Kocher, P., and Naccache, D. (2001). Statistics and secret leakage. In Frankel, Y., editor, *Proc. Financial Cryptography 2001*, pages 157–173. LNCS 1962.

Daemen, J. and Rijmen, V. (2002). *The design of Rijndael.* Springer Series on Information Security and Cryptography. Springer.

den Hartog, J., Verschuren, J., de Vink, E., de Vos, J., and Wiersma, W. (2003). PINPAS: a tool for power analysis of smartcards. In Gritzalis, D., Samarati, P., and Katsikas, S., editors, *Proc. SEC 2003*, page 5pp. Wolters-Kluwer. IFIP WG 11.2 Small Systems Security.

Dhem, J.-F., F. Koeume, P.-A. Leroux, Mestré, P., Quisquater, J.-J., and Willems, J.-L. (1998). A practical implementation of the timing attack. In Quisquater, J.-J. and Schneier, B., editors, *Proc. Smart Card Research and Applications*, pages 167–182. LNCS 1820.

Dobbertin, H. (1998). Cryptanalysis of MD4. *Journal of Cryptology*, 11:253–271.

Dusart, P., Letourneux, G., and Vivolo, O. (2003). Differential fault analysis on AES. Technical Report 2003–01, LACO, Université de Limoges.

Goguen, J. A. and Meseguer, J. (1982). Security policy and security models. In *Proc. of the 1982 Symposium on Security and Privacy*, pages 11–20, Oakland. IEEE.

Golić, J.D. and Tymen, C. (2003). Multiplicative masking and power analysis of AES. In Jr, B.S. Kaliski, Koç, C.K., and Paar, C., editors, *Proc. CHES 2002*, pages 198–212. LNCS 2523.

Goubin, L. and Patarin, J. (1999). DES and differential power analysis (the "duplication" method). In Koç, C.K. and Naccache, D., editors, *Proc. CHES'99*, pages 158–172. LNCS 1717.

Kocher, P. (1996). Timing attacks on implementations of Diffie-Hellman, RSA, DSS, and other systems. In Koblitz, N., editor, *Proc. CRYPTO'96*, pages 104–113.

Kocher, P., Jaffe, J., and Jun, B. (1999). Differential power analysis. In Wiener, M.J., editor, *Proc. CRYPTO'99*, pages 388–397. LNCS 1666.

Messerges, T.S. (2000). *Power Analysis Attacks and Countermeasures for Cryptographic Algorithms.* PhD thesis, University of Illinois, Chicago.

NIST (2001). *FIPS 197: Announcing the Advanced Encryption Standard.* NIST.

Quisquater, J.-J. and Samyde, D. (2001). Electro-magnetic analysis (EMA) measures and counter-measures for smart cards. In Attali, I. and Jensen, T., editors, *Proc. E-Smart Card Programming and Security*, pages 200–210. LNCS 2140.

R. Focardi, R. Gorrieri, F. Martinelli (2000). Non-interference for the analysis of cryptographic protocols. In Montanari, U., Rolim, J.D.P., and Welzl, E., editors, *Proc. ICALP 2000*, pages 354–372. LNCS 1853.

Rivest, R., Shamir, A., and Adleman, L. (1978). A method for obtaining digital signatures and public-key cryptosystems. *Communication of the ACM*, 21:120–126.

Ryan, P.Y.A. and Schneider, S.A. (2001). Process algebra and non-interference. *Journal of Computer Security*, 9:75–103.

Schramm, K., Leander, G., Felke, P., and Paar, C. (2004). A collision-attack on AES combining sidechannel- and differential attacks. In *Proc. CHES 2004*. LNCS.

Schramm, K., Wollinger, T., and Paar, C. (2003). A new class of collision attacks and its application to DES. In *Proc. FSE 2003*, pages 206–222. LNCS 2887.

FAMILY SECRETS

James Heather and Jonathan Y. Clark
Department of Computing (H3)
University of Surrey
Guildford
GU2 7XH
United Kingdom
j.heather@eim.surrey.ac.uk   j.y.clark@eim.surrey.ac.uk

Abstract

We consider the possibility of secure communications over an insecure channel when the two agents have no verifiable public keys, no shared cryptographic information, and no trusted third party to assist them.

We investigate two scenarios. In the first, the agents are biologically related, and use biological data to construct a shared key; the possibility of using DNA data, shared between the two parties but not readily available to others, is considered. The second concerns unrelated parties who have some printed material, such as a photograph, in common; we explore the possibility of scanning this material at both ends and constructing a secret key from the shared information.

In each case, the two parties can convert their information into approximately equal sequences of bits. We borrow results from coding theory to show how these approximate sequences can be turned into exactly equal shared keys without compromising security in the process.

1.   Introduction

Alice and Bob, as is their wont, are looking to communicate securely over an insecure channel. Usually when they find themselves in this situation, they are spoilt for choice: they can use any of a whole host of well-known cryptographic protocols to agree on a session key by means of a long-term shared secret or their long-term public keys. This time, however, they have been somewhat negligent: they have no cryptographic shared secret and no public keys, and there is no trusted third party who can verify their identities and distribute any public keys that they may choose to create. What to do now?

If they really can find nothing to work with, they will of course be stuck. Alice cannot authenticate herself except by proving that she *knows* something that only Alice is supposed to know—for example, a key she shares with a server; or proving that she can *do* something that only Alice is supposed to be able to do—for example, recovering something from a message encrypted with her public key.

However, they may, for any of several reasons, have access to some store of shared information that is not normally considered 'cryptographic' but is nonetheless accessible only to Alice and Bob. For two arbitrary members of the human race, this is optimistic, to say the least; but if Alice and Bob know each other well, or if they are closely biologically related, there may be cause for hope.

This paper explores these possibilities in detail, presenting two different solutions to this problem. In Section 2 we discuss the feasibility of recovering approximate 'shared secrets' from biological information stored within Alice and Bob themselves, in the case that they are closely related. We then discuss in Section 3 the possibility of generating approximate shared secrets from a shared photograph or similar. Section 4 considers how they can use results from information and coding theory to turn these approximate secrets into an exact shared secret, and provides some indications about the level of security provided by these methods. In Section 5, we briefly consider other possible methods of generating approximate shared secrets. Section 6 discusses future related work; and Section 7 then forms the conclusion.

2.   Biological secrets

There are a number of possible avenues of exploration for finding information shared by siblings that is rare in others. Forensic science has a long history of using fingerprints to identify individuals uniquely. Similarly, retinal images are usually unique to the individual. However, it appears that, even if the individuals are closely related, their fingerprints and retinal images will be substantially different. (Even 'identical' twins have different fingerprints.)

DNA analysis, on the other hand, now in common use in forensic studies, might be exactly what we are looking for: it is very similar in close relatives, but different in those who are unrelated.

Although DNA is modelled as a double helix, the information on the second strand merely mirrors that on the first. The nucleotide bases along the strands are considered as *base pairs*, with **C** (Cytosine) always being paired with **G** (Guanine), and **T** (Thymine) always paired with **A** (Adenine). Each base pair is at a given 'locus' along the strand, and, since there are four possibilities for the nucleotide appearing on the first strand, it can be represented with two binary digits.

The idea is to perform a DNA analysis at each end, and use parts of the analysis that are likely to be similar between close relatives, but different between unrelated people. The DNA in the nucleus of each cell contains about 3.1 billion base pairs. Much of this is shared by other humans (and, indeed, other animals), and is therefore effectively public information. However, if Alice and Bob are siblings, then other possibilities become available. One such possibility involves the DNA contained within the 'powerhouses' of the cell, the *mitochondria*. Mitochondrial DNA ('mtDNA') is identical between siblings in the same family because mitochondria are inherited from the mother. Half-brothers and half-sisters also share the same mtDNA signature provided that they share the same mother. A grandmother and a great grandmother would also share this secret mtDNA code. Blood-relative aunts would have the same mtDNA sequence only if they were sisters of the mother.

The circular human mitochondrial genome consists of about 16,569 base pairs. The best area to consider seems to be the so-called D-loop,because this is the region that contains the greatest variation. The most relevant parts are Hypervariable Region I (HVR-I), a sequence of about 342 base pairs, and Hypervariable Region II (HVR-II), comprising about 268 base pairs. These are the most highly variable regions and are of interest in forensic studies (Isenberg and Moore, 1999). In a famous case, mtDNA was used to confirm the identity of the remains of Tsar Nicholas II, since these were found to have a rare mixture of sequences (Gill et al., 1994; Massie, 1995). As a practical guideline, however, it has been reported by one forensic science laboratory (Tully et al., 1998) that more than one base difference in the mtDNA genome has not been observed by them in any one individual.

Germline mutation in mtDNA—that is, changes in mtDNA between successive generations—occurs about once in every thirty generations (Parsons et al., 1997), so two individuals with a common female ancestor up to thirty generations back would be likely to have roughly the same sequence, provided that there is an unbroken female line linking them. This means that there could be many people with the same sequence, but, one hopes, sufficiently many with different sequences to provide a 'family secret' to form at least one element of an encryption key. Where these mutations do occur, they take the form of a base insertion, a base deletion, or a substitution of one for another.

Of particular interest is an existing study reported in (Handt et al., 1998) in which the degree of variation in the HVR-I and HVR-II areas within a collection of 728 individual sequences has been determined, after careful alignment. Table 1 shows the number of variable loci, together with the number of possible nucleotide permutations. It should be noted that, although the figures are thought to be representative of the human population as a whole, finding exact figures would require all lineages to be represented within the data, which is unlikely to have been the case. The number of bits of entropy has been added by us. The optimistic figures take into account the number of possibilities observed at each locus, according to (Handt et al., 1998); the pessimistic figures assume equal probability of occurrence of any of the four DNA bases.

D-loop	Permutations	Variable loci	Bits (optimistic)	Bits (pessimistic)
HVR-I	2	188	188	376
	3	66	132	132
	4	21	42	42
Total		275	362	540
HVR-II	2	89	89	178
	3	15	30	30
	4	1	2	2
Total		105	121	210
Grand Total		**380**	**483**	**750**

Table 1. Human mtDNA D-loop: variation and representation

The latter would provide the maximum possible entropy. However, since the probabilities are not equal, and further research might improve the optimistic figures, it is more reasonable to consider a point somewhere midway between the two, which would give us around 616 bits of entropy in the variable data from the mtDNA. This is probably enough for our application, but since the data from which this was compiled might not be completely representative of the entire population, it is worthwhile also to consider other options.

Another potential source of information is the DNA in the cell nucleus. The difficulties arise when trying to find sequences unique to Alice and Bob. A possible rich source might be the so-called *short tandem repeats* (STRs), which are commonly used in forensic DNA fingerprinting. These areas are where two or more bases repeat, and the number of times they repeat can be counted. One might expect siblings to have similar lengths of STRs at these loci, and there is at least one study (Biondo, 2000) that showed it was necessary to consider nine different loci in order to separate the profile of two brothers. Although more studies like this are needed for complete confidence, if it is assumed that eight loci in common is typical for siblings, and each locus has a contribution (allele) from each parent, then that would mean 16 attributes in common between brothers out of a possible 26. If it is estimated that the maximum number of permutations per allele is twelve, then each could be represented by four bits. Thus 104 bits would be needed to represent the component of the data stream derived from the STRs in the 'normal' chromosomes.

However, if the two communicating agents are both male, then yet another possibility becomes available. Female humans have a pair of X-chromosomes, so recombination (shuffling or swapping) of genes occurs between the pair. However, the Y-chromosome in a male has no such partner. This makes it as potentially useful a source of data as the mtDNA. A recent paper (Butler et al., 2002) highlights 20 useful loci and describes a method of investigation. Since these loci contain a contribution from only one parent (the father), 80 bits would thus be sufficient to represent this information, using the earlier assumption of around twelve different attribute values at each locus.

It is possible for two close relatives to have their mtDNA and their STRs sequenced (at a modest cost), and for each of them to turn the analysis into two bit sequences, one for the mtDNA and one for the STRs. Depending on decisions taken as to how much of the mtDNA information to use, the lengths of these sequences will be around 610 bits for the mtDNA, and 104 bits for the STRs. Whilst this data is applicable to all siblings wishing to exchange information, two brothers could also take advantage of STRs on the Y-chromosome, in which case another 80 bits could be used to provide a greater level of security.

3. Photography

Another potential source of shared data that does not require the communicants to be related is possession of a shared photograph (or other printed material). Clearly two agents who each have a copy of the same photograph should be considered to share information in some sense; and if the photograph is unavailable to others, they may be able to use this information to generate a shared key. The question is how they are to 'unlock' the photograph and agree on a shared key.

As with the biological data, what we give here is a method for obtaining approximately equal bit strings. The technique for turning these into an exact agreed secret key will be left for Section 4.

The procedure is very simple: roughly speaking, each end should scan the photograph, at an agreed resolution, reduce the colour depth, and treat the pixel information as a string of bits.

In experiments, we have managed to construct bit strings of about 700,000 bits in length, with an error rate of around 1.6%, using a moderate-sized photograph. This is more than adequate here.

There are, however, various considerations that need to be taken into account when attempting this, in order to lower the error rate and increase the chances of successfully agreeing on a shared secret. For one, each scanner has different characteristics, and care must be taken to reduce the discrepancies. Paint Shop Pro's *Histogram Equalize* filter is particularly helpful here: it normalises the data in each colour plane in the image, removing any colour or contrast bias.

Secondly, it is best to reduce each colour plane to a depth of two bits per pixel before constructing the sequence. This is still enough information to provide for 'unguessability', but drastically reduces the error rate. It is possible even to reduce this to one bit per pixel per colour plane.

Thirdly, by pushing the photograph up into the corner of the scanner's bed, it is easy enough to avoid inadvertent rotation of the image. However, it is not so easy to avoid a small translation of the image. But since the procedure outlined below for converting these approximate sequences into an exact secret is fairly quick, it is possible to try various different offsets into the image in order to find a good match.

In Section 4, we shall find Alice sending Bob a relatively short message from which Bob can discover Alice's exact sequence, thus enabling them to agree on a shared key. If Bob ends up with the wrong key, he will need to try the procedure a few times trying different offsets until he alights on the correct key. In our experience, the required offsets have been very small (2 or 3).

Fourthly, one can reduce the effect of rotations and translations by blurring the image a little before converting into a bit sequence. Paint Shop Pro's *Gaussian Blur* has proved useful here.

4.   Approximations

Let us suppose that Alice and Bob have followed the suggestions of Section 2 or Section 3. By this point, they each have a sequence of bits of roughly the same length. These sequences will be approximately the same, in the sense that it will be possible to convert one into the other by a short sequence of steps, each step involving inserting a new bit, deleting a bit, or substituting one bit for another. (A substitution can be thought of as a deletion followed by an insertion, but it will help us to consider this case separately.)

Of course, they cannot directly use these sequences to construct a shared key, because the sequences are not exactly the same, and there is nothing to be gained by encrypting a message under similar but not equal keys. What is required is to find a method of using these approximately equal sequences to agree on an exactly equal sequence, but without giving too much information away to eavesdroppers.

The exact sequence on which Alice and Bob will eventually agree need not be equal to Alice's sequence or Bob's sequence; it may be some amalgamation of the two. However, the easiest approach is to get them to agree on either Alice's sequence or Bob's sequence; we shall assume henceforth, without loss of generality, that they will attempt to agree on Alice's sequence.

4.1   Dealing with substitutions

Let us start by considering a situation in which there are known to be no insertions or deletions, but only substitutions. In that case, the sequences will be of the same length l, and if the approximations have worked well, we shall be able to choose some k with $k \ll l$ such that there is a high probability of not more than k differences between the two sequences.

Alice has the exact sequence; Bob has an approximation to it; Alice wants to send as little as possible to Bob to enable him to establish the exact sequence. This situation is exactly the same as if Bob had known nothing about Alice's sequence, and Alice had just sent her sequence to Bob over a *noisy channel*— that is, over a channel that has a tendency to corrupt data.

The usual way of communicating over a noisy channel is to use an *error-correcting code*. (See (Welsh, 1988) for a good introduction to the general topic of coding theory.) If we wish to communicate a message from $\{0, 1\}^l$, we can construct a set $C \subseteq \{0, 1\}^{l+p}$ of *codewords* such that changing d elements of a codeword $x \in C$ never produces another codeword. (The number of changes required to turn codeword c_1 into codeword c_2 is termed the *Hamming distance* of c_1 and c_2.) By doing this, we increase the length of the transmission along the channel (from l to $l + p$), but provide some error detection and error correction capabilities.

The code described above is *d-error-detecting*. If there are at most d errors in a codeword, the receiver will be able to detect that errors have occurred, because the errors cannot result in a distinct codeword having been received.

If $d = 2z$ then the code is also said to be *z-error-correcting*. If there are no more than z errors in a transmission, the receiver will be able to determine which codeword was intended. The received vector cannot be within z errors of two distinct codewords, or otherwise these codewords would differ by at most $2z = d$ places, and the code has been constructed to make this impossible.

Alice can make use of such a code to tell Bob how to convert his approximation into the exact sequence that Alice holds. Their sequences are of length l, and there is a high probability that there are no more than k errors. They need to make use of a code that has l possible codewords and that is k-error-correcting. They will want to make the codeword length as short as possible. They also need a code in which the codeword representing c is of the form $(c|e)$; that is, where the codeword always starts with the message that is to be communicated, and then follows this up with the error-correcting information. Codes with this property are called *systematic*; not all codes are systematic.

As an example, let us take $l = 4$, $p = 7$, $k = 1$. (The numbers in practice will, of course, be much bigger.) Consider the following code, discovered by Hamming, and first published in (Shannon, 1949):

$\langle 0, 0, 0, 0, 0, 0, 0 \rangle$	$\langle 0, 1, 0, 0, 1, 0, 1 \rangle$	$\langle 1, 0, 0, 0, 1, 1, 0 \rangle$	$\langle 1, 1, 0, 0, 0, 1, 1 \rangle$
$\langle 0, 0, 0, 1, 1, 1, 1 \rangle$	$\langle 0, 1, 0, 1, 0, 1, 0 \rangle$	$\langle 1, 0, 0, 1, 0, 0, 1 \rangle$	$\langle 1, 1, 0, 1, 1, 0, 0 \rangle$
$\langle 0, 0, 1, 0, 0, 1, 1 \rangle$	$\langle 0, 1, 1, 0, 1, 1, 0 \rangle$	$\langle 1, 0, 1, 0, 1, 0, 1 \rangle$	$\langle 1, 1, 1, 0, 0, 0, 0 \rangle$
$\langle 0, 0, 1, 1, 1, 0, 0 \rangle$	$\langle 0, 1, 1, 1, 0, 0, 1 \rangle$	$\langle 1, 0, 1, 1, 0, 1, 0 \rangle$	$\langle 1, 1, 1, 1, 1, 1, 1 \rangle$

The first $l = 4$ bits in each codeword are the message (making this code systematic); the last $p - l = 3$ are the error-correcting bits. Any two distinct codewords differ in at least three places, so that if there is a single error in a codeword transmission, it can be corrected. The code is thus 1-error-correcting.

4.2   Security by photograph

If Alice and Bob are using a scanned photograph as the basis for their shared key, this is all they need. Following the principles set out in Section 3, they can easily each get a large sequence of bits, with an error rate of under 10%.

Alice must then choose the systematic code that they will use, and tell Bob (over a possibly insecure channel) what the code is. She should then send him the error-correcting digits corresponding to the message formed by her sequence; Bob can append these error-correcting digits to the sequence that he has, and decode the resulting codeword to recover Alice's.

Alice and Bob now have the same sequence. It is likely that this sequence will be too long for use directly as a shared key; however, they can each apply a hash function to the sequence to get something of a more appropriate length. The output of a hash function is often of the order of 100–200 bits, which is ideal for symmetric cryptography. A good hash function will also ensure, provided there is enough entropy in the bit sequence, that the resulting shared key is uniformly distributed in the key space.

This, we believe, is secure against a Dolev-Yao-style intruder who can engage not only in passive attacks but also in attacks requiring spoofing, interception or manipulation of messages. The intruder cannot break security by changing the code, or modifying the codeword. If he changes anything, Bob's decoding will not result in the same sequence as Alice's, and they will not agree on the shared key. However, this will quickly become obvious to them when they try to use it, and the intruder will not have managed to learn either of the keys in any case. Clearly if the intruder has control over the communications medium then he can stop them from successfully agreeing on a shared key; but there is nothing that can be done about this. An intruder who has control over the communications medium can always stop agents from communicating.

4.3   Choosing a code

If the codewords are p bits long, and Alice's sequence itself is l bits long, she will need to transmit $p - l$ bits over the insecure channel in order for Bob to be able to establish her sequence.

It is not immediately clear exactly how much information about Alice's sequence can be deduced by the intruder from these $p - l$ bits. However, if only $p - l$ bits have been transmitted, then certainly at most $p - l$ bits of information can have been leaked to the intruder concerning Alice's sequence.

The quantity of information that remains secret from the intruder is, then, at least the amount of secret information in Alice's sequence less $p - l$. Getting an acceptable level of security depends, therefore, on keeping this quantity of information as high as possible. Alice and Bob will want to find a code to minimise $p - l$.

Bounds on $p - l$. Hamming's lower bound on the codeword size gives

$$2^l \leqslant \frac{2^p}{V(p,k)} \qquad \text{where} \qquad V(n,r) = \sum_{i=0}^{r} \binom{n}{i}$$

Rough working figures for this are that if Alice's sequence is l bits long, with $10^2 < l < 10^5$, a lower bound on the number of error-correcting bits required will be somewhere around $0.66l$ to correct an 8% error rate, $0.4l$ to correct a 5% error rate, or $0.25l$ to correct a 3% error rate. These factors get smaller as l increases, but not significantly so in the range that fits our purposes.

A code that meets exactly this theoretical lower bound is called *perfect*. Perfect codes do exist for many values of l, p and k, but they are hard to find.

Gilbert, Shannon and Varshamov's upper bound, alongside work in (Garcia and Stichtenoth, 1995), gives a method for constructing codes such that

$$2^l \geqslant \frac{2^p}{V(p,2k)}$$

This will halve the allowable error rate in the figures given above, so that if Alice's sequence is l bits long, with $10^2 < l < 10^5$, we can construct a code with the number of error-correcting bits at somewhere around $0.66l$ to correct a 4% error rate, $0.4l$ to correct a 2.5% error rate, or $0.25l$ to correct a 1.5% error rate.

Practical implications. In practice, for the photograph technique, results similar to ours would result in Alice and Bob agreeing on a sequence of around 700,000 bits, by sending somewhat less than 250,000 bits of error-correcting data. Running a suitable hash function on the agreed 700,000-bit sequence will create a secret key of about 128 bits, depending on the hash function; this is a decent size of key to use for symmetric-key cryptography.

Whether this method should be regarded as secure hinges critically on the information content of a photograph. Unfortunately, objective answers are difficult to find here: it largely depends on what sort of photograph is used—and how can one possibly determine the information content of, say, a photograph of a tree by a lake?

The information content is certainly much lower than the simple size of the photograph in pixels multiplied by the colour depth: JPEG compression can reduce the file size by a factor of ten without significant loss of image quality. In addition, much of the information will be lost by the reduction in colour depth, and the Gaussian blur applied to the image. This notwithstanding, our belief is that the number of bits in the sequence is so high that the information content will still exceed the 128-bit key that results from the hash function. For instance, if one imagines a photograph of a man standing in a busy high street, it would not be difficult to think of 128 independent factors that could be varied (angle of shot, distance to subject, number of people in background, name of third shop on the left) and that would affect the image and hence the agreed bit sequence. However, these things are admittedly difficult to quantify.

Additionally, of course, it relies on the accuracy of Alice and Bob's beliefs about who holds (or can get hold of) what photograph. If the photograph that they believe to be secret is in fact available to an attacker, or if an attacker can persuade Alice to use a photograph that he holds, then clearly security is lost. This procedure can be used only with a photograph where its distribution is known to the participants.

4.4   Security by biology

The codes referred to above will not be of great help with genetic 'secrets', where the differences between one sequence and the other are attributable not only to substitutions but also to insertions and deletions. Clearly an insertion or deletion near the start of the sequence will cause a match failure from that point onwards, and the Hamming distance between the two sequences will be high even though the sequences may be intuitively very similar.

Fortunately, there are measures of distance between sequences other than the Hamming distance. The *Levenshtein distance*, first proposed in (Levenshtein, 1966), takes into account the minimum number of substitutions, insertions, deletions and transpositions (swapping of two consecutive elements) required to turn one sequence into the other. It is the basis of automatic spelling correction techniques, where, for instance, we should want to be able to correct URPLE to PURPLE without naïvely attempting to match the words letter by letter and rejecting the match. Work in (Schulman and Zuckerman, 1997), among others, building on previous work in (Levenshtein, 1966; Levenshtein, 1992), (Spielman, 1995), (Okuda et al., 1976), (Varshamov and Tenengolts, 1965), and (Calabi and Hartnett, 1969), allows for construction of efficient error-correcting codes that correct insertions and deletions as well as substitutions. The detail of these codes is beyond the scope of this paper; however, Alice does by means of these codes have an efficient means of transmitting error-correcting information to Bob, again enabling him to recover her genetic sequence.

Also, since there is a low expected error rate between the two sequences when using genetic data, the number of error-correcting bits will be small.

The method given in Section 2 allows Alice and Bob to create sequences totalling over 700 bits in length. The discussion there indicates that we can expect at most one error (insertion, deletion or substitution) in the mtDNA part of the sequence, and at most a 10% error rate in the STR part. Using any of several of the available codes that allow for correction of insertions and deletions, Alice should be able to communicate her exact mtDNA sequence to Bob by sending less than 50 bits of error-correcting data; she can then communicate the exact bit sequence constructed from her STRs (which may differ from Bob's by substitution, but not by insertion or deletion) by sending a similar amount of error-correcting data using the code suggested in Section 4.3.

Practical implications.   As in the case of the photograph, it is difficult to quantify the information content in the bit sequences obtained by DNA analysis. Here, it is not any lack of objective criteria that cause the difficulty, but simply that although the science of DNA analysis has produced remarkable results, it is still too young for firm answers to many questions to be available. Not enough people have had their complete DNA sequenced. However, there are few indications at present that there are 'patterns' in the DNA considered here that would reduce the information content drastically. Until some drastic 'decoding' of this DNA demonstrates otherwise, it appears that the information content is reasonably high.

Alice and Bob would then, as with the photograph, apply a hash function to the bit sequence in order to generate a shared key. With current information, we believe that the information content of the secret data agreed upon by Alice and Bob is at least as high as the number of bits produced by the hash function for use as the secret key. However, it is acknowledged that future advances in human biological science may either support or contradict this position.

The security of this method clearly relies on making certain that an attacker cannot get hold of enough genetic material from Alice or Bob to be able to reproduce the DNA sequence for himself. In the short to medium term, depending on the circumstances and the importance of the secret to the attacker, this may well be realistic: the attacker would need a reasonable quantity of genetic material, and would also need to be able to collect it without contaminating the samples. In the long term, if the attacker has significant funds at his disposal or is geographically close to either party, it is possible that he could gather enough material to find the encryption key. This method is therefore probably most applicable in situations in which it is vital that something remain secret, but only for a limited time. It is an emergency measure rather than a suggested pattern for everyday life! It should also be noted that this is a procedure that Alice and Bob cannot use more than once to generate a session key. If they use the procedure twice, they will end up with the same key.

5.   Other possibilities

The connection between the photograph and the DNA analysis is simply that each provides a mechanism for extracting an approximate secret shared between the two participants. It may be that there are other ways of constructing such an approximate sequence; however, it is worth noting that two of the 'easy' options have significant problems.

Text from a book (and similar).   Alice and Bob cannot simply agree to use the text "on page 53 from Barbara Cartland's latest novel": the point is that they will be agreeing this over an insecure channel, and an attacker may be listening in. If he hears them decide which book to use, it will usually be a simple matter for him to obtain a copy of the book. Of course, Alice and Bob may have ways of alluding to the book without saying its title; but this just pushes the issue back a stage. Here, the allusion that they understand but the attacker doesn't is itself the shared secret. They will need to be sure how much information content there is in this shared secret before they commit to using it for cryptographic purposes.

Challenge and response.   It may be that Alice and Bob can get somewhere by using information relating to past common experiences: maybe they are the only ones who know the answer to certain questions about their past.

Two scenarios need to be carefully distinguished here. In one, they authenticate each other by means of various questions until they are satisfied that they really are speaking to each other, after which they have their private conversation; in the other, they use answers to such questions to create a shared key.

The former is not appropriate here. If the approach is to be able to deal with Dolev-Yao attackers then there can be no guarantee that the attacker will not wait for the authentication to take place and then subsequently break in and masquerade as one party or the other. Indeed, even if he does nothing active, he may still overhear the private conversation.

Construction of a shared key using answers to such questions may work; however, it would require immense care and patience. To construct a key with, say, 128 bits of entropy may need a lot of questions. Even 128 yes/no questions will not be sufficient unless the probability of a yes for each question is 0.5 and is independent of probabilities for all the other questions. Other questions may have more information content, but assessing the information content and the secrecy of the answer will be very difficult.

6.   Future work

It may be that there are more efficient ways of turning approximately equal sequences into exactly equal ones. Efficiency here is well worth striving for, since its consequence is that less error-correcting data will be transmitted, and so less information about the secret key will be leaked to any eavesdropper.

If improvements are to be found, there are four promising lines of enquiry.

In the first place, Alice and Bob's agreed sequence need not be either Alice's or Bob's original sequence. It may be that there is a way for them to agree on some combination of the sequences with less communication than is required for them to agree on Alice's sequence. It may also be possible for them to exchange a small quantity of information that would enable them to determine which parts of the sequence are likely to be the same and which parts are not. If so, then they would be able to drop the different parts of the sequence and exchange error-correcting data just on the parts likely to be the same; this would reduce the length of the agreed sequence, but with a possibly significantly reduced error rate.

Secondly, Wyner in (Wyner, 1975) and Csiszár and Körner in (Csiszár and Körner, 1978) conducted work on secure key agreement over noisy channels. Their models may shed light on the techniques discussed in this paper; for, as we have already shown, the problem of converting approximate shared secrets to exact shared secrets is closely related to the problem of communicating secrets over noisy channels.

In addition, there is recent work by Maurer and Wolf (see (Maurer and Wolf, 1997; Maurer and Wolf, 2000) among others) on *privacy amplification*, in which two agents hold a secret about which a Dolev-Yao attacker knows partial information; they discuss how to convert this into a secret about which almost nothing is known by the attacker. Their analysis also includes consideration of noisy channels. The work they present differs from ours in that in their scenario the information is fully shared but partially secret, whereas in ours the information is only partially shared. However, this, we believe, will provide interesting avenues for further exploration. In particular, it may be possible to use their results to allow for and remove any information known to the attacker resulting from less than perfect entropy in DNA and in photographs.

Thirdly, the codes discussed here are all designed to cope with errors that can appear anywhere in the codeword, including in the error-correction data. This is more robust than is required for our purposes. We need to allow for errors in Bob's version of Alice's sequence, but we do not need a code that allows for transmission errors in the error-correcting part of the code. This, of course, reduces the number of cases that our error-correcting part needs to be able to distinguish, and so might allow for a reduction in the size of the error-correcting part itself. A code of this nature would be highly specialised; in fact, it is difficult to think of any possible applications of it other than this one. It is not surprising, then, that there seems not to have been any work done on such codes. Investigation of this is the subject of planned future work.

Finally, the notion of *edit distance* may be useful here. Atallah, Kerschbaum and Du provide a way (Atallah et al., 2003) of enabling Alice and Bob to calculate the edit distance of their similar sequences without revealing to each other any more information than is contained in the edit distance itself. This could certainly be used by Alice and Bob initially to determine the similarity of their sequences and give a guide for how much error-correcting information is needed; the technique could possibly be adapted to find an efficient way of agreeing on a common sequence.

7.   Conclusion

In this paper, we have given two methods by which two agents may be able to agree on a secret key even when they have no previously agreed cryptographic data with which to work, and no trusted third party who can verify their identities and distribute public keys for them. In one case, where the agents are closely biologically related, they can construct approximately equal bit sequences by using the information stored in certain parts of their DNA; in the other case, agents who have a shared photograph can extract the information from this photograph and manipulate the information so as to construct approximately equal bit sequences.

Regardless of which method is used, they can then use the techniques of Section 4 to convert this into an exact shared secret that can be used for cryptographic purposes. Although the approaches discussed here relate to DNA and to photographs, any other approach that generates approximate shared secrets could equally use the techniques of this section to construct a shared key.

It is worth observing that although the paper has been phrased in terms of two agents who wish to share secret information between them, the approach could be trivially extended to cover generation of a 'group key' for three or more siblings, or three or more agents who all have the same photograph.

Much of what is presented here is admittedly speculative, and may often be inapplicable to the two agents in question. However, it is sufficient to demonstrate that the usual assumption in this regard—essentially, that one cannot generate something from nothing—may not always hold.

Some of the more 'cloudy' issues will become clearer over time. There is still much to be learnt about DNA, its information content, and its variation throughout the population; the cost and difficulty of sequencing will also come down over time. Biometric information will undoubtedly come to play a large part in the world of security. Research is also ongoing into the discovery of efficient codes; new light shed on this area may allow agents to generate and use codes whose information rate is much closer to Hamming's lower bound.

Acknowledgements.   Thanks are due to the anonymous referees for their insightful comments, and also to the FAST 2004 participants for a lively, interesting and useful discussion following presentation of the paper.

References

Atallah, Mikhail J., Kerschbaum, Florian, and Du, Wenliang (2003). Secure and Private Sequence Comparisons. In *Proceedings of the ACM workshop on Privacy in the electronic society*, pages 39–44. ACM Press.

Biondo, R. (2000). The impact of CODIS software in criminal investigations in the Italian police. In *Eleventh International Symposium on Human Identification*. Available from www.promega.com/geneticidproc/ussympllproc/content/biondo.pdf.

Butler, J. M., Schoske, R., Vallone, P. M., Kline, M. C., Redd, A. J., and Hammer, M. F. (2002). A novel multiplex for simultaneous amplification of 20 Y chromosome STR markers. *Forensic Science International*, 129:10–24.

Calabi, L. and Hartnett, W. E. (1969). A family of codes for the correction of substitution and synchronization errors. *IEEE Transactions on Information Theory*, IT-15:102–106.

Csiszár, I. and Körner, J. (1978). Broadcast channels with confidential messages. *IEEE Transactions on Information Theory*, 24(3):339–348.

Garcia, A. and Stichtenoth, H. (1995). A tower of Aritin-Schreier extensions of function fields attaining the Drinfed-Vladut bound. *Inventiones Mathematicae*, 121(1):211–222.

Gill, P., Ivanov, P. L., Kimpton, C., Piercy, R., Benson, N., Tully, G., Evett, L., Hagelberg, E., and Sullivan, K. (1994). Identification of the remains of the Romanov family by DNA analysis. *Nature Genetics*, 6:130–135.

Handt, O., Meyer, S., and von Haeseler, A. (1998). Compilation of human mtDNA control region sequences. *Nucleic Acids Research*, 26(1):126–129.

Isenberg, A. R. and Moore, J. M. (1999). Mitochondrial DNA Analysis at the FBI Laboratory. *Forensic Science Communications*, 1(2). Available from http://www.fbi.gov/hq/lab/fsc/backissu/july1999/dnatext.htm.

Levenshtein, V. I. (1966). Binary Codes Capable of Correcting Deletions, Insertions, and Reversals. *Soviet Physics—Dolkady*, 10(8):707–710.

Levenshtein, V. I. (1992). On perfect codes in deletion and insertion metric. *Discrete Mathematics and its Applications*, 2(3):241–258.

Massie, R. K. (1995). *The Romanovs: The Final Chapter*. Random House, New York.

Maurer, Ueli and Wolf, Stefan (1997). Privacy amplification secure against active adversaries. In Jr., Burton S. Kaliski, editor, *Advances in Cryptology—CRYPTO '97*, volume 1294 of *Lecture Notes in Computer Science*, pages 307–321. Springer-Verlag.

Maurer, Ueli and Wolf, Stefan (2000). Information-theoretic key agreement: From weak to strong secrecy for free. In *Advances in Cryptology—EUROCRYPT 2000*, volume 1807 of *Lecture Notes in Computer Science*, pages 351–368. Springer-Verlag.

Okuda, T., Tanaka, E., and Kasai, T. (1976). A method for the correction of garbled words based on the Levenshtein metric. *IEEE Transactions on Computing*, C-25(2):172–176.

Parsons, T. J., Muniec, D. S., Sullivan, K., Woodyatt, N., Alliston-Greiner, R., Wilson, M. R., Berry, D. L., Holland, K. A., Weedn, V. W., Gill, P., and Holland, M. M. (1997). A high observed substitution rate in the human mitochondrial dna control region. *Nature Genetics*, 15:363–368.

Schulman, Leonard J. and Zuckerman, David (1997). Asymptotically Good Codes Correcting Insertions, Deletions, and Transpositions. In *Symposium on Discrete Algorithms*, pages 669–674.

Shannon, Claude (1949). Communication Theory of Secrecy Systems. Technical report, Bell Systems.

Spielman, Daniel A. (1995). Linear-time encodable and decodable error-correcting codes. pages 388–397.

Tully, G., Morley, J. M., and Bark, J. E. (1998). Forensic analysis of mitochondrial DNA: application of multiplex solid-phase - fluorescent minisequencing to high throughput analysis. In *Second European Symposium on Human Identification*, pages 92–96. Online at http://www.promega.com/geneticidproc/eusymp2proc/20.pdf.

Varshamov, R. R. and Tenengolts, G. M. (1965). Codes which correct single asymmetric errors. *Automatika i Telemekhanika*, 26(2):288–292.

Welsh, Dominic (1988). *Codes and Cryptography*. Oxford University Press.

Wyner, A. D. (1975). The wire-tap channel. *Bell System Technical Journal*, 54(8):1355–1387.

AN INTERACTIVE TRUST MANAGEMENT AND NEGOTIATION SCHEME*

Hristo Koshutanski and Fabio Massacci

Dip. di Informatica e Telecomunicazioni - Univ. di Trento
via Sommarive 14 - 38050 Povo di Trento (ITALY)

{hristo, massacci}@dit.unitn.it

Abstract   Interactive access control allows a server to compute on the fly missing credentials needed to grant access and to adapt its responses on the basis of client's presented and declined credentials. Yet, it may disclose too much information on *what credentials a client needs*. Automated trust negotiation allows for a controlled disclosure on *what credentials a client has* during a mutual disclosure process. Yet, it requires pre-arranged policies and sophisticated strategies. How do we bootstrap from simple security policies a comprehensive interactive trust management and negotiation scheme that combines the best of both worlds without their limitations? This is the subject of the paper.

Keywords: Trust Management; Trust Negotiation; Interactive Trust Management; Interactive Access Control; Credential-Based Systems; Internet Computing; Logics for Access Control;

1.   Introduction

The new business hype of the moment – virtual organizations based on Web Services [1] – is particularly challenging for security research in access control. In a nutshell, the idea is to orchestrate into a coherent business process the Web Services (WS for short) offered by different partners. The functional orchestration is not trivial but the orchestration of security policies of partners even less, even if we take for granted the usage of Trust Management systems [3, 2].

First, the client may have no idea on the right set of credentials that have to be presented to each partner and the process may bring different

---

*This work is partially funded by the IST programme of the EU Commission FET under the IST-2001-37004 WASP project and by the FIRB programme of MIUR under the RBNE0195K5 ASTRO Project and RBAU01P5SS Project.

partners on the forefront depending on the actual business execution path. So, business partners must have a way to find out what credentials are required (missing) for clients to get access to their resources. Second, the client, once asked for the missing credentials, may be unwilling to disclose them unless the server discloses some of its credentials first, i.e. negotiates the need to disclose his own credentials.

Solution for the first problem has been proposed by Koshutanski and Massacci [7, 8]: interactive access control. Assuming a logical formalization (actually a rule-based policy is enough) and using some advanced inference services, it is possible for the server to compute the missing credentials on the fly. Credentials that may not be straightforwardly deduced from the security policy, as approached by the trust negotitation paradigm, but may require a more sophisticated reasoning service.

Solution for the second problem is trust negotiation, for instance as advocated by Winslett et al. [11]. Here, we can structure a security policy to specify what credentials a client must have already shown to get access to our own credentials, i.e. we specify the sequence of disclosable credentials that gradually establish trust.

Notice that the two problems are related but different. For sake of example consider the view point of a server. In the first one, we help the server to compute the *missing set* of foreign credentials that a client needs to get access to a service. The second approach helps the server, in response to some counter requests, to control the disclosure of its own credentials by stipulating what *foreign credentials* a client must supply to get access to the server's local ones.

Both approaches in their core have limitations: the first approach does not allow for a piecemeal disclosure to the clients of what they eventually need. The second one requires a sophisticated and rigid structuring of policies to work.

1.1   The Contribution of this Paper

If we merge the two frameworks we have the following problems:

1 Alice wants to access some service of Bob

2 Alice does not know exactly what credentials Bob needs, so

   (a) Bob must compute what is missing and ask Alice,
   (b) Alice must send to Bob all credentials he requested.

3 In response to 2b, Alice may want to have some credentials from Bob before sending hers, so

   (a) She must tell Bob what he needs to provide,

    (b) Bob must have a policy to decide how access to his credentials is granted.

4 In response to 2a, Bob may not want to disclose all that is missing at once but may want to ask Alice first some of the less sensitive credentials, so

    (a) Bob must have a way to request in a piecewise fashion the missing credentials.

Here we combine the best of the both worlds under the limited assumptions that we have just three policies:

(i) a policy for determining the credentials needed by a client to get access to a service,

(ii) a policy for determining the credentials needed by a client to access (see) server's credentials,

(iii) a policy for specifying what credentials are disclosable whose need can be potentially demanded from a client.

The policies can be arbitrarily complex with almost everything that is on the (Datalog for) Access Control market (say with negation as failure, constraints on separation of duties, or other fancy credentials such as those by Li et al. [9]). We only need deduction and its sister abduction[1]

Out of these two services we have constructed an algorithm that first evaluates a client's request by checking whether the client can access the requested service – using policy (i). If the client is not enough trusted (i.e. he does not have enough credentials), the algorithm computes a (minimal, trusted enough) set of missing credentials, from policies (i) and (iii), that unlocks the desired resource. Then it starts a negotiation process in which needed credentials are disclosed in a piecewise manner according to policy (iii) and requested credentials are disclosed according to policy (ii). The process continues until enough trust is established and the service is granted. In a negotiation process a client, itself, may also run the algorithm to control access to its own credentials.

2.   Interactive Access Control for Web Services

In the framework introduced by Koshutanski and Massacci [7, 8] each partner has a *security policy for access control* $\mathcal{P}_A$ and a *security policy for disclosure control* $\mathcal{P}_D$. The policy for access control is used for making decision about usage of all web services offered by a partner. The

---

[1]Note that if the former is decidable within complexity class $\mathcal{C}$, the latter is decidable within complexity class $\Sigma^{\mathcal{C}}$ or at worst $\Pi^{\mathcal{C}}$ if minimality of abductive solutions is requested.

Role: $R_i \succ$ Role: R_j when role Role: R_i dominates role Role: R_j.

Role: $R_i \succ_{\text{WebServ} S}$ Role: R_j when role Role: R_i dominates, just for service WebServ: S, the role Role: R_j.

assign (P, WebServ: S) when an access to the service WebServ: S is granted to P. Where P can be either a Role: R or User: U.

forced (P, WebServ: S) when access the service WebServ: S must be forced to P (P can be either a Role: R or User: U).

(a) Predicates for assignments to Roles and Services

declaration (User: U) it is a statement by the User: U for its identity.

credential (User: U, Role: R) when User: U has a credential activating Role: R.

credentialTask (User: U, WebServ: S) when User: U has the right to access WebServ: S.

(b) Predicates for Credentials

Figure 1.   Predicates used in the model

policy for disclosure control is used to decide the credentials whose need can be potentially disclosed to a client.

To execute a service, under the control of a partner, a user will submit a *service request* r and a set of *credentials* C_r. When the user sends the request r the server starts a negotiation session and creates a client's profile. The client's profile consists of two sets – the set of *presented credentials* C_P and the set of *declined credentials* C_N. Both sets are kept up-to-date by the server as at each interaction step, C_P is updated with the credentials the client currently sends, while C_N is updated as a difference between the *missing credentials* C_M, the client was asked in the previous interaction, and the ones presented in the current step.

For the syntax we have three disjoint sets of constants: one for users identifiers denoted by User: U; one for roles denoted by Role: R; and one for services denoted by WebServ: S.

The predicates can be divided into three classes: predicates for assignments of users to roles and services (Fig. 1a), predicates for credentials (Fig. 1b), and predicates describing the current status of the system. The last class of predicates keeps track on the main activities done by users and services, such as: successful activation of services by users; successful completion of services; abortion; etc. We refer to [8] for additional details on the model.

We note here that the model, presented in the this section, can be adapted to *any* generic policy framework. Since the information we need from the underlying policy model, for our basic reasoning services, is shown in Figure 1 and that infromation can be found in (extracted from) most policy languages.

Below are the definitions of the basic reasoning services used in our formal framework.

DEFINITION 1 (LOGICAL CONSEQUENCE AND CONSISTENCY) *We use the symbol* $P \models L$, *where P is a policy and L is either a credential or a service request, to specify that L is a logical consequence of a policy P. P is consistent ($P \not\models \bot$) if there is a model for P.*

DEFINITION 2 (1-STEP DEDUCTION) *We use the symbol $P \models_1 A$, where P is a policy with a predefined set of ground atoms $\mathscr{A}$ and A is a positive literal, if for some literals $L_1, \ldots, L_n$ holds the following:*
(i) $A \leftarrow L_1, \ldots, L_n$ is in ground(P),
(ii) $\mathscr{A} \models L_1, \wedge \ldots \wedge, L_n$.

DEFINITION 3 (ABDUCTION) *Abduction solution (see Fig. 2(b)) over a policy P, a set of predicates H (with a defined p.o. over subsets of H) and a ground literal L is a set of ground atoms E such that:*
(i) $E \subseteq H$,
(ii) $P \cup E \models L$,
(iii) $P \cup E \not\models \bot$,
(iv) any set $E' \prec E$ does not satisfy all conditions above.

Traditional p.o.s are subset containment or set cardinality.

The core of our interactive trust management protocol, introduced in the next section, is shown in Figure 2. The basic computations of deduction (Def. 1) and abduction (Def. 3) are shown in Figure 2(b). The global variables C_N and C_P represent the client's profile (as described earlier). The protocol takes as input the request r and the partner's policies for access and disclosure control – P_A, P_D. The output is either *grant* r, or *deny* r, or *ask*(C_M) – the set of missing credentials that the client needs to provide in order to get r.

The intuition behind the algorithm is the following. First (in step 1) it is checked whether the client's credentials C_P are enough to get access to service r according to policy P_A. In the case of failure, the algorithm runs the abduction process (step 3) to compute what is missing (complement) to C_P that unlocks r. A preliminary step to abduction is computing the set of disclosable and not declined credentials C_D (step 2). The set C_D stores those credentials that are disclosable by P_D and C_P and does not contain any credential of C_N. Then the abduction process computes all possible subsets of C_D that are consistent with the access policy P_A and, at the same time, grant r. Out of all these sets

Global vars: $\mathcal{C_N}, \mathcal{C_P}$;
Protocol input: $r, \mathcal{P_A}, \mathcal{P_D}$;
Protocol output: grant/deny/ask($\mathcal{C_M}$);

InteractiveAccessControl($r, \mathcal{P_A}, \mathcal{P_D}$){

    1: if doDeduction($r, \mathcal{P_A} \cup \mathcal{C_P}$) then return *grant*

    2: else compute the set of *disclosable credentials* $\mathcal{C_D} = \{c \mid \mathcal{P_D} \cup \mathcal{C_P} \models c\} \backslash \mathcal{C_N}$;

    3: *result* = doAbduction($r, \mathcal{C_D}, \mathcal{P_A} \cup \mathcal{C_P}$);

    4: if *result* == $\emptyset$ then return *deny*

    5: else $\mathcal{C_M}$ = *result* and return *ask($\mathcal{C_M}$)*;

}

(a) Interactive Access Control Algorithm

doDeduction(R: Query, P: LogProgram){ // check for $P \models R$?

    1: run DLV* in deduction mode with input: P, R? ;

    2: check output: if R is deducible then return *true* else return *false*;

}

doAbduction(R: Observation, H: Hypotheses, P: LogProgram){

    1: run DLV in abduction diagnosis mode with input: R, H, P ;

    2: DLV output: all sets C_i that (i) $C_i \subseteq H$, (ii) $P \cup C_i \models R$, (iii) $P \cup C_i \not\models \bot$;

    3: if no C_i exists then return $\bot$

    4: else select a minimal C_{min} and return C_{min};

}

*DLV System – www.dlvsystem.com

(b) Basic Functionalities of Deduction and Abduction

Figure 2.   Basic Trust Management Protocol

(if any) the algorithm selects the minimal one. Here we point out that the minimality criterion could be different for different contexts. We have identified two criteria: minimal set cardinality and role minimality (least privilege).

When the abduction is finished the protocol either returns *ask($\mathcal{C_M}$)* or denies r if no $\mathcal{C_M}$ was computed.

3.   Automated Trust Negotiation

The main idea in a trust negotiation process is to gradually disclose sensitive credentials between negotiation participants until sufficient trust is established.

In Winslett et al framework [11, 12] a policy protects a resource, being it access to a service or disclosure of a credential, by stipulating what the requestor should satisfy to be authorized for that resource. They require, first, a policy to be monotonic – if a set of credentials unlocks a service also a superset unlocks it – and, second, for each resource there should be exactly one solution (set of statements) that unlocks it.

One can abstract from any policy language by wrapping it in a *policy compliance checker* module and treat it as a black box, encapsulating a decision engine for the underlying policy language. It accepts as an input a set of credentials and a policy and returns as output the subset of the credentials that satisfy the policy. However, the actually used policy language can be easily casted into a set of negation-free Datalog rules. Each alternative set of credentials that unlock a resource can be casted in a Datalog rule having a predicate corresponding to the resource in the head and the needed credentials in the body.

Winslett et al define a TrustBuilder *negotiation protocol* and, running on top of it, *families of strategies* that address the requirements and needs of each party to negotiate in a way best suited for it. The protocol defines message type and ordering while the strategy controls the content of negotiation messages. Both the negotiation protocol and the families of strategies are located in a *negotiation strategy* module – the TrustBuilder.

So, whenever two parties want to negotiate, they first choose (agree on) negotiation strategies that guarantee a successful interoperation and completion of the process. Once they chose the strategies, they run the TrustBuilder protocol.

Abstracting from the concrete strategy and family, in its essence, the relevant strategy for selecting the next set of credentials (message) is the following: for every credential relevant to the service request, if the credential is disclosable by the client's presented set of credentials it is added to the output else its policy (the part that protects the resource) is added instead. Then in the final output of the current strategy step the client can find the newly unlocked credentials together with policies for the others (not disclosed ones) that the client should satisfy in order to continue the process. The process continues with parties swapping roles until all requirements are satisfied and the resource is granted or a consensus was not reached by one of the parties and terminated.

4.   Bootstrapping Trust Negotiation

To combine automated trust negotiation and interactive access control we only assume that both a client and a server have some logical security policies. In particular we assume available:

1 a policy for access to *own* resources $\mathcal{P}_{AR}$ on the basis of *foreign* credentials,

2 a policy for access to *own* credentials $\mathcal{P}_{AC}$ on the basis of *foreign* credentials,

3 a policy for disclosure the need of (missing) *foreign credentials* $\mathcal{P}_D$.

Here $\mathcal{P}_{AR}$ is a logic program over the predicates defined in Section 2 in which no credential and no execution atom can occur in the head of a rule and role hierarchy atoms occur as facts. Respectively, $\mathcal{P}_{AC}$ and $\mathcal{P}_D$ are logic programs in which no role hierarchy atom and no execution atom can occur in the head of a rule.

Technically speaking we could merge 1 and 2 into a flat policy for protecting sensitive resources. We believe that a structured approach is better because the criteria behind (and likely the administrator of) each policy are different. Resource access is decided by the business logic, whereas credential access is due to security and privacy considerations.

So, a client and server do not need to worry about interoperable strategies but can simply run the trust negotiation protocol shown in Fig. 3. The intuition behind the protocol is the following:

- A client, Alice, sends a service request r and (optionally) a set of credentials C_r to a server, Bob (steps 1 and 2).

- Then Bob looks at r and if it is a request for a service he calls InteractiveAccessControl with his policy for access to resources and his policy for disclosure of foreign credentials $< \mathcal{P}_{AR}, \mathcal{P}_D >$ (step 6) and we fall back in the case of Section 2.

- If r is a request for a credential then he calls InteractiveAccessControl with his policy for access to own credentials and again his policy for disclosure of foreign credentials $< \mathcal{P}_{AC}, \mathcal{P}_D >$ (step 9).

- In the case of computed missing credentials C_M (in step 11), he transforms that into requests for credentials (askCredentials(...) function in Figure 3) and waits until receives all responses. At this point Bob acts as a client, requesting Alice the set of credentials C_M. Alice will run the same protocol swapping roles.

- When Bob's main process receives all responses it checks whether the missing credentials have been supplied by Alice (step 13).

Global vars: C_N, C_P:: initially set up to $\emptyset$ when the main process is started;
```
InteractiveTrustManagement(){ // runs in a new thread.
```
  1: $r = $ `receiveRequest()`;

  2: $C_r = $ `receiveCredentials()`;

  3: $C_P = C_P \cup C_r$;

  4: repeat

  5:   if `isService(r)` then

  6:     $result = $ `InteractiveAccessControl(r, $\mathcal{P}_{AR}$, $\mathcal{P}_D$)`;

  8:   else // `isCredential(r(c))`

  9:     $result = $ `InteractiveAccessControl(r, $\mathcal{P}_{AC}$, $\mathcal{P}_D$)`;

  11:   if $result == $ `ask($C_M$)` then

  12:     `askCredentials($C_M$)`;

  13:     if $C_M \subseteq C_P$ then $result = $ grant;

  14: until $result == $ grant or $result == $ deny;

  15: if $result == $ grant and `isCredential(r)` then

  16:     `sendResponse(cred(r))`;

  17: else

  18:     `sendResponse(result)`;

}
```
askCredentials($C_M$){
```
  1: parfor each $c \in C_M$ do

  2:     `sendRequest(r(c))`;

  3:     if `receiveResponse()` $==$ `cred(c)` then

  4:       $C_P = C_P \cup \{c\}$;

  5:       $C_N = C_N \setminus \{c\}$;

  6:     else if $c \notin C_P$ then

  7:       $C_N = C_N \cup \{c\}$;

  8: done

}

Figure 3. Interactive Trust Negotiation Protocol

- If C_M was not reached, Bob restarts the loop and consults the `InteractiveAccessControl` algorithm for a new decision.

- When a final decision is taken, a respective response (steps 16 and 18) is sent back to Alice.

The server initiates the main trust negotiation process when a client initially submits a request for a service. Then each counter request from the client side is run in a different thread that shares the same globally accessible client's profile (C_P, C_N) with other threads running under the same negotiation process.

Technicality in the protocol is in the way the server requests missing credentials back to the client. As indicated in the figure, we use the keyword **parfor** for representing that the body of the loop is run each time in a parallel thread under the thread that has computed C_M. At that point of the protocol, it is important that each of the finished threads updates the presented and declined set of credentials appropriately. So, we avoid the situations where some running parallel threads ask the client already asked credentials or already declined ones computed in other running threads under the same main process.

Also an important point here is to clarify the way we treat decliend and not yet released credentials. In a negotiaition process, declining a credential is when an entity is asked for it and the same entity replies to the same request an empty set (saying no). In the second case, when the entity is asked for a credential and, insted of reply, there is a counter request for more credentials, then the thread, started the original request, awaits the client for an explicit reply and treats the requested credential as not yet released. In any case, at the end of a (sub) negotiation process a client either supplies the originally asked credential or declines it.

The thread based implementation (with shared C_P and C_N) is necessary to allow for a *polynomial execution time* of the trust negotiation protocol in the number of queries to the abduction algorithm. Indeed, without a shared memory for received credentials it is possible to structure the policies in a way that a credential will be asked far too many times. In this way the protocol queries to P_{AC} are bounded by the number of credentials in the policy.

REMARK 1 *It can be proved that if policies are negation free then the algorithms on the client and server sides interoperate.*

It is possible to run the TrustBuilder by Yu et al. [12] on top of our mechanism so that our framework abstracts away the requirements on policies and strategies that should be imposed on the user's disclosure policy if using TrustBuilder directly.

However, we have not solved the problem of piecewise disclosure of missing foreign credentials yet. This turns out to be also possible as we shall see in the next section.

```
Global vars: C_N, C_P;
InteractiveTrustManagement(){ ...
}
PiecewiseDisclosure(C_M, P_D){
```

1: $C_{D1} = \{c \mid P_D \cup C_P \models_1 c\} \setminus C_N;$

2: $P_{D1} = \{\hat{c} \leftarrow B \mid c \leftarrow B \in P_D\} \cup$
  $\{c \leftarrow \hat{c} \mid c \notin C_{D1} \text{ and } c \leftarrow B \in P_D \text{ for some } B\};$

3: $Q = \left\{q \leftarrow \bigwedge_{c \in C_M} c\right\};$

4: $C_{M1} = \text{doAbduction}(q, C_{D1}, P_{D1} \cup C_P);$

5: return $C_{M1};$

```
}
askCredentials(C_M, P_D){
```

1: repeat

2:    C_{M1} = PiecewiseDisclosure(C_M, P_D);

3:    if $C_{M1} == \perp$ then return;

4:    parfor each $c \in C_{M1}$ do

5:       sendRequest($r(c)$);

6:       if receiveResponse() == cred(c) then

7:          $C_P = C_P \cup \{c\};$

8:          $C_N = C_N \setminus \{c\};$

9:       else if $c \notin C_P$ then

10:        $C_N = C_N \cup \{c\};$

11:    done

12:   $C_M = C_M \setminus C_P;$

13: until $C_M \subseteq C_N;$

```
}
```

Figure 4. Piecewise Trust Management Protocol

5. Controlled Disclosure of Missing Credentials

The intuition here is that Bob may not want to disclose the missing credentials all at once or directly to Alice. Instead he may want to ask Alice first some less sensitive credentials[6] assuring him that Alice is

---

[6]Here we point out that the stepwise approach may concern credentials that are not directly related to a specific resource but needed for a finer-grained disclosure control.

enough trustworthy to disclose her other credentials and so on continuing until the missing ones are disclosed.

To address this issue we extend the protocol in Section 4 with an algorithm for piecewise disclosure of missing credentials. The basic intuition is that the logical policy structure itself tells us which credentials must be disclosed to obtain the information that other credentials are missing. So, we simply need to extract this information automatically. We perform a step-by-step evaluation on the policy structure. For that purpose we use one step deduction (Def. 2) over the disclosure policy $\mathcal{P_D}$ to determine the next set of potentially disclosable credentials.

Essentially, the protocol replaces the `askCredentials` function with a new version of it using the piecewise disclosure algorithm and adds the disclosure policy to its arguments, see Figure 3.

With its new version the `askCredentials` function (Figure 4) takes as input the set of missing credentials $\mathcal{C_M}$ (as the old one) together with the policy for disclosure control $\mathcal{P_D}$ that $\mathcal{C_M}$ was computed from. In a nutshell, the algorithm requests the client all missing credentials supplied in the input, but with the difference of stepwise awaiting for each of the computed steps by the `PiecewiseDisclosure` algorithm. In other words, when a next step of missing credentials is computed (step 2) the algorithm waits until the client responds to all current requests. Again here the client's profile is updated on each request/response to facilitate other threads' access decisions. Then the check in step 3 for $\mathcal{C_{M1}}$ comprises two cases: either the set of presented credentials $\mathcal{C_P}$ has been updated (indirectly) by other running threads such that now $\mathcal{C_M}$ is satisfied and there is no next step or the client has declined some credentials that stop his way further to $\mathcal{C_M}$.

The task of the `PiecewiseDisclosure` is to determine at each interaction step exactly the relevant credentials that are needed to reach at the end the set $\mathcal{C_M}$.

Basically, we compute the set of abducible credentials in one step as $\mathcal{C_{D1}}$ (compare with the corresponding step 2 in Figure 2(a)). Out of those, we extract only the minimal set of credentials that is actually necessary to derive $\mathcal{C_M}$. To this extent, we modify policy $\mathcal{P_D}$ by adding a new atom q that can be derived if all (and only) $\mathcal{C_M}$ credentials are derived. Additionally, we also change syntactically the structure of $\mathcal{P_D}$ rule so that relevant credentials in $\mathcal{C_{D1}}$ must be abduced and can no longer be derived from chaining other rules.

We do that by changing a rule of the from $c \leftarrow c_1, \ldots, c_n$ into a pair of rules $\hat{c} \leftarrow c_1, \ldots, c_n$ and $c \leftarrow \hat{c}$, where $\hat{c}$ is a new symbol. The informal meaning of the first rule is that c is disclosable if all c_i are. So, we now say that the need for the fictitious $\hat{c}$ is disclosable if the need for all c_i

is disclosable and that the need for credential c is disclosable if the need for c_i is.

Then if we remove the $c \leftarrow \hat{c}$ for all c in $\mathcal{C}_{\mathcal{D}1}$ there will be no rule to infer that the need for c is disclosable so we must abduce c as a primitive atom (if it is actually needed to derive q, i.e. some of the $\mathcal{C}_{\mathcal{M}}$).

6.   Implementation

For the implementation of the framework we have chosen Collaxa[8] manager. Collaxa server supports many standards as BPEL4WS, WSDL, SOAP, etc. and interoperates with platforms as BEA's WebLogic and Microsoft .NET. So, this makes it well-suited for the purposes of the framework. The main idea of the work is that using BPEL4WS specification [5] we can orchestrate the requirements and communications between client and partners in an automatic and transparent way via a main authorization server.

For the implementation of the algorithms and protocols, presented in the paper, we need at a lower level a suitable engine for the basic reasoning services of deduction and abductiom. For that purpose we have done a wrapper (a set of interfaces) to the DLV system that manages all internal computations, queries and transformations to and from the DLV's defined front-ends.

For the actual crypto infrastructure we decided to use PERMIS[9] [4]. We chose PERMIS because it implements RBAC using entirely X.509 Identity and Attribute Certificates [6]. It allows for creating, verifying and validating attribute certificates and for storing and allocating them using LDAP directories [10]. For the integration with PERMIS, we extend the PERMIS's Access Decision Function (ADF) with the functionality of our model such that PERMIS validates and gathers client's credentials on its own and then asks our algorithm for an access decision (next possible step) presenting the newly collected credentials.

7.   Conclusions

In this paper we have proposed a framework for leveraging trust management and negotiation scheme between a client and a service provider in the WS world. We proposed a basic access control algorithm that evaluates a client's request with respect to a partner's policies and in the case of failure it computes what is necessary for the client to get the desired resource. Then we devised an interactive trust management

---

[8]www.collaxa.com | www.oracle.com/technology/bpel
[9]www.permis.org

protocol that communicates and negotiates the missing credentials in a piecewise manner until enough trust is established and the service is granted or the negotiation failed and the process was terminated.

The protocol can be run on both the client and server side so that they understand each other and automatically interoperate until a desired solution is reached or denied.

It is also possible to run the TrustBuilder by Yu et al. [12] on top of the protocol with the only requirement of transforming each time the protocol input/output to a syntax understandable by TrustBuilder.

One of the advantages in our approach is that we do not pose any restrictions on partner's policies since the basic computations performed on the policies are deduction and abduction, which do not require any specific policy structure.

References

[1] BENATALLAH, B., CASATI, F., AND TOUMANI, F. Web service conversation modeling: a cornerstone for e-business automation. *IEEE Internet Computing 8*, 1 (Jan/Feb 2004), 46–54.

[2] BLAZE, M., FEIGENBAUM, J., IOANNIDIS, J., AND KEROMYTIS, A. *The KeyNote Trust-Management System Version 2*, 1999. RFC 2704.

[3] BLAZE, M., FEIGENBAUM, J., AND LACY, J. Decentralized trust management. In *Proc. of IEEE Symposium on Security and Privacy* (1996), pp. 164–173.

[4] CHADWICK, D. W., AND OTENKO, A. The PERMIS X.509 role-based privilege management infrastructure. In *7th ACM SACMAT* (2002), pp. 135–140.

[5] FRANCISCO CURBERA, ET AL. *Business Process Execution Language for Web Services (BPEL4WS)*. BEA, IBM, Microsoft, May 2003. http://www-106.ibm.com/developerworks/webservices/library/ws-bpel/.

[6] ITU-T RECOMMENDATION X.509:2000(E) | ISO/IEC 9594-8:2001(E). The directory: Public-key and attribute certificate frameworks.

[7] KOSHUTANSKI, H., AND MASSACCI, F. Interactive access control for Web Services. In *19th IFIP Information Security Conference (SEC 2004)*, pp. 150–166.

[8] KOSHUTANSKI, H., AND MASSACCI, F. A logical model for security of Web services. Tech. rep., 1st International Workshop on Formal Aspects of Security and Trust (FAST), Pisa, Italy, September 2003.

[9] LI, N., AND MITCHELL, J. C. RT: A role-based trust-management framework. In *Proc. of 3rd DARPA Information Survivability Conference and Exposition (DISCEX III)* (Los Alamitos, California, April 2003), pp. 201–212.

[10] WAHL, M., HOWES, T., AND KILLE, S. Lightweight Directory Access Protocol (v3), December 1997. RFC 2251.

[11] WINSLETT M, ET AL. Negotiating trust in the Web. *IEEE Internet Computing 6*, 6 (Nov/Dec 2002), 30–37.

[12] YU, T., WINSLETT, M., AND SEAMONS, K. E. Supporting structured credentials and sensitive policies through interoperable strategies for automated trust negotiation. *ACM TISSEC 6*, 1 (2003), 1–42.

COMPLEMENTING COMPUTATIONAL PROTOCOL ANALYSIS WITH FORMAL SPECIFICATIONS*

Kim-Kwang Raymond Choo, Colin Boyd, Yvonne Hitchcock, and Greg Maitland
Information Security Research Centre
Queensland University of Technology
GPO Box 2434, Brisbane, QLD 4001, Australia
{k.choo,c.boyd,y.hitchcock,g.maitland}@qut.edu.au

Abstract   The computational proof model of Bellare and Rogaway for cryptographic protocol analysis is complemented by providing a formal specification of the actions of the adversary and the protocol entities. This allows a matching model to be used in both a machine-generated analysis and a human-generated computational proof. Using a protocol of Jakobsson and Pointcheval as a case study, it is demonstrated that flaws in the protocol could have been found with this approach, providing evidence that the combination of human and computer analysis can be more effective than either alone. As well as finding the known flaw, previously unknown flaws in the protocol are discovered by the automatic analysis.

1.   Introduction

Cryptographic protocols are fundamental security tools for electronic communications and a high level of assurance is needed in the correctness of such protocols. Techniques to verify the correctness of security proofs for cryptographic protocols have been directed in two distinct directions, namely the formal methods approach [1, 4] and the computational complexity approach [5, 6, 10, 17].

In the formal methods approach, emphasis is placed on model checking and automatic theorem proving. Usually the abstract formal specification is in the tradition of the model of Dolev and Yao [12]. This means that a 'black box' model of cryptographic operations is used, which ignores different cryptographic properties and possible loss of partial information. Therefore it is quite possible to have flaws in protocols that were proven secure in the Dolev-

*This work was partially funded by the Australian Research Council Discovery Project Grant DP0345775.

Yao sense [3, 15] and we cannot be entirely confident that such a protocol can be implemented securely.

In the computational complexity approach, emphasis is placed on a proven reduction from the problem of breaking the protocols to another problem believed to be hard. Such proofs are invariably generated by humans. Application of the computational complexity approach to protocol analysis was initiated by Bellare and Rogaway in 1993, with a proof for a simple two party entity authentication and key exchange protocol [6]. They formally defined a model of adversary capabilities with an associated definition of security. Since then, the model has been further revised several times. In 1995, Bellare and Rogaway analysed a three-party server-based key distribution protocol [7] using an extension to the 1993 model. The most recent revision to the model was proposed in 2000 by Bellare, Pointcheval and Rogaway [5], hereafter referred to as the BPR2000 model.

A complete mathematical proof with respect to cryptographic definitions provides a strong assurance that a protocol is behaving as desired. However, the difficulty of obtaining correct computational proofs of security has been illustrated dramatically by the well-known problem with the OAEP mode for public key encryption [17]. Although OAEP was one of the most widely used and implemented algorithms, it was several years after the publication of the original proof that a problem was found (and subsequently fixed in the case of RSA). Problems with proofs of protocol security have occurred too. In this paper, we will use the original version of a protocol due to Jakobsson and Pointcheval [13] which carried a claimed proof in the Bellare-Rogaway model but was later found to be flawed by Wong and Chan [18].

In recent years a number of researchers have started to recognize the disparity in the two different approaches to protocol analysis. Previous efforts in unifying the two domains have been devoted towards providing abstract models of cryptographic primitives which are suitable for machine analysis and yet can be proven to be functionally equivalent (in some well-defined sense) to the real cryptographic primitives that they model. Abadi and Rogaway [2] started this trend, and more recently comprehensive efforts have been under way in two different but related projects by Canetti [9] and by Backes *et al.* [3].

In this work we take a different, more pragmatic, approach to the problem. We are motivated by the observation that so far no researchers have tried to utilize the communication and adversary model from computational proofs in a machine specification and analysis. Although we cannot capture the complexity-based definitions for security and cryptographic primitives, we can ensure that the same protocol and adversary capabilities are specified in both the human-generated proofs and the machine analysis. In other words, rather than trying to unify the two approaches, we treat them as complementary but ensure that, as far as possible, they are analysing the same objects.

Our thesis is that the human proof will take care of the cryptographic details lacking in the machine analysis, while the machine analysis will help to ensure that human error resulting in basic structural mistakes is avoided.

We provide a formal specification and machine analysis of the adversary model from the BPR2000 model as shown in Figure 1. The Bellare-Rogaway model is the most widely used model for human-generated security proofs of protocols. As a case study we analyse the protocol of Jakobsson and Pointcheval. The original version appeared in the unpublished pre-proceedings of Financial Cryptography 2001 with a claimed proof of security in the Bellare-Rogaway model. Nevertheless, a flaw in the protocol was discovered by Wong and Chan. In the published paper [13], the flaw in the protocol has been fixed.

Our choice of formalism for this work is Asynchronous Product Automata (APA), a universal state-based formal method [16]. APA is supported by the Simple Homomorphism Verification Tool (SHVT) [14] for analysis and verification of cooperating systems and communicating automata. Once the possible state transitions of each automaton have been specified, SHVT can be used to automatically search the state space of the model. SHVT provides a reachability graph of the explored states. In our APA specification, the abstract communication model captures the representation of the protocol, the message transmission, and the communication channels. The automated state space analyses performed with SHVT reveal the known attack on the Jakobsson-Pointcheval protocol and also two other previously unpublished attacks.

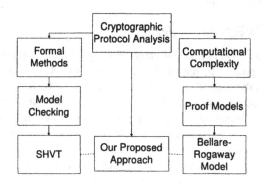

Figure 1. Our proposed approach

This work differs significantly from related earlier work of Boyd and Viswanathan [8], as their formal specification did not capture the entire Bellare-Rogaway model. In addition, no automatic searching was performed and no new attack was revealed in their earlier work.

We regard the main contributions of this paper to be confirmation of the feasibility of using formal specifications to identify problems in human-generated computational complexity proofs, demonstration of the use of SHVT in an automated manner to find unknown attacks in protocols, and a re-usable framework for automatic analysis of protocols proven secure in the BPR2000 model.

The remainder of this paper is structured as follows: Section 2 briefly explains the adversarial model used in our formal specification framework and the Bellare-Rogaway adversarial model. Section 3 describes the original version of the mutual authentication and key exchange protocol (MAKEP) due to Jakobsson and Pointcheval, and the hijacking attack first mentioned by Wong and Chan. Section 4 briefly outlines the state-based APA specification, followed by the results of the protocol analysis using SHVT. Section 5 presents the conclusions.

2. Overview of Our Formal Specification Framework

In this section, we present an overview of the BPR2000 model, followed by a definition of an adversary in our APA formal specification framework. We follow the general adversarial formalism of the BPR2000 model, except that the probabilistic characteristics of the BPR2000 adversary are not explicitly modelled in our formal specification due to the deterministic nature of SHVT. However, since our thesis is that the human proof will take care of the cryptographic details lacking in the machine analysis, this does not present an obstacle to our protocol analysis.

2.1 The BPR2000 Model

The BPR2000 model defines provable security for entity authentication and key distribution goals. In the model, the adversary $\mathcal{A}_{BR}$ is a probabilistic machine that has the capability to read, delay, replay, modify, delete, and fabricate messages between communicating principals and to start new instances of communicating principals. $\mathcal{A}_{BR}$ controls all the communications that take place between parties by interacting with a set of oracles at any time in any order. Each of the oracles represents an instance of a principal (Π_U^i denotes the i-th instance of a principal U) in a specific protocol run. The predefined oracle queries are described informally as follows.

- The SendClient and SendServer queries allow the adversary to simulate the actions of the principals according to the protocol by sending some message of her choice to any client or server oracle at will. The client or server oracle, upon receiving the query, will compute what the protocol specification demands and send back the response.

- The Reveal query allows the adversary to expose an old session key which has been previously accepted. Any oracle receiving this query, if it has accepted and holds some session key, will send this session key back to the adversary. This query enables the modelling of the requirement that loss of a session key should only affect the session that used the key, and not any other session. In addition, some session keys may not need to be kept secret after the completion of a session, e.g. keys used for message authentication.

- The Corrupt query allows the adversary to corrupt any principal at will, and thereby learn the complete internal state of the corrupted principal. The Corrupt query also gives the adversary the ability to overwrite the long-lived key of the corrupted principal with any value of her choice. This query can be used to model the real world scenarios of an insider cooperating with the adversary and an insider who has been completely compromised by the adversary.

- The Test query is the only oracle query that does not correspond to any of $\mathcal{A}_{BR}$'s abilities. If the oracle being asked a Test query has accepted with some session key, and depending on the randomly chosen bit b, $\mathcal{A}_{BR}$ is given either the actual session key or a session key drawn randomly from the session key distribution. $\mathcal{A}_{BR}$ may only make one Test query during a game simulation. The use of the Test query is explained in Section 2.1.3.

The definition of security depends on the notions of partnership of oracles and indistinguishability. The definition of partnership is used in the definition of security to restrict the adversary's Reveal and Corrupt queries to oracles that are not partners of the oracle whose key the adversary is trying to guess.

2.1.1   Definition of Partnership.   Partnership is defined using the notion of session identifiers (*SIDs*). *SIDs* are defined as the concatenation of messages exchanged during the particular protocol run in question. An oracle who has accepted will hold the associated session key, a *SID* and a partner identifier (*PID*).

DEFINITION 1 *Two oracles,* Π_A^i *and* Π_B^j, *are partners if, and only if, both oracles have accepted the same session key with the same SID, have agreed on the same set of principals (i.e., the initiator and the responder of the protocol), and no other oracles besides* Π_A^i *and* Π_B^j *have accepted with the same SID.*

2.1.2   Definition of Freshness.   Definition 2 describes the notion of freshness, which depends on the notion of partnership in Definition 1.

DEFINITION 2 *Oracle* Π_A^i *is fresh (or it holds a fresh session key) at the end of execution, if, and only if, oracle* Π_A^i *has accepted with or without a partner oracle* Π_B^j, *both oracle* Π_A^i *and its partner oracle* Π_B^j *(if such a partner oracle exists) are unopened (i.e., have not been sent a* Reveal *query), and none of the players are corrupted (i.e., no one has been sent a* Corrupt *query).*

2.1.3 Definition of Security.   Security is defined using the game $\mathcal{G}$, played between a malicious adversary $\mathcal{A}_{BR}$ and a collection of oracles. $\mathcal{A}_{BR}$ runs $\mathcal{G}$ and is able to send any oracle queries at will. At some point during $\mathcal{G}$, $\mathcal{A}_{BR}$ will choose a fresh session on which to be tested and send a Test query to the fresh oracle associated with the test session. Depending on the randomly chosen bit b, $\mathcal{A}_{BR}$ is given either the actual session key or a session key drawn randomly from the session key distribution. $\mathcal{A}_{BR}$ continues making any oracle queries of its choice. Eventually, $\mathcal{A}_{BR}$ terminates the game and outputs a bit b', which is its guess of the value of b.

Success of $\mathcal{A}_{BR}$ is measured in terms of $\mathcal{A}_{BR}$'s advantage in distinguishing whether $\mathcal{A}_{BR}$ receives the real key or a random value. $\mathcal{A}_{BR}$ wins if, after asking a Test query, $\mathcal{A}_{BR}$'s guess bit b' equals the bit b selected during the Test query. If the advantage of $\mathcal{A}_{BR}$ is denoted by $\mathsf{Adv}^{\mathcal{A}_{BR}}$, then $\mathsf{Adv}^{\mathcal{A}_{BR}} = 2 \times \Pr[b = b'] - 1$.

DEFINITION 3 *A protocol is secure if both the following requirements are satisfied: (1) when the protocol is run between two oracles in the absence of a malicious adversary, the two oracles accept the same key, and (2) for all probabilistic, polynomial-time adversaries* $\mathcal{A}_{BR}$, *the advantage* $\mathsf{Adv}^{\mathcal{A}_{BR}}$ *is negligible and the advantage that any adversary has in violating entity authentication is negligible. An adversary is said to violate entity authentication if some fresh oracle terminates (i.e., accepts a session key and completes the protocol) with no partner.*

2.2   Our Formal Specification Framework

In our formal framework using APA specification, protocol principals are modelled as a family of elementary automata. The various state spaces of the principals are modelled as a family of state sets. The channel through which the elementary automaton communicates is modelled by the addition and removal of messages from the shared state component Network, which is initially empty. Each of the elementary automata only has access to the particular state components to which it is connected. In addition to the regular protocol principals, we specify an adversary $\mathcal{A}$, which has access to the shared state component Network, but no access to the internal states of the principals.

Adopting the adversary formalism from the BPR2000 model, we consider an adversary $\mathcal{A}$ who is able to intercept messages in the Network, swap data components in the intercepted messages to form new messages, remove messages from the Network, or fabricate new messages. $\mathcal{A}$ is then able to send these messages to the client or server oracles via the Network (corresponding to SendClient and SendServer queries in the BPR2000 model). Also, once an oracle, Π_U^i, has accepted and holds a session key, the (SID, PID) pair associated with that oracle becomes visible to the adversary $\mathcal{A}$ via the shared state component Transcript. If $\mathcal{A}$ so chooses, $\mathcal{A}$ is then able to obtain the session key of Π_U^i via a Reveal query or a Corrupt query. The shared state component Transcript also contains a log of all sent messages and is equivalent to a transcript in the Bellare-Rogaway model. The graphical illustration of MAKEP in APA specification is shown in Figure 2.

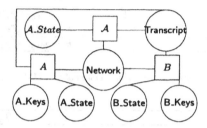

Figure 2.   Graphical illustration of MAKEP in APA specification

The advantage of $\mathcal{A}_{BR}$ is not explicitly modelled in our specification due to its probabilistic nature. Instead of modelling the attack to distinguish between the real key and a random value, we simplify the game $\mathcal{G}$ defined in Section 2.1.3 by assuming that $\mathsf{Adv}^{\mathcal{A}_{BR}} = 1$ if $\mathcal{A}_{BR}$ can obtain a fresh session key, otherwise $\mathsf{Adv}^{\mathcal{A}_{BR}} = 0$. Consequently, some attacks might be left out while analysing the game $\mathcal{G}$. However, since our aim is to leave computational matters to the human-generated proof, this does not present an obstacle to our protocol analysis.

When using formal specification tools, insecurity is commonly specified in terms of the unreachability of the desired states or reachability of insecure states and a "secure" protocol in a formal specification does not necessarily imply that the protocol is secure. Hence, we find it more natural to define insecurity in our formal framework as given in Definition 4. Protocols proven insecure in our formal specification model will also be insecure in the Bellare-Rogaway model. Definition 4 depends on the notions of partnership in Definition 1 and freshness in Definition 2.

DEFINITION 4 *A protocol is insecure in our formal framework if:*

    1 two fresh non-partner oracles accept the same key, or

2 *some fresh oracle accepts some key, which has been exposed (i.e., is known to A), or*

3 *some fresh oracle accepts and terminates with no partner.*

3. Original Version of Jakobsson-Pointcheval MAKEP

Client $A\ (a, g^a)$		Server $B\ (b, g^b)$
$r_A, t_A \in_R \mathbb{Z}_q, K = y_B^{r_A} = g^{br_A}$		
$k = h_0(g^b, g^{r_A}, K), r = h_1(g^{t_A})$		
$k_2 = h_2(g^b, g^{r_A}, K)$	$\xrightarrow{g^{r_A}, r}$	$K = (g^{r_A})^b, k_2' = h_2(g^b, g^{r_A}, K)$
$k_2 \stackrel{?}{=} k_2'$	$\xleftarrow{k_2', e}$	$e \in_R \{0, 1\}^k$
$d = t_A - ae \bmod q$	$\xrightarrow{d}$	$r \stackrel{?}{=} h_1(g^d(g^a)^e),$
		$k = h_0(g^b, g^{r_A}, K)$
$k = h_0(g^b, g^{r_A}, K)$		$k = h_0(g^b, g^{r_A}, K)$

Figure 3.   Original version of MAKEP

$A\ (a, g^a)$		A		$B\ (b, g^b)$
$r_A, t_A \in_R \mathbb{Z}_q$				
$K = y_B^{r_A} = g^{br_A}$				
$k = h_0(g^b, g^{r_A}, K)$				
$r = h_1(g^{t_A})$				
$k_2 = h_2(g^b, g^{r_A}, K)$	$\xrightarrow{g^{r_A}, r}$			$K_1 = (g^{r_A})^b$
	$\xrightarrow{g^{r_E}, r}$			$K_2 = (g^{r_E})^b$
			$\xleftarrow{k_{2,1}, e_1}$	$k_{2,1} = h_2(g^b, g^{r_A}, K_1)$
				$e_1 \in_R \{0, 1\}^k$
			$\xleftarrow{k_{2,2}, e_2}$	$k_{2,2} = h_2(g^b, g^{r_E}, K_2)$
				$e_2 \in_R \{0, 1\}^k$
$k_2 \stackrel{?}{=} k_{2,1}$		$\xleftarrow{k_{2,1}, e_2}$		
$d = t_A - ae_2 \bmod q$	$\xrightarrow{d}$		$\xrightarrow{d}$	
				$r \stackrel{?}{=} h_1(g^d(g^a)^{e_2})$
$k_{AB} = h_0(g^b, g^{r_A}, (g^b)^{r_A})$				$k_{BA} = h_0(g^b, g^{r_E}, (g^{r_E})^b)$

Figure 4.   A hijacking attack on original version of MAKEP

There are two communicating principals in MAKEP shown in Figure 3, namely the server and the client of limited computing resources, A. The security goals of the protocol are mutual authentication and key agreement between the two communicating principals. A and B are each assumed to know the public key of the other party. Prior to the protocol run, A can pre-compute the session key k which is a hash of the shared secret with B using Diffie-Hellman key exchange, the value r used for client authentication and B's public key (i.e., $k = h_0(g^b, g^{r_A}, K)$). In the protocol, the notation $r_A \in_R \mathbb{Z}_q$ denotes that r_A is randomly drawn from $\mathbb{Z}_q$.

Despite claims of the original version of MAKEP being proven secure in the Bellare-Rogaway model, a hijacking attack on the protocol was discovered by Wong and Chan [18] which breaks the client authentication as shown in Figure 4. The result of the attack is that B actually shares a key with a malicious adversary $\mathcal{A}$ when B believes the key is being shared with A. This attack is revealed by the SHVT analysis explained in Section 4.2.1.

4. Protocol Specification and Analysis

In this section, using the original version of MAKEP as a case study, we specify the protocol using APA. We demonstrate that SHVT can be used to find the hijacking attack first mentioned by Wong and Chan, and two previously unknown flaws in the protocol. For the remainder of this section, E denotes the adversary.

4.1 Protocol Specification

		Examples of some basic types
Agents	::=	set of all the principals (i.e., A, B) and $\mathcal{A}$ (i.e., E)
A_State	::=	A's internal state
A_Keys	::=	set of A's public and private keys
Accepted	::=	set of all oracles who had accepted (visible to $\mathcal{A}$)
		Examples of some functions
gFunction(g, m)	::=	denotes g^m, where m is some value (e.g., gFunction(g, rA) denotes g^{r_A} shown in Figure 3)
verifyGFun(m1, m2)	::=	the verification function used to verify if $g^{m1'} \overset{?}{=} g^{m2'}$ for some $m1'$ and $m2'$. (e.g., verifyGFun(gFunction(gFunction(g, a), b), gFunction(gFunction(g, b), a)) will return true)

Figure 5. Examples of basic types and functions

The first phase of our formal specification is to specify the basic types and the functions as shown in Figure 5. In order to increase run-time efficiency, and to overcome storage restrictions, we replace each unique data item in any message with a unique numeric message identifier (MID) in our specification. For example, the message in message flow 1 sent by A consists of two data items, g^{r_A} and r, whose message identifiers are $MID = 1$ and $MID = 2$ respectively. SID is then the concatenation of these unique $MIDs$ (e.g. $SID = [1, 2, \ldots]$) instead of the concatenation of messages from the BPR2000 model.

Initial State of the Original Version.   The initial state of MAKEP is shown in Figure 6. The left-hand column shows the SHVT specification of the various initial states, and an explanation is given in the right-hand column.

A_State:=	{(B,server),(start,B), (publicK,gFunction(b),B)};	*A* knows that *B* is a server, can start a protocol session run with *B* (indicated by the keyword *start*), and knows the public key of *B* (i.e., g^b).
A_Keys:=	{(publicK,gFunction(a)),(privateK,a)};	*A* owns a key pair (a,g^a).
B_State:=	{(A,agent),(respond,A), (publicK,gFunction(a),A)};	*B* knows that *A* is an agent, can respond to a protocol run initiated by *A* (indicated by the keyword *respond*), and knows the public key of *A* (i.e., g^a).
B_Keys:=	{(publicK,gFunction(b)),(privateK,b)};	*B* owns a key pair (b,g^b).
E_State:=	{(publicK,gFunction(a),A),publicK, gFunction(b),B)};	*A*(Eve) knows the public keys of *A* and *B*.
Network:=	∅;	Network is initially empty.
Transcript:=	∅;	Transcript is initially empty.

Figure 6.   Initial state

Step 1 of the Original Version.   Starting from the initial state shown in Figure 6, SHVT computes all reachable states. The first state transition of the initiator client *A* is explained in Figure 7. To ensure uniqueness of the values r_A, t_A and MID in the APA specification, once these values are assigned, they are removed from the pre-defined sets *new_random_nonce* and *MIDs*. We assume that (SID_A, PID_A) cannot be modified by the adversary. The (SID_A, PID_A) tuple is required to enable the SHVT analysis to define partnership.

A Malicious State Transistion.   An active adversary $\mathcal{A}$ is able to intercept message (g^{r_A}, r) meant for *B* from *A*, to fabricate a new message (g^{r_E}, r) and to send the fabricated message (g^{r_E}, r) to *B* via the Network. This state transition as shown in Figure 8 is equivalent to a SendServer query in the BPR2000 model. Due to space contraints, details of other possible state transitions for the adversary and the protocol are omitted.

4.2   Protocol Analysis

Having formally specified the protocol in APA, we analyse the protocol specification using SHVT as shown in the sections below. The analyses were run on a Pentium IV 2.4 GHz computer with 512 Mb of RAM and the anal-

def_trans_pattern A step_1	Definition of a state transition
B,gb,rA,tA,rAA,r,k,k2,K,SIDA,PIDA,MID	Variables used in this step
['start',B] ? A_State,	Precondition: A can start protocol run with B.
[B,'server'] ? A_State,	Precondition: A knows B is the server.
['publicK',gb,B] ? A_State,	Precondition: A knows B's public key gb. (gb is a variable that takes the value $gFunction(b)$.)
rAA « new_random_nonce, rA := head(rAA), tA := head(tail(rAA)), tail(tail(rAA)) » new_random_nonce, MID « SIDs, tail(tail(MID)) » SIDs, SIDA := [head(MID),head(tail(MID))],	Random unique nonce values are drawn from the pre-defined set new_random_nonce and assigned to r_A and t_A respectively. Random unique $MIDs$ are drawn from the pre-defined set $SIDs$ are assigned to g^{r_A} and r respectively. SID is the concatenation of these unique $MIDs$.
PIDA := B,	PID of A is set to B.
K := ['KFunction',gb,rA],	A computes a new $K = (g^b)^{r_A}$.
k := ['hash0',gb,['gFunction',g,rA],K],	A computes the new shared secret k using the hash function h_0 (i.e., $k = h_0(g^b, g^{r_A}, K)$).
r := ['hash1',['gFunction',g,tA]],	A computes $r = h_1(g^{t_A})$.
k2 := ['hash2',gb,['gFunction',g,rA],K],	A computes $k_2 = h_2(g^b, g^{r_A}, K)$.
['start',B] « A_State,	A initiated one session with B, so one tuple enabling a session to start is removed from A's state.
[SIDA,PIDA,[tA,k,k2,K]] » A_State,	A stores the information that she shares with B for this protocol run.
(A,B, [head(SIDA1), head(tail(SIDA1))], [['gFunction',g, rA], r]) » Network;	A sends message g^{r_A}, r to the Network.

Figure 7. State transition - step 1

ysis statistics are shown in Figure 9. We set the break condition to terminate the SHVT analysis if any of the requirement(s) in Definition 4 are violated. The attack sequence and the internal states can be examined by viewing the reachability graph produced by SHVT.

For run-time efficiency, and to avoid enormous branching factors in the search space, we restrict the actions of the adversary so that certain actions are possible for only some message types. Running SHVT with adversaries having various restrictions and also restricting A to only two protocol runs results in SHVT finding the attacks shown in Figures 4, 10, and 11.

def trans pattern E SendServer	Definition of a state transition
(ga,gb,A,B,M,SIDE,S,rE)	Variables used in this step
['publicK',ga,A] ? E_State,	Precondition: A knows A's public key.
('publicK',gb,B) ? E_State,	Precondition: A knows B's public key.
[A,'agent'] ? E_State,	Precondition: A knows A exists.
[B,'server'] ? E_State,	Precondition: A knows B exists.
$A \neq B$,	Precondition: A and B are two different principals.
(A,B,S,M) ? Network,	Precondition: Checks if there exists any message from A intended for B in the network.
rAA « new_random_nonce, rA := head(rAA), tA := head(tail(rAA)), tail(tail(rAA)) » new_random_nonce, SIDE « SIDs, tail(tail(SIDE)) » SIDs,	Random unique nonce values are drawn from the pre-defined set *new_random_nonce* and assigned to r_A and t_A respectively. Random unique *MIDs* are drawn from the pre-defined set *SIDs* and assigned to grE and rE respectively.
['fabricated','mf1',[head(SIDE),elem(2,S)], [['gFunction',g, head(rE)]]» E_State,	A stores information in her internal state.
(A,B,[head(SIDE),elem(2,S)], [['gFunction', g,head(rE)], elem(2,M)])» Network;	A sends a fabricated message to B via the Network.

Figure 8. A malicious state transition

Protocol Analysis	# Players	# Runs	# Nodes	Run-Time	Flaws?
Hijacking Attack	2	1	34	2 secs	Yes
New Attack 1	2	2	144	3 secs	Yes
New Attack 2	2	2	1538	79 secs	Yes

Figure 9. Analysis statistics

4.2.1 Hijacking Attack. State space analysis performed in the SHVT analysis reveals that both requirements 2 and 3 of Definition 4 can be violated. This attack was first mentioned by Wong and Chan [18] as shown in Figure 4.

4.2.2 New Attack 1. State space analysis in SHVT reveals that requirement 1 of Definition 4 is violated. The internal state of the final node in the reachability graph reveals that the following four oracles have accepted some session key: $\Pi_A^{[1,2,7,10,12])}$ belonging to A and having $SID = [1,2,7,10,12]$ accepted $h_0(g^{rA1}, g^{tA1}, (g^{rA1})^{tA1})$, $\Pi_A^{[3,4,9,8,11])}$ belonging to A and having $SID = [3,4,9,8,11]$ accepted $h_0(g^{rA1}, g^{tA2}, (g^{rA1})^{tA2})$, $\Pi_B^{[1,4,7,8,11])}$ belonging to B and having $SID = [1,4,7,8,11]$ accepted $h_0(g^{tA1}, g^{rA1}, (g^{tA1})^{rA1})$, and $\Pi_B^{[3,2,9,10,12])}$ belonging to B and having $SID = [3,2,9,10,12]$ accepted $h_0(g^{tA1}, g^{rA2}, (g^{tA2})^{rA1})$. By Definition 1, none of these oracles have any partner oracles since their *SIDs* are different. However, we observe that the pairs $(\Pi_A^{[1,2,7,10,12]}, \Pi_B^{[1,4,7,8,11]})$ and $(\Pi_A^{[3,4,9,8,11]}, \Pi_B^{[3,2,9,10,12]})$ have accepted with the same session keys as shown in Figure 10.

$A\,(a, g^a)$	A	$B\,(b, g^b)$
$r_{A,1}, t_{A,1} \in_R \mathbb{Z}_q$ $K_{A,1} = y_B^{r_{A,1}} = g^{b r_{A,1}}$ $k_{A,1} = h_0(g^b, g^{r_{A,1}}, K_{A,1})$ $r_1 = h_1(g^{t_{A,1}})$ $k_{2(S1(A))} = h_2(g^b, g^{r_{A,1}}, K_{A,1})$ $r_{A,2}, t_{A,2} \in_R \mathbb{Z}_q$ $K_{A,2} = y_B^{r_{A,2}} = g^{b r_{A,2}}$ $k_{A,2} = h_0(g^b, g^{r_{A,2}}, K_{A,2})$ $r_2 = h_2(g^{t_{A,2}})$ $k_{2(S2(A))} = h_2(g^b, g^{r_{A,2}}, K_{A,2})$	$\overset{g^{r_{A,1}}, r_1}{\longrightarrow}$ $\overset{g^{r_{A,2}}, r_2}{\longrightarrow}$	
	$\overset{g^{r_{A,1}}, r_2}{\longrightarrow}$ $\overset{g^{r_{A,2}}, r_1}{\longrightarrow}$	$K_1 = (g^{r_{A(1)}})^b$ $K_2 = (g^{r_{A(2)}})^b$
	$\overset{k_{2,1}, e_1}{\longleftarrow}$ $\overset{k_{2,2}, e_2}{\longleftarrow}$	$k_{2,1} = h_2(g^b, g^{r_{A,1}}, K_1)$ $e_1 \in_R \{0,1\}^k$ $k_{2,2} = h_2(g^b, g^{r_{A,2}}, K_2)$ $e_2 \in_R \{0,1\}^k$
$k_{2(S1(A))} \overset{?}{=} k_{2,1}$ $k_{2(S2(A))} \overset{?}{=} k_{2,2}$ $d_1 = t_{A,1} - a e_2 \bmod q$ $d_2 = t_{A,2} - a e_1 \bmod q$	$\overset{k_{2,1}, e_2}{\longleftarrow}$ $\overset{k_{2,2}, e_1}{\longleftarrow}$ $\overset{d_1}{\longrightarrow}$ $\overset{d_2}{\longrightarrow}$	$e_2 \in_R \{0,1\}^k$ d_1 d_2 $r_2 \overset{?}{=} h_1(g^{d_1}(g^a)^{e_2})$ $r_1 \overset{?}{=} h_1(g^{d_2}(g^a)^{e_1})$
$k_{AB_{(1)}} = h_0(g^b, g^{r_{A,1}}, (g^b)^{r_{A,1}})$ $k_{AB_{(2)}} = h_0(g^b, g^{r_{A,2}}, (g^b)^{r_{A,2}})$		$k_{BA_{(1)}} = h_0(g^b, g^{r_{A,1}}, (g^{r_{A,1}})^b)$ $k_{BA_{(2)}} = h_0(g^b, g^{r_{A,2}}, (g^{r_{A,2}})^b)$

Figure 10. New attack 1

This implies that by revealing one oracle in any pair, the adversary $\mathcal{A}$ is able to distinguish the session key held by the other oracle in the same pair. Hence, the protocol state is not secure since the adversary $\mathcal{A}$ can find a fresh session key. In addition, mutual authentication is violated since both the client and server oracles terminate without a partner.

The attack sequence is shown in Figure 10, and is revealed by following the reachability graph to the insecure state. The attack sequence is as follows: the adversary $\mathcal{A}$ intercepts and removes the two original messages from the Network, swaps the components in these two messages to form two new messages, and sends these two modified messages to B impersonating A via the Network. B, upon receiving these two messages, will respond as per the protocol specification. $\mathcal{A}$ intercepts the messages in protocol flow 2 sent by B to A, and swaps the components in these two messages to form new messages and again sends these two modified messages back to the Network, impersonating B. If A authenticates the server, she will respond with some value d as per the protocol specification. B receives the messages d_1 and d_2 in protocol flow 3. Once some oracle has accepted and holds some session key, the particular (SID, PID) pair will be made visible to the adversary via the shared state component Transcript. $\mathcal{A}$ is then able to send Reveal queries to the oracles of B, and receive the session keys held by the associated fresh oracles of A.

$A\,(a, g^a)$	A	$B\,(b, g^b)$
$r_{A,1}, t_{A,1} \in_R \mathbb{Z}_q$ $K_{A,1} = y_B^{r_{A,1}} = g^{br_{A,1}}$ $k_{A,1} = h_0(g^b, g^{r_{A,1}}, K_{A,1})$ $r_1 = h_1(g^{t_{A,1}})$		
$k_{2(S1(A))} = h_2(g^b, g^{r_{A,1}}, K_{A,1})$ $r_{A,2}, t_{A,2} \in_R \mathbb{Z}_q$ $K_{A,2} = y_B^{r_{A,2}} = g^{br_{A,2}}$ $k_{A,2} = h_0(g^b, g^{r_{A,2}}, K_{A,2})$ $r_2 = h_2(g^{t_{A,2}})$	$\xrightarrow{g^{r_{A,1}}, r_1}$	
$k_{2(S2(A))} = h_2(g^b, g^{r_{A,2}}, K_{A,2})$	$\xrightarrow{g^{r_{A,2}}, r_2}$ $\xrightarrow{g^{r_{A,1}}, r_E}$	$K_1 = (g^{r_{A,1}})^b$
	$\xrightarrow{g^{r_E}, r_1}$	$K_2 = (g^{r_E})^b$
	$\xrightarrow{g^{r_E}, r_2}$	$K_3 = (g^{r_E})^b$
	$\xrightarrow{g^{r_{A,2}}, r_E}$	$K_4 = (g^{r_{A,2}})^b$
	$\xleftarrow{k_{2,1}, e_1}$	$k_{2,1} = h_2(g^b, g^{r_{A,1}}, K_1)$ $e_1 \in_R \{0,1\}^k$
	$\vdots$	$\vdots$
	$\xleftarrow{k_{2,4}, e_4}$	$k_{2,4} = h_2(g^b, g^{r_{A,2}}, K_4)$ $e_4 \in_R \{0,1\}^k$
$k_{2(S1(A))} \overset{?}{=} k_{2,1}$	$\xleftarrow{k_{2,1}, e_2}$	
$k_{2(S2(A))} \overset{?}{=} k_{2,4}$	$\xleftarrow{k_{2,4}, e_3}$	
$d_1 = t_{A,1} - ae_2 \bmod q$	$\xrightarrow{d_1}$ $\xrightarrow{d_1}$	$r^E \overset{?}{=} h_1(g^{d_1}(g^a)^{e_2})$
$d_2 = t_{A_2} - ae_3 \bmod q$	$\xrightarrow{d_2}$ $\xrightarrow{d_2}$	$r^E \overset{?}{=} h_1(g^{d_2}(g^a)^{e_3})$
$k_{AB_{(1)}} = h_0(g^b, g^{r_{A,1}}, (g^b)^{r_{A,1}})$ $k_{AB_{(2)}} = h_0(g^b, g^{r_{A,2}}, (g^b)^{r_{A,2}})$		$k_{BA_{(1)}} = h_0(g^b, g^{r_E}, (g^{r_E})^b)$ $k_{BA_{(2)}} = h_0(g^b, g^{r_E}, (g^{r_E})^b)$

Figure 11. New attack 2

4.2.3 New Attack 2.

State space analysis in SHVT reveals that requirements 2 and 3 of Definition 4 are violated and the internal state of the final node in the reachability graph reveals that fresh oracles of B, $\Pi_B^{[3,2,5,6,9]}$ and $\Pi_B^{[5,2,7,8,16]}$, have accepted with no partner. In addition, the adversary $\mathcal{A}$ is able to compute both the session keys accepted by B since both session keys are computed based on the random number g^{r_E} chosen by the adversary $\mathcal{A}$.

Hence A is able to decrypt all messages sent by B to A encrypted with these session keys. The attack sequence is shown in Figure 11, and is revealed by following the reachability graph to the insecure state.

5.   Conclusion and Future Work

We have described a formal model which can complement computational complexity proofs in the Bellare-Rogaway model. In our model the adversary capabilities match those in the Bellare-Rogaway model. Through a detailed study of the Jakobsson-Pointcheval protocol we have demonstrated that this approach can capture structural flaws in protocols. We were able to find both existing and previously unknown flaws in the protocol using SHVT. Such a tool is useful in checking the hand-generated Bellare-Rogaway proofs. We may speculate that if Jakobsson and Pointcheval had access to such a tool when constructing their original proof of security they could have spotted the flaw in the protocol.

Further directions for this work include extending it to other cryptographic protocols with proofs of security in order to gain better confidence in their correctness. In so doing we should be able to re-use the basic adversary model already developed. We would also like to explore other computational complexity models, in particular the Canetti-Krawczyk modular approach [10], to gain a better understanding of the uses of a complementary model. Finally, we would like to make use of the recent work of Canetti *et al.* [9, 11] and/or Backes *et al.* [4] in order to incorporate abstract cryptographic properties with a sound computational basis.

Acknowledgments

Thanks are due to Dr Carsten Rudolph of Fraunhofer Institute for Secure Telecooperation for his invaluable feedback on earlier drafts of this paper and also the anonymous referees for their critical feedback.

Notes

1. This work was partially funded by the Australian Research Council Discovery Project Grant DP0345775.

2. This work was partially funded by the Australian Research Council Discovery Project Grant DP0345775.

3. This work was partially funded by the Australian Research Council Discovery Project Grant DP0345775.

4. This work was partially funded by the Australian Research Council Discovery Project Grant DP0345775.

5. This work was partially funded by the Australian Research Council Discovery Project Grant DP0345775.

6. This work was partially funded by the Australian Research Council Discovery Project Grant DP0345775.

References

[1] M. Abadi and A.D. Gordon. A Calculus for Cryptographic Protocols: The Spi Calculus. In *4th ACM Conference on Computer and Communications Security*, pages 36–47. ACM Press, 1997.

[2] M. Abadi and P. Rogaway. Reconciling Two Views of Cryptography (The Computational Soundness of Formal Encryption). In *IFIP International Conference on Theoretical Computer Science - IFIP TCS2000*, pages 3–22. Springer-Verlag, 2000.

[3] M. Backes and C. Jacobi. Cryptographically Sound and Machine-Assisted Verification of Security Protocols. In *20th International Symposium on Theoretical Aspects of Computer Science - STACS 2003*, pages 310–329. Springer-Verlag, 2003.

[4] M. Backes, C. Jacobi, and B. Pfitzmann. Deriving Cryptographically Sound Implementations Using Composition and Formally Verified Bisimulation. In *Formal Methods - Getting IT Right*, pages 310–329. Springer-Verlag, 2002.

[5] M. Bellare, D. Pointcheval, and P. Rogaway. Authenticated Key Exchange Secure Against Dictionary Attacks. In *Advances in Cryptology – Eurocrypt*, pages 139 – 155. Springer-Verlag, 2000. LNCS Volume 1807/2000.

[6] M. Bellare and P. Rogaway. Entity Authentication and Key Distribution. In *Advances in Cryptology*, pages 110–125. Springer-Verlag, 1993. LNCS Volume 773/1993.

[7] M. Bellare and P. Rogaway. Provably Secure Session Key Distribution: The Three Party Case. In *27th ACM Symposium on the Theory of Computing*, pages 57–66. ACM Press, 1995.

[8] C. Boyd and K. Viswanathan. Towards a Formal Specification of the Bellare-Rogaway Model for Protocol Analysis. In *Formal Aspects of Security - FASec 2002*, pages 209–223. British Computer Society Press, Dec 2002.

[9] R. Canetti. Universally Composable Security: A New Paradigm for Cryptographic Protocols. Cryptology ePrint Archive, Report 2000/067, 2000.

[10] R. Canetti and H. Krawczyk. Analysis of Key-Exchange Protocols and Their Use for Building Secure Channels. In *Advances in Cryptology - Eurocrypt 2001:*, pages 453–474. Springer-Verlag, May 2001. LNCS Volume 2045/2001.

[11] R. Canetti and H. Krawczyk. Universally Composable Notions of Key Exchange and Secure Channels (Extended Version). Cryptology ePrint Archive, Report 2002/059, 2002.

[12] D. Dolev and A.C. Yao. On the Security of Public Key Protocols. *IEEE Transaction of Information Technology*, 29(2):198–208, 1983.

[13] M. Jakobsson and D. Pointcheval. Mutual Authentication and Key Exchange Protocol for Low Power Devices. In *Financial Cryptography*, pages 178–195. Springer-Verlag, 2001.

[14] P. Ochsenschlager, J. Repp, and R. Rieke. Abstraction and a Verification Method for Cooperating Systems. *Journal of Experimental and Theoretical Artificial Intelligence*, 12:447–459, Jun 2000.

[15] B. Pfitzmann, M. Schunter, and M. Waidner. Cryptographic Security of Reactive Systems. In Steve Schneider and Peter Ryan, editors, *Electronic Notes in Theoretical Computer Science*, volume 32. Reed Elsevier, 2000.

[16] R. Rieke. Implementing the APA Model for the Symmetric Needham-Schroeder Protocol in State Transition Pattern Notation in the SH Verification Tool. Technical report, Fraunhofer Institute for Secure Telecooperation SIT, 26 July 2002.

[17] V. Shoup. OAEP Reconsidered. In *Advances in Cryptology - CRYPTO 2001*, pages 239–259. Springer-Verlag, 2001. LNCS Volume 2139/2001.

[18] D.S. Wong and A.H. Chan. Efficient and Mutually Authenticated Key Exchange for Low Power Computing Devices. In *Advances in Cryptology - Asiacrypt 2001*. Springer-Verlag, 2001.

A Trust Model with Statistical Foundation

Jianqiang Shi[1] , Gregor v. Bochmann[2] and Carlisle Adams[2]
[1]*Systems Science;* [2]*School of Information Technology and Engineering (SITE)*

University of Ottawa

Ottawa, Ontario, Canada K1N 6N5

{jianqshi, bochmann, cadams}@site.uottawa.ca

Key words: trust, utility, decision making

Abstract: The widespread use of the Internet signals the need for a better understanding of trust as a basis for secure on-line interaction. In the face of increasing uncertainty and risk, users and machines must be allowed to reason effectively about the trustworthiness of other entities. In this paper, we propose a trust model that assists users and machines with decision-making in online interactions by using past behavior as a predictor of likely future behavior. We develop a general method to automatically compute trust based on self-experience and the recommendations of others. Furthermore, we apply our trust model to several utility models to increase the accuracy of decision-making in different contexts of Web Services.

1. INTRODUCTION

With the expansion of the Internet, users and services are often required to interact with unknown entities. This is so in application areas such as e-commerce, knowledge sharing, and even game playing. Because the entities are autonomous and potentially subject to different administrative and legal domains, it is important for each user to identify trustworthy entities or correspondents with whom he/she should interact, and untrustworthy correspondents with whom he/she should avoid interaction [6].

Trust models have emerged as an important risk management mechanism in such online communities. The goal of a trust model is to assist users with decision-making in online interactions by using past behavior as a predictor of likely future behavior. Most electronic marketplaces on the Internet, such as eBay, Yahoo Auction, Amazon, and Epinions, support some form of trust management mechanism. eBay, for example, encourages both parties of each transaction to rate the other participant with a positive (+1), neutral (0), or negative (-1) rating. eBay makes the cumulative ratings of its members publicly known to every registered user [10]. Epinions provides a mechanism to weave "the web of trust", a network of members whose reviews and ratings have been consistently found valuable. Each member can write a review on any topic and product. Reviews can be rated as "Not Helpful", "Somewhat Helpful", "Helpful", and "Very Helpful". The Web of Trust mimics the way people share word-of-mouth advice every day. Shareaza, a P2P file sharing system, allows members to write comments and ratings with respect to shared files. Thus, Shareaza allows members to avoid those that are fakes and download good quality, accurately represented files.

Our goal is to develop a general trust model that can be used for making rational decisions in order to make optimal choices. It should be usable in the context of Web Services and online transactions that meet real people's needs. We have opted for a trust model that is based on stochastic models of Web Services. We will explain how trust can be built up from experimental evidence and how statistical methods can be applied, together with utility functions, to make rational choices between different service providers or different strategies for problem solving. Our trust model is scalable in the number of users and services, and is usable, both for people and artificial autonomous agents.

The rest of this paper is organized as follows. Section 2 summarizes some related work on trust models. Section 3 introduces our approach, a trust model with a statistical foundation, giving the key definitions for the state space of possible outcomes of actions, trust update, and outcome space mapping. Section 4 presents some decision models. Section 5 briefly introduces recommendations and their evaluation. Section 6 concludes the paper and discusses potential directions for future work.

2.   EXISTING DEFINITIONS OF TRUST AND RELATED WORK

Due to limited space, this section is abridged from the full paper (available at http://www.site.uottawa.ca/~cadams/papers/TrustStat.pdf).

We write $T_a(\beta,\delta)$ for the trust an entity α has in another entity β with respect to a given situation δ. General trust represents the trust an entity α has in an entity β over all situations. We write $T_a(\beta)$ for the general trust of entity α in entity β. Basic trust is the general trusting disposition of the entity. We write T_a for the basic trust of entity α.

3.   A TRUST MODEL WITH A STATISTICAL FOUNDATION

In this section we propose a statistical foundation for a trust model. Such a foundation is intuitive and useful in many practical situations, as will be shown in Section 4.

3.1   A model of the trusted entity

Our trust model is based on a model of the trusted entity β. We discuss the space of possible outcomes with respect to a service performed by β and then propose a stochastic model for β.

3.1.1 The space of possible outcomes

Our trust model is based on an abstract model of the trusted entity. We assume that the trust concerns the execution of a certain action by the entity. In most cases, the execution of the action corresponds to a specific service that is provided by the trusted entity. There may be different outcomes of the action. The trust is concerned with some form of prediction of what the outcome will probably be. In the case of situational trust, we are concerned with a particular action in a certain situation; in the case of general trust, the action represents any action of the trusted entity that may be of interest.

It is important to identify the space of possible outcomes. This space determines the nature of the associated trust model. We note that the granularity of this space determines the precision with which any prediction of future behavior can be made. We give in the following some typical examples.

a) Discrete categories

In this case, the outcomes are classified into a finite set of categories. For instance, the eBay trust model foresees the three categories: "positive", "neutral", and "negative". In the case of trust concerning the quality of the food in a restaurant, the categories may be "excellent", "good", "average", "bad", and "very bad". The case of two-valued outcomes is a special case of discrete categories; here the outcomes are classified into two categories, which may be called "good" and "bad".

While in the above examples, the different categories were ordered according to some intuitive "goodness" relationship ("good" being better than "average", for instance), there are cases in which such an ordering does not necessarily exist. We may consider the example where the outcomes are classified into the following categories: "normal: all options OK", "option A failed", and "option B failed". Here it is not clear which of the last two categories would be better.

b) Numeric outcomes

There are many cases in which the outcome can be characterized by a numerical value. For instance, the trust may concern the response time of a Web server, or the delivery delay of a parcel delivery service. In these cases, we are interested in the delay for completing the action, and this delay may be measured in fractions of seconds, minutes, or hours, depending on the precision that is reasonable for the application. In these cases, the number of different outcomes is in principle infinite.

Other examples where the outcomes can be classified by a numerical value are the following: (1) What percentage of cost overruns can one expect in a construction contract? – or (2) What is the expected quality of a video obtained from a video-on-demand service?

c) Multidimensional outcome characterization

In many situations, the outcome of the action of interest has several parameters that are important to consider. Each of these parameters can usually be characterized either by a value from discrete value space, or a numerical (integer or real) value. In this case, we say that the space of the possible outcomes is multi-dimensional (one dimension for each parameter). Here are two examples:

1. Restaurant service with several evaluation criteria: (i) quality of food, (ii) service, and (iii) environment. For each of these three criteria, the restaurant may be classified into a certain number of discrete values, such as "excellent" down to "very bad". Therefore, the outcome of a restaurant experience may be classified as a point in this three-dimensional space, where each coordinate in this space is defined by a value between "excellent" and "very bad".

2. Multimedia presentation quality: As explained in [14] and [15], the quality of a multimedia presentation may be characterized by three values: (i) frame rate (in video frames per second), (ii) resolution (number of pixels within a frame), and (iii) color quality (number of colors distinguished per pixel). Therefore, the outcome of a video presentation obtained from a video-on-demand service may be characterized by three numerical values corresponding to these three quality of service parameters.

3.1.2 A stochastic model of the trusted entity

We assume that the trusted entity behaves like a stochastic process, in the sense that the outcome of an action of interest cannot be predicted exactly, that the outcome of one execution of an action of interest is statistically independent of the outcome of previous executions of that action, and that, over the long run, the probability that the outcome for the next execution of the action will be a particular point within the space of possible outcomes is described by a probability distribution, which we call the **outcome distribution** of the trusted entity, and which we represent by D_β. The value of D_β for a particular outcome $o \in O$ (where O is the space of possible outcomes) is written as $D_\beta(o)$. The outcome distribution is a distribution over the space of possible outcomes. Therefore the sum over all possible outcomes of the outcome distribution must be equal to one.

In the case of discrete outcome spaces, one usually does not make any assumptions about relationships between the outcome probabilities for different outcomes (except that they must sum to one). However, in the case of numerical outcomes, one may introduce additional assumptions. For instance, in Figure 1, a Gaussian outcome distribution is assumed, and the parameters of the Gaussian distribution are determined from a histogram of the outcomes observed during multiple experiments.

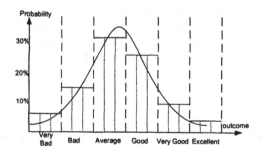

Figure 1

3.2   Building trust from experience

We now define trust and propose a model to build trust from prior experiences.

3.2.1   Definition of trust

Definition of trust: The trust of an entity α in the outcome of an action of entity β is an estimation of the outcome distribution D_β for the execution of the action by entity β.

The basic mechanism for building trust is by experience, that is, by observing the execution of the action of interest by the entity β a certain number of times. Let us assume that the space of possible outcomes O is finite and that N observations have been made, where the outcome of the *i-th* observation was o_i. If we make no assumptions about relationships between outcome probabilities for different outcomes, then the best estimation of D_β, the trust of the observing entity α, is given by the formula

$T_\alpha(\beta)$ (o) = (number of times that the outcome o_i was equal to o) / N (for all $o \in O$)

In the case that the space of possible outcomes includes a dimension with a numerical coordinate, the set of possible outcomes becomes infinite. In this case, the above simple average value calculation is not possible. Instead, the numerical coordinate is usually partitioned into a discrete number of intervals, as shown in Figure 1. Each interval is then treated like a discrete value and the above formula can be applied. If the model of the trusted entity includes an assumption about the functional form of the outcome distribution function D_β then the trust should be of the same form, and the parameters of this function should be adjusted to best fit the experimental data.

Instead of keeping in memory all previous experimental outcomes, one may use an incremental trust update formula. The following incremental formula is equivalent to the comprehensive formula above. For calculating the trust incrementally, we keep in memory the current trust $T_\alpha(\beta)(o)$ for each $o \in O$ and the number of observations to date. When a new experience yielding outcome o is observed, the values of $T_\alpha(\beta)$ and N will be updated as follows:

T_α (β) (o) = $(T_\alpha$ (β) (o) * N+ 1 $)$ / $(N + 1)$

T_α (β) (o') = T_α (β) (o') * N / $(N + 1)$ for o' different from o

$N = N + 1$

Note that the incremental formula and the comprehensive formula are applicable to both situational trust and general trust. In the case of the independent multidimensional outcome space, $T_\alpha(\beta)(o) = P(o) = \prod_{k=1}^{K} P(o_k)$ where $P(o)$ is the probability of outcome o, $o= (o_1, o_2, ..., o_K)$ and o_k is the outcome in k-th dimension. Here the marginal distribution of o_k can be used instead of the joint distribution of o because the dimensions are independent.

Consider the example of restaurant service β whose three-dimensional outcomes are independent. Entity α has situational trust in restaurant β based on nine experiences ($N=9$) as follows

Table 1

Distribution $T(o)$	Quality of food $T1(o)$	Service $T2(o)$	Environment $T3(o)$
excellent	6/9	2/9	4/9
good	2/9	4/9	3/9
bad	1/9	2/9	1/9
very bad	0	1/9	1/9

After entity α obtains one outcome such as $o=$ *("Quality of food"= "excellent", "service"="good", "environment"="bad")*, entity α updates situational trust according to the incremental trust update formula and obtains the following trust ($N=10$)

Table 2

Distribution $T(o)$	Quality of food $T1(o)$	Service $T2(o)$	Environment $T3(o)$
excellent	7/10	2/10	4/10
good	2/10	5/10	3/10
bad	1/10	2/10	2/10
very bad	0	1/10	1/10

3.2.2 Estimating the error of the trust value

Generally the trusting entity estimates the true trust value with some uncertainty, both because of inherent product or service variability and because of imperfect information. Thus, it is necessary to have a method of determining the standard error of experimental outcomes. The main objective is to obtain both a desirable accuracy and a desirable confidence level with minimum cost – number of experiences.

For an outcome with a score of 0 or 1 for no or yes (Bernoulli Distribution), the standard error (SE) of the estimated proportion p, based on random sample observations, is given by: $SE = [p(1-p)/N]^{1/2}$ where p is the proportion obtaining a score of 1, and N is the sample size [16]. This SE is the standard deviation of the range of possible estimate values. The SE is at its maximum when $p = 0.5$, therefore the worst case scenario occurs when 50% are yes, and 50% are no. Under this extreme condition, the sample size, N, can then be expressed as the largest integer less than or equal to $0.25/SE^2$. To have some notion of the sample size, note that for *SE* to be 0.04 (i.e. 4%), a sample size of 156 will be needed; 5%, 100; 10%, 25.

3.2.3 Considering trusted entities with evolving performance

If it can be assumed that the performance of the trusted entity is not constant, but evolving over time, then the basic assumption about a given outcome distribution for the actions of the entity, valid over all times, is not true any more. In this case, we must take into account that the outcome distribution of the trusted entity evolves over time. If the trusting entity knows the speed of this evolution, possibly defined by a given characteristic time delay, then the trusting entity may include in the trust calculation only recent experiments not older than the characteristic time delay.

It is also possible to give different weights to the different experiments, either according to their age or their order. The following incremental trust update formula based on the order of the experiments may be used:

$T_\alpha (\beta) (o) = (T_\alpha (\beta) (o) + \gamma) / (1 + \gamma)$

$T_\alpha (\beta) (o') = T_\alpha (\beta) (o') / (1 + \gamma)$ for o' different from o

where the value of γ determines the weight of the last experience compared with the previous trust estimation.

3.2.4 Initial trust values

In two cases, entity α needs to set his/her initial trust values in entity β. (i) When entities α and β have no previous relationship (in any situation) and entity α has no knowledge about entity β, then entity α needs to initialize his/her general trust and situational trust in entity β. (ii) When entities α and β have no previous relationship in a new situation but entity α has general trust in entity β, then entity α needs to initialize his/her new situational trust in entity β. To address these problems, a mapping between different spaces is needed. Mapping to initial trust for a particular entity or situation depends on the space of possible outcomes of that situation.

3.2.5 Mapping between spaces

In many cases, entity α needs to map between different spaces. (i) In the case of setting initial trust values, entity α needs to map his/her basic trust space to his/her general trust space, as well as his/her general trust space to his/her situational trust space. (ii) In the case of general trust update, entity α needs to map his/her situational trust space to his/her general trust space. (iii) There may also be cases in which entity α will update his/her basic trust as a result of a large number of general or situational trust experiences. We focus in the following two mappings:

1. Generalization mapping: from situational trust space to general trust space for the purpose of general trust update. We write $G(o)$ for the outcome of general trust when the situational trust outcome is o. Using $G(o)$ one can update his/her general trust $T_\alpha(\beta)(G(o))$. Note that this kind of generalization mapping causes information loss since the general trust would be more "general" (abstract) in nature and the mapping is usually a many-to-one mapping, which implies that the number of discrete outcomes of general trust space must be no more than that of the situational trust space.

2. Specialization mapping: from basic trust space to general trust space and from general trust space to situational trust space for the purpose of setting initial trust values. We write $S(o)$ for the outcome of situational trust when the general trust outcome is o. We also write $S(o)$ for the outcome of general trust when the basic trust outcome is o. Using $S(o)$ one can set initial situational trust $T_\alpha(\beta,\delta)(S(o))$ and initial general trust $T_\alpha(\beta)(S(o))$. Note that the specialization mapping is the reverse process of the generalization mapping. It usually is a one-to-many mapping. An example of a mapping from the general trust to the situational trust is illustrated in the following figure.

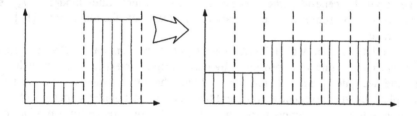

Figure 2

In this example, the entity α will map his/her general trust to situational trust by defining the mapping $S(o)$:

– outcome "Good" in general trust maps to outcomes "average" or higher in situational trust

– outcome "Bad" in general trust maps to outcomes "Bad" or lower in situational trust

Note that the areas must be the same; that is, $T_\alpha(\beta)(o) = T_\alpha(\beta,\delta)(S(o))$. Thus

$T_a(\beta)("Good")$ $=$ $T_a(\beta,\delta)("Excellent")+$ $T_a(\beta,\delta)("Very$ $Good")+$
$T_a(\beta,\delta)("Good") + T_a(\beta,\delta)("Average") = 80\%,$ and
$T_a(\beta)("Bad")$ $= T_a(\beta,\delta)("Bad")+ T_a(\beta,\delta)("Very Bad") = 20\%.$

This histogram is then the initial set of values for situational trust outcomes (i.e., $N = N_{init}$) that will be updated over time as entity α has further interactions with service β.

4.   DECISION MAKING

Decision making is often a question of selecting the optimal choice among a number of alternatives. It is therefore important to understand how different alternatives are evaluated in order to determine which is optimal. This means that for each alternative, a utility must be defined so that the alternative with the highest utility can be chosen. These kinds of approaches have been used in different areas.

In this section, we apply our trust model to several utility models to show how our trust model can be used for rational decision making. For most economic scenarios, the highest expected current utility model [13] is appropriate. For some critical scenarios, the lowest expected failure rate model [17] is appropriate. For some service scenarios, the total satisfaction model [14] is appropriate.

Expected Utility Theory (EUT) [12] states that the decision maker (DM) chooses between risky or uncertain prospects by comparing their expected utility values, i.e., the weighted sums obtained by adding the utility values of outcomes multiplied by their respective probabilities. The most popular expected utility function is the linear compensatory model in which preference for a product or service is represented by $x_j = \sum_{k=1}^{K} w_k y_{jk}$ where x_j is the preference for a product or service j, y_{jk} is the amount of attribute k in product or service j, and w_k is the importance weight assigned to attribute k [13]. In quality of service negotiation [14], a user satisfaction function plays a similar role.

Based on our trust model, we propose the following: if entity α wants to use his/her trust for decision making, the entity should first establish the utility of the action of a trusted entity β for each possible outcome. We write $U_a(o)$ for the utility when the outcome is o. Then it is clear that the expected utility obtained from the execution of an action by entity β for which the trust is $T_a(\beta,\delta)$ can be calculated by the formula

$$U_a(\beta) = \sum_{o \in O} T_\alpha(\beta, \delta)(o) \times U_\alpha(o)$$

In the case of multi-dimensional outcome spaces, the different dimensions may have their own utility mapping functions, and the overall utility may be the sum of the single-dimension utilities, adjusted with weight factors for the different dimensions. We then get an analogous formula to the one given in [13]. If all dimensional outcomes are independent, then the above expected utility formula

can be generalized to $U_\alpha(\beta) = \sum_{k=1}^{K} U_\alpha^{(k)}(\beta) \times w_\alpha^{(k)}$ where $U_\alpha^{(k)}(\beta)$ is the

expected *k-th* dimensional utility, $w_\alpha^{(k)}$ is the subjective weight of *k-th* dimension (we assume that the sum of all weights is equal to 1).

We note that the latter formula corresponds to the formula for the expected utility quoted from [13] above. $U_\alpha^{(k)}(\beta)$ in our formula corresponds to the value y_{jk} in the formula above.

We give three examples of making decisions and choosing the utility mapping function $U_\alpha(o)$.

1. Consider the example of restaurant service β. Entity α assumes that all three evaluation criteria are independent. Let us assume that entity α adopts the following mapping functions and dimensional weights with the following values: $W^{(1)} = 0.6$; $W^{(2)} = 0.3$; $W^{(3)} = 0.1$.

Table 3

Utility Mapping $U(o)$	Quality of food $U^{(1)}(o)$	Service $U^{(2)}(o)$	Environment $U^{(3)}(o)$
excellent	5.6	3	2
good	2.7	1	1
bad	0	-0.5	0
very bad	-4	-2	-1

The weighted "quality of food" dimension utility can be calculated using the trust values from the table in Section 3.2.1 as follows

$U1$ = sum over all o in dimension "quality of food" of ($U^{(1)}(o)$ * $T1(o)$ * $W^{(1)}$) = (5.6 * (7/10) + 2.7 * (2/10) + 0.0 * (1/10) + (-4) * 0) * 0.6 = 2.676

Similarly, the weighted "service" dimension utility $U2$ has the value 0.24, and the weighted "environment" dimension utility $U3$ has the value 0.1. Therefore the utility for entity α of this restaurant service β is $U_\alpha(\beta) = U1 + U2 + U3 = 2.676 + 0.24 + 0.1 = 3.016$

Following the same process, entity α can calculate the utility of other restaurant services. Entity α would choose the restaurant service with the highest utility value.

2. Consider the example of multimedia presentations. Based on the multi-dimensional outcome space discussed at the end of Section 3.1.1, we could use the above formula to calculate the overall utility. However, Richards et al. [14] propose another formula. They call satisfaction s_k what we call utility $U^{(k)}$, and they assume that the values of satisfaction range between zero (unacceptable quality) and one (ideal quality). Instead of the weighted summation formula above, they propose to calculate the overall satisfaction by $S_{total} = K / \sum_{k=1}^{K} \frac{1}{s_k}$. The reason for proposing this formula is the following argument: If the satisfaction for one dimension is zero, then the total satisfaction should be zero (which is not satisfied by our formula). Both formulae satisfy the following property: If the satisfaction for all dimensions has the same value, then the overall satisfaction has that same value. Richards' formula can be extended to include weights.

3. Consider the previous example of restaurant service β. Entity α, this time, uses a failure probability model similar to failure rate as proposed in [17] for decision making. Entity α first maps the outcome space to a consideration space which consists of 2 outcomes, namely "success" and "failure"; for instance, we may assume that we have "failure" when the value of $U_\alpha(o)$ is less than zero. The service failure probability is the proportion of outcome "failure" and can be represented by $P_f = \sum_{U_\alpha(o)="failure"} T_\alpha(\beta,\delta)(o)$. The service with the lowest failure probability can be chosen. Note that one can consider this model as a special case of expected utility model in which the utility mapping has only two values, "success" and "failure".

5.   ISSUES RELATED TO RECOMMENDATIONS

Entity α can build up his/her situational and general trust from past experiences, as has been discussed in the previous sections. Due to the limitation of resources, entity α may need to rely on recommendations from other entities in order to obtain trust with sufficient confidence. Entity α could get many independent recommendations from different entities. Some of these recommendations will probably conflict with each other. To address the conflict, a recommendation evaluation and combination algorithm is necessary. A recommendation need not necessarily represent the real belief of the recommending entity. In fact, recommenders may lie or give out contradictory recommendations to different entities.

Following Yu and Singh [11], we define *local trust* and *global trust (reputation).* An entity's *local trust* with respect to another entity is from his/her direct experiences. The *local trust* consists of situational trust which can be propagated to others upon request. An entity's *global trust (reputation)* with respect to another entity combines the *local trust* (if any) with recommendations received from other entities.

How to find recommenders is another issue. Yu and Singh [11] proposed an algorithm to find acyclic paths between a querying entity and recommenders. The number of possible paths is related to the connections between entities. If the entities are densely connected, the number of paths is quite large. If the entities are sparsely connected, the number of paths could be quite small or even zero.

6.   CONCLUSIONS AND FUTURE WORK

We have addressed the problem of building a general trust model for online entities based on their direct experiences and the recommendations of other entities. Considering trust a complex and multi-faceted thing, we use the estimated distribution in a multidimensional outcome space to represent trust. The statistical characterizations of trust (incremental trust update, estimated error, outcome space mapping) are discussed. Our trust model can be used by different decision models (utility, failure probability, satisfaction) for rational decision making in different scenarios.

For future research, we plan to investigate how the recommendations from different entities can be combined, how malicious recommendations can be detected, and how recommenders can be found. We intend to test the behavior of our trust model using simulations.

7.   REFERENCES

[1] Stephen Paul Marsh. *Formalising Trust as a Computational Concept.* Ph.D. Thesis, University of Stirling, April 1994

[2] Catholijn M. Jonker, Jan Treur. *Formal Analysis of Models for the Dynamics of Trust based on Experiences.* 2nd Workshop on Deception, Fraud and Trust In Agent Societies, pp. 221 – 231, 1999

[3] Greg Elofson. *Developing Trust with Intelligent Agents: An Exploratory Study.* In Proceedings of the 1st International Workshop on Trust, pp. 125 – 139, 1998

[4] Miquel Montaner, Beatriz López, Josep Lluís de la Rosa. *Opinion-Based Filtering Through Trust.* In proceedings of the 6th International Workshop on Cooperative Information Agents VI, pp. 164 – 178, 2002

[5] Alfarez Abdul-Rahman, Stephen Hailes. *Supporting Trust in Virtual Communities.* In Proceedings of the 33rd Hawaii International Conferences on System Sciences - Volume 6, 2000

[6] Bin Yu, Munindar P. Singh. *An Evidential Model of Distributed Reputation Management*. In Proceedings of the first international joint conference on Autonomous agents and multiagent systems, pp. 294 – 301, July 2002

[7] Thomas Tran, Robin Cohen. *Learning Algorithms for Software Agents in Uncertain and Untrusted Market Environments*. In Proceedings of the Eighteenth International Joint Conference on Artificial Intelligence (IJCAI-03), pp. 1475 – 1476, August 2003

[8] Mao Chen, Jaswinder Pal Singh. *Computing and Using Reputations for Internet Ratings*. EC'01, pp. 154 – 162, October 2001

[9] Y.H. Tan and W. Thoen. *Towards a Generic Model of Trust for Electronic Commerce*. In Proceedings of the 12th International Bled Electronic Commerce Conference, Vol. 1, pp. 346 – 359, Bled Slovenia, 1999

[10] Chrysanthos Dellarocas. *Immunzizing Online Reputation Reporting Systems Against Unfair Ratings and Discriminatory Behavior*. EC'00, pp. 150 – 157, October 2000

[11] Bin Yu, Munindar P. Singh. *Detecting Deception in Reputation management*. AAMAS'03, pp. 73 – 80, July 2003

[12] Philippe Mongin. *Expected Utility Theory*.
http://expected-utility-theory.behaviouralfinance.net/Mong.pdf

[13] John H. Roberts, Glen L. Urban. *New Consumer Durable Brand Choice: Modeling Multiattribute Utility, Risk, and Dynamics*. Management Science Volume 34, Issue 2, 1988

[14] Antony Richards, Glynn Rogers, Mark Antoniades, Varuni Vitana. *Mapping User Level QoS from a Single Parameter*. In proceedings of the 2nd IFIP/IEEE International Conference on Management of Multimedia Networks and Services'98, Nov. 1998

[15] Abdelhakim Hafid, Gregor v. Bochmann. *An Approach to Quality of Service Management in Distributed Multimedia Application: Design and an Implementation*. Multimedia Tools Appl. 9(2), 1999, pp. 167-191

[16] Hossein Arsham. *Statistical Thinking for Managerial Decision Making*.
http://home.ubalt.edu/ntsbarsh/Business-stat/opre504.htm#rssss

[17]   NIST/SEMATECH.   *Engineering   Statistics   Handbook*
http://www.itl.nist.gov/div898/handbook/apr/section1/apr181.htm

MODELLING DYNAMIC OPACITY USING PETRI NETS WITH SILENT ACTIONS

Jeremy W. Bryans, Maciej Koutny and Peter Y.A. Ryan
School of Computing Science, University of Newcastle,
Newcastle upon Tyne, NE1 7RU, U.K.

Abstract

In a previous work, [1], we presented a Petri Net based framework in which various confidentiality properties may be expressed in terms of predicates over system state and abstraction mappings from the reachable states and transitions of the underlying Petri Net. Here we extend that work by generalising these mappings by allowing them to be state dependent. This provides a natural framework in which to model various situations of importance in security, for example key compromise and refresh, downgrading of secrecy labels and conditional anonymity. We also show how global changes in the abstraction mappings can be used to model how some secrecy requirements depend on the status of the observer. We illustrate this by modelling the various flavours of anonymity that arise in the dining cryptographers example.

A further development on the earlier work is to provide a more complete treatment of silent actions. We also discuss the expressiveness of the resulting framework and the decidability of the associated verification problems. [1]

Keywords: opacity, non-deducibility, anonymity, Petri nets, observable behaviour, silent actions.

1. Introduction

The notion of opacity with respect to a given system predicate, see for example [10], formalises the idea that an observer of a system may never be able to establish the truth of that predicate. As such it appears to be very general and flexible and to allow a wide class of well-established notions of secrecy to be captured.

In a previous paper, [1], we presented a Petri Net based framework in which various opacity properties may be expressed in terms of predicates over system state and abstraction mappings from the reachable states and transitions of an underlying Petri Net. in this paper we extend this earlier work in a number of respects:

- Rather than just considering a static abstraction mapping we allow the transition labels to depend on the markings, i.e., the system state.

- We give a more satisfactory treatment of silent actions.

- We introduce a further Petri Net based notion of opacity, namely *total opacity*.

- We give a more extensive discussion of the notion of anonymity in this framework. In particular we illustrate, using the full dining cryptographers example, how flavours of anonymity may change with the observer viewpoint, i.e., with the abstraction mapping.

- The decidability results of [1] are extended to this richer model.

Our earlier framework allowed us, via the notion of opacity, to capture a number of situations of importance in security but that sit awkwardly with the more familiar information flow concepts such as non-interference [3]. These include, for example, anonymity and encrypted channels in which there is inevitably some partial information flow. The extended framework presented here allows us to go further and capture situations in which the information flow may vary with the state of the system. Note that we can include the state of an adversary in our system model. Thus we can now model key compromise or refresh as well as classification downgrades.

The new form of opacity, *total opacity*, that we introduce here further allows us to capture the notion of *non-inference*.

Using the framework of Petri nets gives us access to a raft of existing results and tools that have been developed in the Petri net community.

2.   Petri nets

In this section, we introduce Petri nets with weighted arcs [12], and give their operational semantics in terms of step sequences[2].

A (weighted) *net* is a triple $N = (P, T, W)$ such that P and T are disjoint finite sets, and $W : (T \times P) \cup (P \times T) \to \mathbb{N}$. The elements of P and T are respectively the *places* and *transitions*, and W is the *weight function* of N. In diagrams, places are drawn as circles, and transitions as rectangles. If $W(x, y) \geq 1$ for some $(x, y) \in (T \times P) \cup (P \times T)$, then (x, y) is an *arc* leading from x to y. As usual, arcs are annotated with their weight if this is 2 or more. We assume that, for every $t \in T$, there is a place p such that $W(p, t) \geq 1$.

The *pre-* and *post-multiset* of a transition $t \in T$ are multisets of places, $\text{PRE}_N(t)$ and $\text{POST}_N(t)$, respectively given by $\text{PRE}_N(t)(p) = W(p, t)$ and $\text{POST}_N(t)(p) = W(t, p)$, for all $p \in P$. Both notations extend to finite multisets of transitions U: $\text{PRE}_N(U) = \sum_{t \in U} U(t) \cdot \text{PRE}_N(t)$ and $\text{POST}_N(U) = \sum_{t \in U} U(t) \cdot \text{POST}_N(t)$.

A *marking* of a net N is a multiset of places. Following the standard terminology, given a marking M of N and a place $p \in P$, we say that p is marked if $M(p) \geq 1$ and that $M(p)$ is the number of tokens in p. In diagrams, M will be represented by drawing in each place p exactly $M(p)$ tokens (black dots).

Transitions represent actions which may occur at a given marking and then lead to a new marking. Here we define this dynamics in terms of multisets of (simultaneously occurring) transitions.

A *step* is a non-empty finite multiset of transitions, $U : T \to \mathbb{N}$. It is *enabled* at a marking M if $M \geq \text{PRE}_N(U)$. Thus, in order for U to be enabled at M, for each place p, the number of tokens in p under M should at least be equal to the total number of tokens that are needed as an input to U, respecting the weights of the input arcs.

If U is enabled at M, then it can be *executed* leading to the marking $M' = M - \text{PRE}_N(U) + \text{POST}_N(U)$. This means that the execution of U 'consumes' from each place p exactly $W(p, t)$ tokens for each occurrence of a transition $t \in U$ that has p as an input place, and 'produces' in each place p exactly $W(t, p)$ tokens for each occurrence of a transition $t \in U$ with p as an output place. If the execution of U leads from M to M' we write $M[U\rangle M'$.

An *execution* from a marking M to a marking M' is a sequence $\mu = M U_1 M_1 \ldots M_{n-1} U_n M'$ such that $M [U_1\rangle M_1 \cdots M_{n-1} [U_n\rangle M'$. We also say that M' is *reachable* from M.

3. Observing Petri net behaviour

In this section, we introduce a specific device aimed at modelling various observation capabilities based on the executed behaviours of a Petri net. Our framework is deliberately general to allow one to deal with a wider range of observation scenarios. We also extend the previous scheme, by allowing even greater discriminating power on the observer's side.

We start by making a small (but important from the point of view of applications) adjustment of the standard notion of a marked net, by assuming that the system specification we are given at the outset is a pair $\Sigma = (N, \mathcal{M}_0)$, where N is a net as defined in the previous section and $\mathcal{M}_0$ is a non-empty finite set of initial markings. This allows us to easily model situations where only partial information of the initial state of the system is available to an observer.

We will denote by $[\mathcal{M}_0\rangle$ the set of all markings reachable from any of the markings in $\mathcal{M}_0$, and by $RG(\Sigma)$ the reachability graph of Σ defined as the labelled directed graph whose nodes are the markings in $[\mathcal{M}_0\rangle$, and the labelled arcs represent all steps executed at these markings according to the rules from the previous section We will denote by $RG_{steps}(\Sigma)$ the set of all the steps labelling the arcs of $RG(\Sigma)$.

3.1   Visibility of reachable markings and executed steps

In our approach, we assume that there is a mapping *obs* which for each reachable marking in $[\mathcal{M}_0\rangle$ returns some label $obs(M)$ which is meant to capture the observable or visible aspects of system's global states. We further assume that the mapping is defined for steps of executed transitions; more precisely, for each reachable marking M and a step of transitions U enabled by M, $obs(M, U)$ issome label which is meant to capture the observable or visible aspects of executing step U at the global state M.

We do not place any restrictions on the nature of the *obs* mapping at this point; indeed, it is left under-specified deliberately to accommodate a wide range of observation scenarios. We only assume that markings and steps are visible through different sets of labels (i.e., $obs(M) \neq obs(M', U)$, for all $M, M' \in [\mathcal{M}_0\rangle$ and U enabled at M').

We employ a special label τ which is returned as the value of $obs(M, U)$ in cases when U is a step invisible to the observer in the system state M.

Notice that, unlike in [1], we do not define the mapping *obs* for steps, i.e., $obs(U)$ is not assumed to be given (clearly, if $obs(M, U)$ returns the same label ℓ for all markings M enabling U, then we can define $obs(U) = \ell$ and we have exactly the setup from [1]). The motivation for this is that we envisage application when the observability of executed transitions would depend on the current state of the system (for example, after breaking one of the cryptographic keys used by a system under attack, the adversary would typically be able to deduce more from the observed message exchange).

Suitable choices of *obs* mapping can be used to encode the various levels of visibility of system behaviour that we attribute to the environment or adversary. Thus transitions visible only to a secret user might be mapped to a τ label. Such events would be completely invisible to the environment, i.e., the environment would not be aware that any transition had occurred (and, if all the transitions in an executed step are invisible, then the whole step is mapped to τ). Transitions corresponding to the transmission of encrypted values could be mapped to a single label. Transitions deemed visible to the adversary may be left unchanged by the *obs* mapping.

Note that, in particular, *obs* allows us to 'detect' properties like deadlock-freeness or acceptance sets. The theory is rich enough to incorporate and reason about them. It is another matter, of course, how deadlocks would be detected or observed in the real life system, but these issues are beyond the scope of the current paper.

Having defined the observable aspects of individual markings and steps of transitions, we can define the effect of the observation mapping on the executions of the marked net Σ.

Let $\mu = M_0 U_1 M_1 \ldots M_{n-1} U_n M_n$ be an execution from a marking $M_0 \in \mathcal{M}_0$. We first introduce two auxiliary notations:

- $obs'(\mu) = \ell_0 \ell_1' \ell_1 \ldots \ell_n' \ell_n$ is the sequence obtained from μ by replacing each M_i by $\ell_i = obs(M_i)$ and each U_i by $\ell_i' = obs(M_{i-1}, U_i)$.

- $obs''(\mu)$ is obtained from $obs'(\mu)$ by replacing each maximal subsequence $\ell_i \ell_{i+1}' \ell_{i+1} \ldots \ell_j' \ell_j$ such that $i \leq j$ and $\ell_i = \cdots = \ell_j$ and $\ell_{i+1}' = \cdots = \ell_j' = \tau$, by ℓ_i^S, where $S = \{M_i, M_{i+1}, \ldots, M_j\}$.

obs'' collapses sequences of the same (observable) states interspersed with τ's into a single state, since this is what will be observable to the user.

Suppose now that $obs''(\mu) = \hat{\ell}_1^{S_1} \hat{\ell}_1' \hat{\ell}_2^{S_2} \ldots \hat{\ell}_m^{S_m}$. Then the *observation* of μ is given by $obs(\mu) = \hat{\ell}_1 \hat{\ell}_1' \hat{\ell}_2 \ldots \hat{\ell}_m$. Moreover, for each $i \leq m$, $obs^i(\mu) = S_i$ and $obs^{init}(\mu) = S_1$, $obs^{fin}(\mu) = S_m$, $obs^{all}(\mu) = S_1 \cup \ldots \cup S_m$.

For example, if $\mu = M_0 U_1 M_1 U_2 M_2 U_3 M_3$ is such that $obs'(\mu) = z\tau z b w \tau y$ then $obs(\mu) = z b w \tau y$, $obs^{init}(\mu) = \{M_0, M_1\}$, $obs^{fin}(\mu) = \{M_3\}$ and $obs^{all}(\mu) = \{M_0, M_1, M_2, M_3\}$.

Note that one could have deleted from $obs(\mu)$ all the remaining τ's without changing any of the subsequent results, but this would have led to a more complicated definitions and constructions in proofs.

Examples.   The two basic forms of defining the *obs* mapping are *transition labelling* and *marking projection*. In the first case, we assume that each transition t has its own (not necessarily unique) label $\ell(t)$ and then the visibility of a step $U = \{t_1, \ldots, t_k\}$ is defined as the multiset

$$\ell(U) = \begin{cases} \tau & \text{if } \ell(t_1) = \cdots = \ell(t_k) = \tau \\ \{\ell(t_i) \mid \ell(t_i) \neq \tau\} & \text{otherwise}. \end{cases}$$

In the case of marking projection, we assume that $Vis \subseteq P$ is a set of places on which we can always see the tokens, and all places in $P \setminus Vis$ are hidden from us (in the extreme case, $Vis = \emptyset$ which effectively means that no information about the tokens is available). Then, for every marking M, we define $M|_{Vis}$ as a multiset over Vis such that $M|_{Vis}(p) = M(p)$ for every place $p \in Vis$.

Dynamic observation functions can be encoded using these projections. We simply include information that the observer has as part of the net. For example, in Figure 1, the net on the left represents the transmitting of messages encrypted using a key k. The net on the right represents the observers state of knowledge of the encryption key. Before the inverse key (k^{-1}) is known is represented by state S_2 and after the inverse key is known by state S_3. The key may be refreshed (modelled by the *ref* transition); this moves the observer back to the initial state. We include the possibilty that the *ref* transition may also occur before the key is compromised.

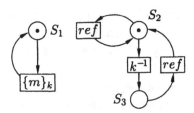

Figure 1.   An encoding of a dynamic observation mapping.

The (relevant part of the) *obs* mapping can then be defined as
$$obs(M) = M \,, \quad obs(\{S_1, S_2\}, \{m\}_k) = \{m\}_k \,, \quad obs(\{S_1, S_3\}, \{m\}_k) = m$$
and so when the observer has the inverse key he can read any messages which pass on this channel.

Of course, once the observer has the inverse key he can go back to any previously read messages which he has saved, and decode them offline. It is possible that the observation function could also take this *post-hoc* analytic ability into consideration, but we do not pursue that idea further in this paper.

The same construction also seems suitable to model the notion of a *downgrader*: Once the appropriate downgrade action takes place an uncleared user may observe the messages or read the files which have been downgraded.

Figure 2 is an example of using the τ transitions to model information flow. Consider two system users, *high* and *low*. *high* is able to execute either of two large processes, initiating them with the action exe_1 or exe_2 as appropriate. *low* is using the same system, but is a lower-priority user. His *work* request will be disallowed if *high* is executing one or other of his processes.

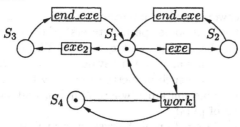

Figure 2. An encoding of an information flow.

We can consider the exe_1 and exe_2 transitions as silent or τ transitions with respect to the low user. If the *high* user is in state S_2 or S_3 then when *low* attempts to *work* he will be unable to perform the transition. This will allow him to deduce that either S_2 or S_3 is occupied, but not which one.

The (relevant part of) the *obs* mapping would then be defined as

$$
\begin{aligned}
obs(M) &= M|_{S_4} \\
obs(\{S_1, S_4\}, \{work\}) &= work \\
obs(\{S_2, S_4\}, \{exe\}) &= \tau \\
obs(\{S_3, S_4\}, \{exe\}) &= \tau \\
obs(\{S_2, S_4\}, \{end\_exe\}) &= \tau \\
obs(\{S_3, S_4\}, \{end\_exe\}) &= \tau
\end{aligned}
$$

Although *low* cannot see the state of *high* directly, some information can be deduced by the willingness of the system to respond to his own *work* requests. Either *high* is in state S_1 and the work request will be granted, or *high* is in one of states S_2 and S_3, and the *work* request will not be granted.

In fact, this approach appears somewhat linked to the CSP refusals semantic model [9]. In that, the semantics of the system is taken to be the observed traces of events, together with the sets of events that may be *refused* to an observer. Here, the semantics of the systems (as observed by *low*) is taken as a trace of states and transitions (events) but some refusal information is captured by our treatment of silent actions.

Exploring and formalising such links to other semantic models is not pursued here, but will be considered in a forthcoming paper.

3.2   Opacity

In the present framework, we are interested in whether an observer can establish a property $\mathcal{P}$ at some specific state(s) of the execution of the system solely on the basis of its visible version. We consider here any state property, i.e., one which can be evaluated at any reachable marking in $[\mathcal{M}_0\rangle$. Clearly, any such property can simply be represented as the set of those reachable markings where it holds, and so we will take $\mathcal{P}$ to be any subset of $[\mathcal{M}_0\rangle$.

Now, given an observed execution of the system, we will be interested in finding out whether the fact that an underlying marking belongs to $\mathcal{P}$ can be deduced by the observer. Note, however, that we are not interested in establishing whether the underlying marking does not belong to $\mathcal{P}$. To do this, we would rather consider the property $\overline{\mathcal{P}} = [\mathcal{M}_0\rangle \setminus \mathcal{P}$.

What it means to deduce a property can mean different things depending on what is relevant or important from the point of view of real application. Below, we formalise four possible ways of defining variants of opacity. The first two properties can be used to capture the fact that we are only interested in the holding of our property in the observed initial or final state, respectively.

- $\mathcal{P}$ is *initial-opaque* if for every execution μ from any marking in $\mathcal{M}_0$, if $obs^{init}(\mu) \cap \mathcal{P} \neq \varnothing$, then there exists an execution μ' from a marking in $\mathcal{M}_0$ such that $obs(\mu) = obs(\mu')$ and $obs^{init}(\mu') \cap \mathcal{P} = \varnothing$.

- $\mathcal{P}$ is *final-opaque* if for every execution μ from any marking in $\mathcal{M}_0$, if $obs^{fin}(\mu) \cap \mathcal{P} \neq \varnothing$, then there exists an execution μ' from a marking in $\mathcal{M}_0$ such that $obs(\mu) = obs(\mu')$ and $obs^{fin}(\mu') \cap \mathcal{P} = \varnothing$.

The next property reflects a view that we are interested in the holding of our property at all the specific observed states of the execution.

- $\mathcal{P}$ is *always-opaque* if for every execution μ from any marking in $\mathcal{M}_0$, if $obs^i(\mu) \cap \mathcal{P} \neq \varnothing$ for some i, then there exists an execution μ' from a marking in $\mathcal{M}_0$ such that $obs(\mu) = obs(\mu')$ and $obs^i(\mu') \cap \mathcal{P} = \varnothing$.

The last property capture the situation that the holding of our property can never be established for sure.

- $\mathcal{P}$ is *total-opaque* if for every execution μ from any marking in $\mathcal{M}_0$ such that $obs^{all}(\mu) \cap \mathcal{P} \neq \varnothing$ there exists an execution μ' from a marking in $\mathcal{M}_0$ such that $obs(\mu) = obs(\mu')$ and $obs^{all}(\mu') \cap \mathcal{P} = \varnothing$.

initial-opacity is illustrated by the dining cryptographers example. It would appear that *initial-opacity* is suited to modelling situations in which initialisation information such as crypto keys, etc., needs to be kept secret. More generally, situations in which confidential information can be modelled in terms of initially resolved non-determinism can be captured in this way. *always-opacity* would seem more appropriate to capture situation in which secret information is input at run time, for example due to high level interactions.

The distinction between *total-opacity* and *always-opacity* can be illustrated in the two diagrams below.

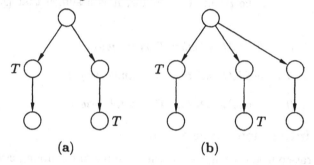

(a)   (b)

Figure 3.   The difference between total-opacity and final-opacity.

Assume that each of the paths through the nets in figure 3 gives rise to the same observation. In figure 3(a), a property which holds at each of the states marked T will be *always-opaque*, because at each of the states where it holds there is a corresponding execution for which the property does not hold *in the corresponding state*. But it is not *total-opaque*, because by the end of whichever execution we observe, we can say that the property has held at some point. For *total-opacity* we would require the extra execution of figure 3(b). Now, at the end of the execution we do not know if the property was ever true.

Informally, the notion of *non-inference*, [11], captures the idea that an observer should never be able to eliminate the possibility that the High user did nothing. More formally:

$$\forall t \in traces(S)\ \exists t' \in traces(S) \bullet$$
$$t \downarrow Low = t' \downarrow Low\ \wedge\ t' \downarrow High = \langle \rangle$$

We will be exploring the application of these formal properties in a future paper.

PROPOSITION 1 *If P is total-opaque then it is initial-opaque, final-opaque and always-opaque. Moreover, if P is always-opaque then it is initial-opaque and final-opaque. No other implication of this kind in general holds.*

THEOREM 2 *For $x \in \{initial, final, always, total\}$, it is the case that $P = \varnothing$ is x-opaque, $P = [M_0\rangle$ is not x-opaque, and if $P \subseteq P'$ and P' is x-opaque then P is x-opaque.*

What now follows are crucial results stating that three of the four notions of opacity are decidable provided that the system has finitely many states. In all the results that follow, it is assumed that $[M_0\rangle$ is finite.[3]

THEOREM 3 *It is decidable whether P is initial-opaque.*

THEOREM 4 *It is decidable whether P is final-opaque.*

THEOREM 5 *It is decidable whether P is total-opaque.*

4.   Dining cryptographers

To illustrate our approach, we use the example of the dining cryptographers, first presented in [4]. A simplified version (involving only two cryptographers) was presented in [1].

This example involves three diners and admits some further anonymity properties, e.g., a paying cryptographer can remain anonymous w.r.t. his or her companions.

The three cryptographers, Anne, Bob and Charlie, enjoy a meal in a restaurant. When they call for the bill, the waiter tells them that it has already been paid. Each cryptographer wishes to know whether the bill was paid by the NSA, or if it was one of them. However, if one of them paid, they do not want an eavesdropper, Yves, on the neighbouring table to know which of them paid. The protocol they choose to solve this problem is as follows:

They each toss a coin, and reveal the result only to the cryptographer sitting one their left. Yves, of course, cannot see any of the coins. If Anne paid, she lies about the parity of the two coins (she calls 'agree' if she sees a head and a tail, and 'disagree' otherwise). If Anne did not pay, she tells the truth about the parity of the coins. Similarly for Bob and Charlie. Now each cryptographer knows if the NSA paid for the meal, or if the bill was settled by one of them. If the number of "disagree" calls is even, then the NSA is paying. If the number is odd, then one of the cryptographers is paying. In this case, the other two cryptographers do not know which of their dining companions has paid for the meal. Yves cannot distinguish the paying cryptographer from the others.

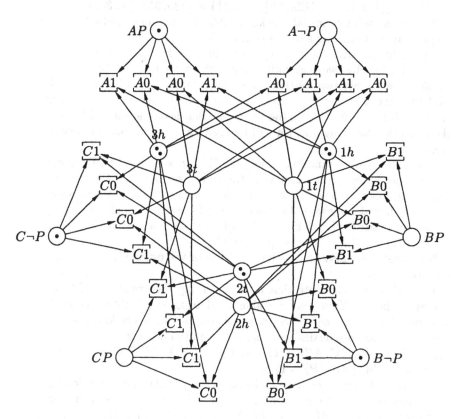

Figure 4.   Net for the 3-way dining cryptographers example with one of the n initial markings.

Figure 4 presents a possible encoding of the protocol. The two places at the top of the diagram represent Anne's initial state (having paid is represented by placing a single token in place AP, and having not paid is represented by placing a single token in place $A\neg P$). The two places at the right represent Bob's initial state (BP and $B\neg P$) and the two places on the left Charlie's initial state (CP and $C\neg P$). The possible initial markings for these places are $\{AP, B\neg P, C\neg P\}$, $\{A\neg P, BP, C\neg P\}$, $\{A\neg P, B\neg P, CP\}$, $\{A\neg P, B\neg P, C\neg P\}$. The three sets of two places in the centre of the diagram represent the three coins (heads is represented by placing tokens in place $c_i h$, and tails is represented by placing tokens in place $c_i t$, for $i = 1, 2, 3$). For each pair, the marked place must contain two tokens. This is because two cryptographers must see each coin. The possible initial markings for the coins are therefore

$$\{\{1h, 1h\}, \{1t, 1t\}\} \times \{\{2h, 2h\}, \{2t, 2t\}\} \times \{\{3h, 3h\}, \{3t, 3t\}\}$$

The set of possible initial markings, $\mathcal{M}_0$, is the cross product of the cryptographer markings and the coin markings.

The eight transitions at the top represent the eight possible scenarios for Anne, given by two possibilities for each coin multiplied by the two possibilities for her own initial state. Each transition is labelled with '$A0$' (if Anne says the coins 'disagree') or '$A1$' (if Anne says the coins 'agree'). Similarly for Bob on the right and Charlie on the left. This gives the transition labelling ℓ which will be used for defining the visibility of steps.

Yves' observation function is simple. He can see none of the places (he does not know the initial state of the cryptographers, nor the state of the coins), but he can see all of the labels of the executed transitions (he can hear all that they say). In other words, for every reachable marking M and executed step U, we have the following (see section 3.1):

$$obs_Y(M) = M|_\varnothing = \varnothing \ , \ obs_Y(U) = \ell(U).$$

Note that Yves also knows the structure of the original net, i.e., the protocol.

We wish to demonstrate that after observing the execution of transitions, although Yves may be able to determine whether the meal was paid for by one of the cryptographers, he can never know which one. The three properties we wish to be initial-opaque are therefore $\mathcal{P}_A = \{M \in \mathcal{M}_0 \mid M(AP) = 1\}$ and $\mathcal{P}_B = \{M \in \mathcal{M}_0 \mid M(BP) = 1\}$. $\mathcal{P}_C = \{M \in \mathcal{M}_0 \mid M(CP) = 1\}$.

Yves cannot determine the satisfaction of any of the above predicates. Note, however, that Yves can in either case determine the satisfaction of the property $\mathcal{P} = \{M \in \mathcal{M}_0 \mid M(AP) + M(BP) + M(CP) = 1\}$, i.e., he knows when one of the cryptographers paid the bill. In terms of our framework, both $\mathcal{P}_1$ and $\mathcal{P}_2$ are initial-opaque, but $\mathcal{P}$ is not.

These properties are similar to the ones which hold for the limited version of the case study, presented in [1]. The difference is that in the situation where one of the cryptographers paid for the meal, the other two do not know who it was. The paying cryptographer remains anonymous with respect to their dining companions. To see this, we model the point of view of one of the cryptographers, by change the *obs* function to model the increased level of knowledge. For example, the observation function of Anne is such that, for every reachable marking

M and executed step U,

$$obs_{Anne}(M) = M|_{\{AP,A\neg P,1h,1t,3h,3t\}}$$
$$obs_{Anne}(U) = \ell(U).$$

Anne knows her own initial state, and can see the state of her coin and the coin on her left. Given this observation function, she learns exactly what she wants to know — did the NSA pay, or was it one of her friends?

5. Conclusions and future work

We have presented an extension of our earlier Petri net framework in order be able to capture a richer class of information flow requirements. In this richer model we can encompass conditional information flow policies (e.g., downgraders) as well as scenarios that include key compromise and key refreshment.

In this paper we model the full dining cryptographers example which allows us to illustrate how various flavours of anonymity can be captured, corresponding to the various observer viewpoints.

A further advance presented here is a full treatment of invisible events.

The decidability results of the earlier paper have been extended to the richer model presented here and for the new *total opacity* property.

In future work we intend to explore the relationship of the approach presented here to process algebraic formulations of generalised non-interference [14] and anonymity [15].

A major challenge in such work is the choice of appropriate abstractions to encode the adversary's observational capabilities. This is particularly delicate where cryptographic mechanisms are involved. Adversary deductions and algebraic manipulations complicate the modelling. We intend to investigate using the dynamic *obs* mappings presented here to address such issues.

A further line of research is to explore analogues in this framework of the notion of *non-deducibility on strategies*, due to Johnson and Wittbold [17]. This seeks to capture the possibility of a secret user and an uncleared user colluding and using adaptive strategies to cause information flows in violation of the policy. This is likely to require more precise modelling of various flavours of non-determinism within the Petri net framework.

We will also investigate the problem of preservation of opacity properties under refinement and composition of Petri nets.

Acknowledgement

This research was supported by the EPSRC GOLD project and DSTL.

Notes

1. A fuller version of this paper, which includes the omitted proofs, can be found at [2].

2. We have already demonstrated in [1] that step and interleaving semantics lead to different notions of opacity (even without the τ labels we introduce later).

3. Note that the finiteness of $[\mathcal{M}_0)$ is decidable, and can be checked using the standard coverability tree construction [12].

References

[1] J.W.Bryans, M.Koutny and P.Y.A.Ryan: Modelling Opacity using Petri Nets. Proceedings of WISP 2004 (2004)

[2] J.W.Bryans, M.Koutny and P.Y.A.Ryan: Modelling Dynamic Opacity using Petri Nets with Silent Actions University of Newcastle Technical Report Series 2004

[3] N.Busi and R.Gorrieri: Structural Non-interference with Petri Nets. Proceedings of WITS 2004 (2004)

[4] D. Chaum: The dining cryptographers problem: unconditional sender and recipient untraceability. Journal of Cryptology, 1, 1988

[5] E.Cohen: Information Transmission in Computational Systems. Proceedings of 6th ACM Symposium on Operating System Principles (1997)

[6] R.J.Feiertag: A technique for Proving Specifications are Multi-level Secure Technical. Report CSL109, CSL, SRI International (1980)

[7] J.Goguen and J.Meseguer: Security Policies and Security Models. Proceedings of IEEE Symposium on Security and Privacy (1982)

[8] J.Goguen and J.Meseguer: Inference Control and Unwinding. Proceedings of IEEE Symposium on Research in Security and Privacy (1984)

[9] C. A. R. Hoare: Communicating Sequential Processes (1985)

[10] L. Mazare: Using Unification for Opacity Properties. Proceedings of WITS 2004 (2004)

[11] C. O'Halloran: A Calculus of Information Flow. Proceedings of ESORICS (1990)

[12] W.Reisig and G.Rozenberg (Eds.): Lectures on Petri Nets. LNCS 1491 & 1492 (1998)

[13] J.Rushby: Noninterference, Transitivity and Channel-Control Security Policies. SRI Techical Report (1992)

[14] P.Y.A.Ryan: Mathematical Models of Computer Security. Proceedings of Foundations of Security Analysis and Design, LNCS 2171 (2000)

[15] S.A.Schneider and A.Sidiropoulos: CSP and Anonymity. Proceedings of ESORICS (2000)

[16] D.Sutherland: A Model of Information, Proceedings of 9th National Computer Security Conference (1986)

[17] J.T.Wittbold and D.M.Johnson: Information Flow in Nondeterministic Systems. Proceedings of the Symposium on Research on Security and Privacy (1990)

REASONING ABOUT SECURE INTEROPERATION USING SOFT CONSTRAINTS

Stefano Bistarelli[1,2], Simon N. Foley[3], Barry O'Sullivan[3,4]

[1]*Istituto di Informatica e Telematica, CNR, Pisa, Italy*
stefano.bistarelli@iit.cnr.it

[2]*Dipartimento di Scienze, Universita degli Studi "G. D'Annunzio", Pescara, Italy*
bista@sci.unich.it

[3]*Department of Computer Science, University College Cork, Ireland*
{*s.foley,b.osullivan*}*@cs.ucc.ie*

[4]*Cork Constraint Computation Centre, University College Cork, Ireland*
b.osullivan@4c.ucc.ie

Abstract   The security of a network configuration is based not just on the security of its individual components and their direct interconnections, but also on the potential for systems to interoperate indirectly across network routes. Such interoperation has been shown to provide the potential for circuitous paths across a network that violate security. In this paper we propose a constraint-based framework for representing access control configurations of systems. The *secure reconfiguration* of a system is depicted as a constraint satisfaction problem.

Keywords: Secure interoperation, constraint satisfaction.

1.   Introduction

In its most general case, determining the security of a system is undecidable [Harrison et al., 1976] (the safety problem). This has led to the design of a wide range of decidable security mechanisms that are based on more restrictive forms of security, for example, [Amman and Sandhu, 1992, Bertino et al., 1998]. These mechanisms decide whether an access by a subject is authorized according to the rules set out in a security policy. A system is secure (upholds its security policy) if it is not possible for a subject to gain unauthorized access.

The composition of secure systems is not necessarily secure. A user may be able to gain unauthorized access to an object by taking a circuitous access route across individually secure but interoperating systems [Gong and Qian, 1996, Foley, 2000]. Determining security is based not just on the individual system authorization mechanisms but also on how the systems are configured to interoperate. For example, if Alice is permitted to have access to Bob's files on the Administration system, and Clare is permitted access Alice's files on the Sales system, then is it safe to support file sharing between these systems? The extent of system interoperation must be limited if the administration security policy states that Clare is not permitted access to Bob's (administration) files.

The computational challenges of secure interoperation for access control systems is considered in [Gong and Qian, 1994, Gong and Qian, 1996]. In their research Gong and Qian represent access control as an abstract graph of system entities (files, users, etc.) with arcs representing (binary) potential for access. System interoperation is defined as a form of graph composition, and determining whether an interoperation is secure can be performed in polynomial time. However, given systems whose interoperation is not secure, then *optimally* re-configuring the interoperation such that composition is secure is NP-complete. Finding an optimal re-configuration is desirable in order to minimize the extent of the additional access restrictions and maximize desired interoperation: reconfiguring access control to deny all access, while secure, is overly restrictive.

We are interested in the development of practical tools for modelling and analyzing complex system configurations. In this paper we describe how constraints [Bistarelli et al., 1997, Bistarelli, 2004, Wallace, 1996] provide a practical and natural approach to modelling and solving the secure interoperation problem. Constraint solving is an emerging software technology for declarative description and effective solving of large problems. The advantages of expressing secure interoperation as a constraint satisfaction problem is that there exists a wide body of existing research results on solving this problem for large systems of constraints in a fully mechanized manner. Section 2 provides a brief introduction to soft constraints.

In Section 3 we propose a constraint-based framework for representing access control configurations of systems. By building on a semiring of permissions, our framework is sufficiently general to be applied to models such as [Gong, 1999, Sandhu et al., 1996]. Section 4 defines what it means to securely reconfigure a system as a constraint satisfaction problem and Section 5 uses this definition to formulate the meaning of secure interoperation. The advantage of taking the constraint approach is that information about all possible interoperation vulnerabilities are effectively available during analysis. This provides the potential for managing tradeoffs between vulnerabilities using techniques such as [Bistarelli and O'Sullivan, 2003]. Conventional tests for interoperation [Gong and Qian, 1994, Gong and Qian, 1996] are designed to find just one vulnerability. Section 6 considers a special case of secure interoperation that is not unlike the approach described in [Gong and Qian, 1994, Gong and Qian, 1996]. In Section 7 a number of concluding remarks are made.

2. Soft Constraints

Constraints have been successfully used in the analysis of a wide variety of problems ranging from network management, for example [Fruehwirth and Brisset, 1997, Aziz et al., 2004], to complex scheduling such as [Bellone et al., 1992]. They have also been used to analyze security protocols [Bella and Bistarelli, 2001, Bella and Bistarelli, 2002, Bella and Bistarelli, 2004], to represent integrity policy [Bistarelli and Foley, 2003a, Bistarelli and Foley, 2003b], for secure systems interoperation [Bistarelli et al., 2004b, Bistarelli et al., 2004a] and in the development of practical security administration tools [Konstantinou et al., 1999]. In [Konstantinou et al., 1999] constraints are used to help the System Administrator to easily describe network configurations and relations among servers, firewalls and services for the final users. Constraints are used to represent, in a declarative manner, the relations among network objects. This permits the use of local propagation techniques to reconfigure the network when hardware/software changes occur (particularly in a wireless environment). Such automatic reconfiguration would not be possible if the network policy was encoded using conventional shell scripts.

The constraint programming process consists of the generation of requirements (constraints) and solution of these requirements, by specialized constraint solvers. When the requirements of a problem are expressed as a collection of boolean predicates over variables, we obtain what is called the *crisp* (or classical) Constraint Satisfaction Problem (CSP). In this case the problem is solved by finding any assignment of the variables that satisfies all the constraints.

Sometimes, when a deeper analysis of a problem is required, *soft* constraints are used instead [Bistarelli et al., 1997, Bistarelli et al., 2002, Bistarelli, 2004]. Soft constraints associate a qualitative or quantitative value either to the entire constraint or to each assignment of its variables. More precisely, they are based on a semiring structure $S \doteq \langle A, +, \times, 0, 1 \rangle$ and a set of variables V with domain D. In particular the semiring operation $\times$ is used to combine constraints together, and the $+$ operator for disjunction, projection and for comparing levels (a partial order $\leq_S$ is defined over A such that $a \leq_S b$ iff $a + b = b$).

Technically, a *constraint* is a function which, given an assignment $\eta : V \rightarrow D$ of the variables, returns a value of the semiring. So $C = \eta \rightarrow A$ is the set of all possible constraints that can be built starting from S, D and V (values in A are interpreted as levels of preference or importance or cost).

When using soft constraints it is necessary to specify, via suitable combination operators, how the level of preference of a global solution is obtained from the preferences in the constraints. The combined weight of a set of constraints is computed using the operator $\otimes : C \times C \rightarrow C$ defined as

$(c_1 \otimes c_2)\eta = c_1\eta \times_S c_2\eta$. Disjunction of constraints $\oplus : C \times C \to C$ is instead defined as follows: $(c_1 \oplus c_2)\eta = c_1\eta +_S c_2\eta$

By using the $\oplus_S$ operator we can easily extend the partial order $\leq_S$ over C by defining $c_1 \sqsubseteq_S c_2 \iff c_1 \oplus_S c_2 = c_2$. In the following, when the semiring will be clear from the context, we will use $\sqsubseteq$.

Moreover, given a constraint $c \in C$ and a variable $v \in V$, the *projection* of c over $V - \{v\}$, written $c \Downarrow_{(V-\{v\})}$ is the constraint c' s.t. $c'\eta = \sum_{d \in D} c\eta[v := d]$.

3. Access Configuration

Let ENT represent the domain of all possible entities (subjects, objects, principals) that are of interest across all systems in a network. Access relationships are defined in terms of the permission that one entity holds for another. The current access constraints in a system are represented as a soft-constraint $C(X, Y)$ over variables X, Y, where for $a, b \in ENT$ then $C(a, b) \in PERM$ is the access permission that entity a holds for entity b.

Permissions are represented using a semiring $S \doteq \langle PERM, +, \times, \bot, \top \rangle$ where $PERM$ represents the set of all possible permissions, $+$ (union) and $\times$ (intersection) are used to combine permissions. $\bot$ represents the no-access permission and $\top$ represents full-access permission. In general, an entity with permission $p \in PERM$ implicitly has permission $p' \leq p$, where $\leq$ is the partial order relation on the semiring S. Encoding permissions using a partial order is common, for example, [Bell and Padula, 1976] is based on a partial order of security classes, Java Security permissions are partially ordered [Gong, 1999] and [Bharadwaj and Baras, 2003] codifies Role and Permission lattices within a semiring.

DEFINITION 1 *Access Configuration.* An access configuration of a system is represented as a constraint on the access permissions between entities from ENT.   □

EXAMPLE 1 Given an arbitrary semiring $S \doteq \langle PERM, +, \times, \bot, \top \rangle$ of permissions, an access configuration that denies all access for all entities in $X, Y \in ENT$ is defined as:

$$C_\bot(X, Y) \doteq \bot$$

A system that places no access restrictions on entities is specified as the null constraint $C_\top$, where $C_\top(X, Y) \doteq \top$ for all X, Y.   △

EXAMPLE 2 Consider a simple system $S1$ with permissions no-access (**F**) and full-access (**T**) that are represented by the Boolean algebra:

$$S_{Bool} \doteq \langle \{\mathbf{F}, \mathbf{T}\}, \vee, \wedge, \mathbf{F}, \mathbf{T} \rangle.$$

$$C_{S1}$$

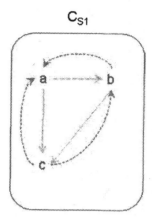

Figure 1.   An access flow permitted through transitivity (Example 2).

The system has entities: a, b and c with access constraints

$$\mathcal{C}_{S1}(\mathsf{c},\mathsf{b}) \; \hat{=} \; \mathbf{F}$$
$$\mathcal{C}_{S1}(\mathsf{b},\mathsf{a}) \; \hat{=} \; \mathbf{F}$$

In this constraint network we can evaluate $\mathcal{C}_{S1}(\mathsf{a},\mathsf{b}) = \mathcal{C}_{S1}(\mathsf{b},\mathsf{c}) = \mathbf{T}$ and, by transitivity, $\mathcal{C}_{S1}(\mathsf{a},\mathsf{c}) = \mathbf{T}$. This situation is depicted in Figure 1. Note that in this figure, and in all others in this paper, solid (light/green) lines represent permitted flows ($\mathbf{T}$ in this case), and dashed (dark/red) lines represent not permitted flow ($\mathbf{F}$ in this case).

In practice, access control need not always be transitive and many interesting and useful requirements can be described by, what are effectively, non-transitive access configurations [Lee, 1988, Foley, 1992, Foley, 1997, Foley, 2000]. To model non-transitive access flows, prohibitions on transitive access must be explicitly specified within the system of constraints. For example, adding the constraint $\mathcal{C}_{S1}(\mathsf{a},\mathsf{c}) \hat{=} \mathbf{F}$ implies that $\mathcal{C}_{S1}(\mathsf{a},\mathsf{c})$ is evaluated as $\mathbf{F}$ (the greatest lower bound on the weights of all paths that connect a to c). The class of all access configurations that are based on the boolean semiring of permissions is equivalent to the set of reflexive policies described in [Foley, 1992, Foley, 1997].   △

EXAMPLE 3 A system supports read and write access control, as defined by the semiring $S_{rw} \; \hat{=} \; \langle\{2^{\{r,w\}}, \cup, \cap, \{\}, \{r,w\}\rangle$. The system has constraints (see Figure 2):

$$\mathcal{C}_{S^1_{rw}}(\mathsf{a},\mathsf{b}) \hat{=} \{r,w\} \quad \mathcal{C}_{S^1_{rw}}(\mathsf{b},\mathsf{c}) \hat{=} \{r\} \quad \mathcal{C}_{S^1_{rw}}(\mathsf{a},\mathsf{c}) \hat{=} \{r\}$$
$$\mathcal{C}_{S^1_{rw}}(\mathsf{b},\mathsf{a}) \hat{=} \{\} \qquad \mathcal{C}_{S^1_{rw}}(\mathsf{c},\mathsf{b}) \hat{=} \{\} \qquad \mathcal{C}_{S^1_{rw}}(\mathsf{c},\mathsf{a}) \hat{=} \{\}$$

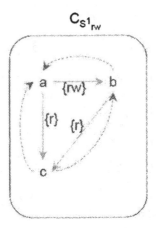

Figure 2.   The access flows in the system described in Example 3.

$\triangle$

4.   Access Reconfiguration

An existing access configuration may be safely re-configured by further re-stricting (decreasing permission levels) the existing access relationships. In-creasing (according to the semiring) permissions between existing system en-tities is not permitted as it may lead to an entity having access that was previ-ously denied.

DEFINITION 2 *Secure Reconfiguration.* We say that $C_{S'}$ is a suitable recon-figuration of access configuration C_S if $C_{S'} \sqsubseteq C_S$, where for any assignment η of variables to domain values from ENT, then $C_{S'}\eta \leq C_S\eta$.   □

It follows by definition that $\sqsubseteq$ is a partial order with most restrictive configu-ration $C_\perp$ and least restrictive configuration $C_\top$. We have for any configuration C_S that $C_\perp \sqsubseteq C_S \sqsubseteq C_\top$.

EXAMPLE 4 Configuration $C_{S_{rw}^1}$ can be securely reconfigured as $C_{S_{rw}^2}$ (see Figure 3), where

$$C_{S_{rw}^2}(a,b) \doteq \{r,w\} \quad C_{S_{rw}^2}(b,c) \doteq \{r\} \quad C_{S_{rw}^2}(a,c) \doteq \{\}$$
$$C_{S_{rw}^2}(b,a) \doteq \{\} \quad C_{S_{rw}^2}(c,b) \doteq \{\} \quad C_{S_{rw}^2}(c,a) \doteq \{\}$$

We have $C_\perp \sqsubseteq C_{S_{rw}^2} \sqsubseteq C_{S_{rw}^1} \sqsubseteq C_\top$. $\triangle$

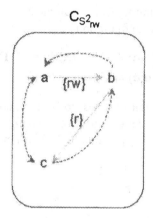

Figure 3. The secure reconfiguration of $C_{S_{r_w}^1}$ as $C_{S_{r_w}^2}$ (Example 4).

5. Access Interoperation

A network is composed of a number of different interoperating systems. For the purposes of this paper we assume that interoperation is represented by entities that are common to the individual systems. For example, a system with user a and a shared filesystem b, interoperates with any system that has the same user a or mounts the same file system b. While a system has control over its own system it has no jurisdiction over access control on other systems. Therefore, when a system interoperates with another, we need to ensure that the interoperation is such that it is not possible for the access rules of the original system to be bypassed by taking a circuitous route through the connected system.

When (securely) composing systems $S1$ and $S2$, the new 'combined' system $S3$ must represent a secure reconfiguration of $S1$ and $S2$, that is, $C_{S3} \sqsubseteq C_{S1}$ and $C_{S3} \sqsubseteq C_{S2}$. It is clear that $C_\perp$ is a secure re-configuration as it prohibits all access. However, $C_\perp$ is overly restrictive; we seek the least restrictive secure re-configuration of $S1$ and $S2$.

DEFINITION 3 *Secure Configuration Composition.* The (secure) configuration of interoperating systems $S1$ and $S2$ is configured as $C_{S1} \otimes C_{S2}$, where for any assignment η of variables to domain values from ENT, then $(c_1 \otimes c_2)\eta = c_1\eta \times_S c_2\eta$. This corresponds to conjunction of constraints. □

The set of all possible secure access configurations forms a lattice, with partial order $\sqsubseteq$, greatest lower bound operator $\otimes$ and unique lowest bound $C_\perp$. Therefore, the configuration specified by $C_{S1} \otimes C_{S2}$ provides the least restrictive secure re-configuration for the interoperation of systems $S1$ and $S2$.

EXAMPLE 5 Using the semiring from Example 2, a system $S3$ manages entities $\{a,c,d\}$ and has access configuration

$$\mathcal{C}_{S3}(a,c) \hateq \mathbf{F} \qquad \mathcal{C}_{S3}(a,d) \hateq \mathbf{F}$$
$$\mathcal{C}_{S3}(d,c) \hateq \mathbf{F} \qquad \mathcal{C}_{S3}(d,a) \hateq \mathbf{F}$$

Since the system does not control access to entity b, no access constraints can
be placed on this entity. The least restrictive re-configuration of the composed
system is depicted as $\mathcal{C}_{S1} \otimes \mathcal{C}_{S3}$ in Figure 4. This new configuration ensures

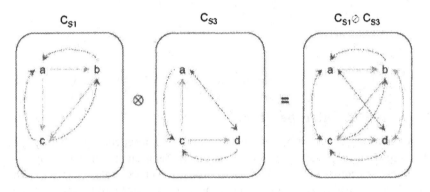

Figure 4.   Configurations $\mathcal{C}_{S1}, \mathcal{C}_{S3}$ and $\mathcal{C}_{S1} \otimes \mathcal{C}_{S3}$ (Example 5).

(under the $\sqsubseteq$ ordering) that the access restrictions of the original configurations
are preserved. For example, while $\mathcal{C}_{S1}(a,c) \hateq \mathbf{T}$ we have $\mathcal{C}_{S1} \otimes \mathcal{C}_{S3}(a,c) = \mathbf{F}$
since $\mathcal{C}_{S3}(a,c) \hateq \mathbf{F}$.

$\triangle$

Configuration intersection can be used to guide the re-configuration of the
original systems. A system $S1$ that is to be (securely) composed with a system
$S2$ should be re-configured using the access restrictions of $(\mathcal{C}_{S1} \otimes \mathcal{C}_{S2})$. Since
$\otimes$ gives the greatest lower bound on configurations according to the secure
reconfiguration ($\sqsubseteq$) relation, then $(\mathcal{C}_{S1} \otimes \mathcal{C}_{S2})$ gives the least restrictive secure
re-configuration of $\mathcal{C}_{S1}$ that also ensures the access restrictions of $\mathcal{C}_{S2}$.

DEFINITION 4 *Strict Secure Interoperation.* Systems $S1$ and $S2$ securely
interoperate in a strict manner if they enforce the access constraints of each
other, that is, if $\mathcal{C}_{S1}$ can be regarded as a secure re-configuration of $\mathcal{C}_{S2}$ and
vice-versa.

To ensure strict secure interoperation, system $S1$ should be (securely) re-
configured as $\mathcal{C}'_{S1} \hateq (\mathcal{C}_{S1} \otimes \mathcal{C}_{S2})$ and, similarly $\mathcal{C}'_{S2} \hateq (\mathcal{C}_{S1} \otimes \mathcal{C}_{S2})$. $\square$

The above definition of secure interoperation is overly restrictive as it requires each system to be able to enforce the access restrictions of the other. While the constraint $(\mathcal{C}_{S1} \otimes \mathcal{C}_{S2})$ represents the best secure (according to $\sqsubseteq$) re-configuration for the 'combined' system (defined in terms of entities from both systems), in practice, the system $S1$ can only enforce the restrictions on the entities that it manages, and similarly for $S2$. It may not be feasible to securely re-configure $S1$ with $\mathcal{C}_{S1} \otimes \mathcal{C}_{S2}$ if $S1$ has no jurisdiction over entities that are managed only by $S2$. We therefore consider a weaker notion of secure interoperation.

Let the *alphabet* $ENT_S \subseteq ENT$ of a system S define the set of entities over which the system S can exercise access control. If we do not require a system to be responsible for access control on entities that are not in its alpabet then for secure interoperation between $S1$ and $S2$ we need only ensure that $\mathcal{C}_{S1}$ enforces the access constraints of the combined system for elements of ENT_{S1}, that is, whenever we have domain entities a,b $\in ENT_{S1}$ then $\mathcal{C}_{S1}(\mathsf{a},\mathsf{b}) \leq (\mathcal{C}_{S1} \otimes \mathcal{C}_{S2})(\mathsf{a},\mathsf{b})$. This can be defined in terms of the secure re-configuration relation as follows.

DEFINITION 5 *Loose Secure Interoperation.* Let $C_S^\top$ represent a system S that places/assumes no access constraint over elements in ENT_S, and completely denies flows among entities when one of them is not in ENT_S. More formally, we have $C_S^\top(X, Y) \doteq \top$ when both X and Y are elements of ENT_S, and $C_S^\top(X, Y) \doteq \bot$ when either X or Y (or both) are not elements of ENT_S. Systems $S1$ and $S2$ loosely securely interoperate if they uphold the constraints (with respect to elements from their alphabet) in their composition, that is,

$$\mathcal{C}_{S1} \otimes \mathcal{C}_{S1}^\top \sqsubseteq (\mathcal{C}_{S1} \otimes \mathcal{C}_{S2})$$
$$\mathcal{C}_{S2} \otimes \mathcal{C}_{S2}^\top \sqsubseteq (\mathcal{C}_{S1} \otimes \mathcal{C}_{S2})$$

To ensure loose secure interoperation, system $S1$ should be (securely) re-configured as $C'_{S1}(X, Y) \doteq (\mathcal{C}_{S1} \otimes \mathcal{C}_{S2})$ when $X, Y \in ENT_S$, and similarly for $S2$. In the case of a boolean semiring, loose secure interoperation corresponds to the lattice of reflexive flow policies defined in [Foley, 1992]. □

EXAMPLE 6 Continuing Example 5, $S1$ and $S3$ are re-configured for loose secure interoperation as depicted in Figure 5. Note that in practice, networks C'_{S1} and C'_{S2} would also include nodes d and b, respectively, but with no connecting arcs (unconstrained permissions, which we assume to be equivalent to permitted accesses/flows).

If systems $\mathcal{C}_{S1}$ and $\mathcal{C}_{S3}$ are reconfigured in this way then we can be confident that their interoperation will be secure. △

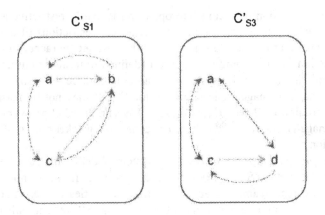

Figure 5.   Re-configurations C'_{S1} and C'_{S3} (Example 6).

6.   Access Transitivity

Reconfiguration for (loose) secure interoperation gives the most permissive reconfiguration (that does not violate the original configurations). If a system does not include an entity in its alphabet then it is assumed that it places no restrictions on access to it.

It is useful to consider variations of this operation for more restrictive scenarios. In particular, some entities that are common to interoperating systems may induce transitive relationships between entities. For example, suppose that c is a service that is shared between systems $S1$ and $S3$ (Example 5), and $C_{S1}(b,c)$ and $C_{S3}(c,d)$. Rather than permitting all accesses between b and d (as computed by $\otimes$, since there are no explicit restrictions these entities), we could instead assume that there is an implicit transitive restriction and weaken the policy by allowing access from b to d, but not vice-versa.

EXAMPLE 7 The system configuration $C_{S2_{rw}}$ (from Example 4) allows accesses $C_{S2_{rw}}(a,b) = \{r,w\}$ and $C_{S2_{rw}}(b,c) = \{r\}$. However, access is not permitted between a and c in $C_{S2_{rw}}$. Regarding b as a transitive entity would induce a transitive access that is the greatest lower bound of the accesses along a path from a to c through b; in this case we would have $\{r\} \cap \{r,w\} = \{r\}$ access from a to c. $\triangle$

DEFINITION 6 *Transitive Weakening.* The transitive weakening of a system configuration C_{S1} with a set of transitive entities A is defined as C_{S1}^{*A}, where

$$C_{S1}^{*A}(X, Z) \ \hat{=} \ (C_{S1}(X, Y) \otimes C'_{S1}(Y, Z)) \Downarrow_{\{X,Z\}}$$

where C'_{S1} is defined as follows:

- for each entity $e \in ENT$, $C'_{S1}(e, e) \hateq \top$;

- if $\langle e, g \rangle \in C_{S_1}$, and $e \in A$ (e is a transitive entity), then $C'_{S1}(e, g) \hateq \top$;

□

In general we have $C_{S1} \sqsubseteq C^{*A}_{S1}$.

THEOREM 1 *Given a system with no transitive entity C_{S1} and the same system C^{*A}_{S1} with a set of transitive entities A, we have $C_{S1} \sqsubseteq C^{*A}_{S1}$.*

The transitive weakening corresponds to a weakening of the configuration constraint: the new configuration may include (transitive) accesses that are not permitted by the original configuration.

DEFINITION 7 *Secure Transitive Reconfiguration.* Configuration C_{S1} is a secure transitive reconfiguration of configuration C_{S2}, with respect to a set of transitive entities A, if its transitive weakening is a secure reconfiguration of C_{S2}, that is,

$$C^{*A}_{S1} \sqsubseteq C_{S2}$$

□

EXAMPLE 8 For Example 7, we have $C^{*\{b\}}_{S^2_{rw}}(a,c) = \{r\}$ and for any $(X, Y) \neq (a, c)$, $C^{*\{b\}}_{S^2_{rw}}(X, Y) = C_{S^1_{rw}}(X, Y)$ (from Example 4) and thus $C_{S^2_{rw}}$ is not a secure transitive reconfiguration of itself. A more strict configuration must be found, for example, the most restrictive $C_\perp$. △

THEOREM 2 *For all systems C_S, and for all sets of transitive entities A, $C_\perp$ is a secure transitive reconfiguration with respect to A of C_S. Also, given $A_1 \subseteq A_2$ easily, $C^{*A_1}_S \sqsubseteq C^{*A_2}_S$.*

In practice, selecting $C_\perp$ as the secure transitive reconfiguration is not useful as the resulting configuration is overly restrictive. In general it is desirable to find the smallest number of changes that must be made on the access links between entities that will ensure a secure transitive reconfiguration. Formally, we search for a least restrictive secure transitive reconfiguration of a configuration C_{S1}, that is, a configuration C_{St} such that there is no other configuration $C_{St'}$ with $C_{St} \sqsubseteq C_{St'} \sqsubseteq C_{S1}$. We are currently exploring constraint-based schemes for solving this type of problem.

DEFINITION 8 *(Loose) Secure Transitive Interoperation.* Systems $S1$ and $S2$ securely interoperate via transitive entities in A if their interoperation is secure when considering transitive weakening (using A).

To ensure secure transitive interoperation we seek the least restrictive secure reconfigurations C_{S1}^t and C_{S2}^t of C_{S1} and C_{S2}, respectively, such that

$$(C_{S1}^t \otimes C_{S1}^{tT})^{\star A} \sqsubseteq C_{S1} \otimes C_{S2}$$
$$(C_{S2}^t \otimes C_{S2}^{tT})^{\star A} \sqsubseteq C_{S1} \otimes C_{S2}$$

$\square$

EXAMPLE 9 The secure transitive interoperation reconfiguration of $S1$ and $S3$ (Example 5) with transitive entity b for permission flows is depicted in Figure 6.

$$(C_{S1} \otimes C_{S3})^{\cdot \{b\}}$$

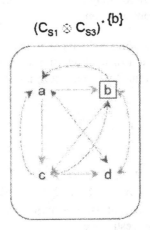

Figure 6. Reconfiguration $(C_{S1} \otimes C_{S3})^{\star \{b\}}$ (Example 9).

Here, we assume that entity b can allow implicit transitive permission. This means that since we have a flow between a and b and between b and c, we must have also a flow between a and c.

The difference in the result is visible by comparing $C_{S1} \otimes C_{S3}$ in Figure 4 and $(C_{S1} \otimes C_{S3})^{\star \{b\}}$ in Figure 6. $\triangle$

7. Discussion and Conclusions

The approach that we present in this paper represents a paradigm shift in the modelling and analysis of interoperability. We present a constraint model that provides a natural description of a network of interoperating systems. While constraint solving is NP-complete in general, this has not detracted from its uptake as a practical approach to solving many real-world problems [Wallace, 1996]. Previous approaches determine secure interoperation in polynomial time, but re-configuring an existing network of systems for secure interoperation, in an optimal way, is NP-complete [Gong and Qian, 1994, Gong and Qian, 1996]. Using a constraint model, we can rely on a significant body of successful techniques from the field of constraint processing for finding the set of secure re-configurations with reasonable effort. As part of our future work in this area we plan to develop an constraint-based implementation with which to demonstrate our approach on some real world data.

References

Amman, P. and Sandhu, R. (1992). The extended schematic protection model. *Journal of Computer Security*, 1(4).

Aziz, B., Foley, S.N., Herbert, J., and Swart, G. (2004). Configuring storage-area networks for mandatory security. In *18th Annual IFIP WG 11.3 Working Conference on Data and Applications Security*.

Bell, D.E. and Padula, L. J. La (1976). Secure computer system: unified exposition and MULTICS interpretation. Report ESD-TR-75-306, The MITRE Corporation.

Bella, G. and Bistarelli, S. (2001). Soft Constraints for Security Protocol Analysis: Confidentiality. In *Proc. of the 3rd International Symposium on Practical Aspects of Declarative Languages (PADL'01)*, LNCS 1990, pages 108–122. Springer-Verlag.

Bella, G. and Bistarelli, S. (2002). Confidentiality levels and deliberate/indeliberate protocol attacks. In *Proc. Security Protocols 10th International Workshop, Cambridge, UK, April, 2002, Revised Papers*, LNCS, pages 104–119. Springer-Verlag.

Bella, G. and Bistarelli, S. (2004). Soft constraint programming to analysing security protocols. *Theory and Practice of Logic Programming (TPLP)*, 4(5):1–28. To appear.

Bellone, J., Chamard, A., and Pradelles, C. (1992). Plane - an evolutive planning system for aircraft production. In *Proc. 1st Interantional Conference on Practical Applications of Prolog (PAP92)*.

Bertino, E. et al. (1998). An authorization model and its formal semantics. In *Proceedings of the European Symposium on Research in Computer Security*, pages 127–142. Springer LNCS 1485.

Bharadwaj, V.G and Baras, J.S. (2003). Towards automated negotiation of access control policies. In *Proc. of IEEE Workshop Policies for Distributed Systems and Networks*, pages 77–80.

Bistarelli, S. (2004). *Semirings for Soft Constraint Solving and Programming*, volume 2962 of *Lecture Notes in Computer Science*. Springer.

Bistarelli, S. and Foley, S.N. (2003a). Analysis of integrity policies using soft constraints. In *Proceedings IEEE 4th International Workshop on Policies for Distributed Systems and Networks (POLICY2003), Lake Como,Italy, June 4-6, 2003*, pages 77–80. IEEE Press.

Bistarelli, S. and Foley, S.N. (2003b). A constraint based framework for dependability goals: Integrity. In *22nd International Conference on Computer Safety, Reliability and Security (SAFECOMP2003), Proceedings, 23-26 September 2003, Edinburgh, Scotland, United Kingdom*, volume 2788 of *Lecture Notes in Computer Science*, pages 130–143. Springer.

Bistarelli, S., Foley, S.N., and O'Sullivan, B. (2004a). Detecting and eliminating the cascade vulnerability problem from multi-level security networks using soft constraints. In *Proceedings Innovative Applications of Artificial Intelligence Conference (IAAI-04)*, pages 808–813. AAAI Press.

Bistarelli, S., Foley, S.N., and O'Sullivan, B. (2004b). Modelling and detecting the cascade vulnerabiliy problem using soft constraints. In *Proc. ACM Symposium on Applied Computing (SAC 2004)*, pages 383–390. ACM Press.

Bistarelli, S., Montanari, U., and Rossi, F. (1997). Semiring-based constraint solving and optimization. *Journal of ACM*, 44(2):201–236.

Bistarelli, S., Montanari, U., and Rossi, F. (2002). Soft concurrent constraint programming. In *Programming Languages and Systems: 11th European Symposium on Programming, ESOP 2002 held as Part of the Joint European Conference on Theory and Practice of Software, ETAPS 2002, Proceedings, Grenoble, France, April 8-12, 2002*, volume 2305 of *Lecture Notes in Computer Science*, pages 53–67. Springer.

Bistarelli, S. and O'Sullivan, B. (2003). A theoretical framework for tradeoff generation using soft constraints. In *Research and Development in Intelligent Systems XX, Proceedings of AI-2003, the Twenty-third SGAI International Conference on Knowledge-Based Systems and Applied Artificial Intelligence*, pages 69–82. Springer, BCS Conference Series "Research and Development in Intelligent Systems xx".

Foley, S.N. (1992). Aggregation and separation as noninterference properties. *Journal of Computer Security*, 1(2):159–188.

Foley, S.N. (1997). The specification and implementation of commercial security requirements including dynamic segregation of duties. In *ACM Conference on Computer and Communications Security*, pages 125–134.

Foley, S.N. (2000). Conduit cascades and secure synchronization. In *ACM New Security Paradigms Workshop*.

Fruehwirth, T. and Brisset, P. (1997). Optimal planning of digital cordless telecommunication systems. In *Proc. PACT97*, London, UH.

Gong, L. (1999). *Inside Java2 Platform Security*. Addison Wesley.

Gong, L. and Qian, X. (1994). The complexity and composability of secure interoperation. In *Proceedings of the Symposium on Security and Privacy*, pages 190–200, Oakland, CA. IEEE Press.

Gong, L. and Qian, X. (1996). Computational issues in secure interoperation. *IEEE Trans. Softw. Eng.*, 22(1):43–52.

Harrison, M., Ruzzo, W., and Ullman, J. (1976). Protection in operating systems. *Communications of the ACM*, 19:461–471.

Konstantinou, A.V., Yemini, Y., Bhatt, S., and Rajagopalan, S. (1999). Managing security in dynamic networks. In *Proc. USENIX Lisa '99*.

Lee, T.M.P. (1988). Using mandatory integrity to enforce 'commerical' security. In *Proceedings of the Symposium on Security and Privacy*, pages 140–146.

Sandhu, R. et al. (1996). Role based access control models. *IEEE Computer*, 29(2):38–47.

Wallace, M. (1996). Practical applications of constraint programming. *Constraints*, 1(1–2):139–168.

A LOGIC FOR AUDITING ACCOUNTABILITY IN DECENTRALIZED SYSTEMS*

R. Corin[1], S. Etalle[1,2], J. den Hartog[1], G. Lenzini[1] and I. Staicu[1]

[1] *Department of Computer Science, University of Twente, The Netherlands*
[2] *CWI, Center for Mathematics and Computer Science, Amsterdam, The Netherlands*
{corin,s.etalle,hartogji,lenzinig,staicu}@cs.utwente.nl

Abstract   We propose a language that allows agents to distribute data with usage policies in a decentralized architecture. In our framework, the compliance with usage policies is not enforced. However, agents may be audited by an authority at an arbitrary moment in time. We design a logic that allows audited agents to prove their actions, and to prove their authorization to posses particular data. Accountability is defined in several flavors, including *agent* accountability and *data* accountability. Finally, we show the soundness of the logic.

1.   Introduction

Consider the following scenario: Alice gives marketing company Big-Brother some personal information (e.g., her spending patterns, music preferences or part of her medical record), in exchange for some bonus miles. In addition, Alice allows BigBrother to sell to a third party a piece of this information, but only if anonimized and under provision that she will receive 10 percent of the revenues. The problem here is, how can we make sure that the data is being used only according to Alice's wishes. Notice that in the above scenario BigBrother might sell Alice's data to BigSister, who in turn might sell part of it to SmallNephew, and so on.

This problem is not only that of privacy protection in a distributed setting. In fact, modern scenarios of digital asset delivery (where a digital asset can be anything ranging from a piece of private information to a movie or a character in a multiplayer game) are departing from the usual schemas in which the assets are equipped with an immutable

---

*This work is partly funded by the EU under project nr. IST-1-507894-IP, by IOP GenCom under project nr. IGC03001 and by Telematica Institute under project nr. 10190

usage policy that applies to the whole distribution chain. Instead, we are moving towards a situation in which information brokers collect, combine and redistribute digital assets. The question that needs to be answered here is how can we describe and enforce usage policies in such a decentralized dynamic, evolving context.

In this paper we present a logic data access and agent accountability in a setting in which data can be created, distributed and re-distributed. Using this logic, the owner of the data attaches a usage policy to the data, which contains a logical specification of what actions are allowed with the data, and under which conditions. This logic allows for different kind of accountability and it is shown to be sound.

Part of problem we are tackling is that of enforcing that agents actually follow the behavior that policies dictate; in general, this is a difficult task, typically requiring continuous monitoring of agents, which is usually infeasible. Therefore, we consider an alternative to policy enforcement, based on an analogy with the real world, where people are not always controlled for correct behavior. Instead, eventually an agent (say Alice) might be *suspected* of incorrect behavior; in that case, an authority would *query* Alice for a justification of her actions. This justification can be supported by *evidence*, that the authority can check.

2.   System, Syntax and running example

Our system consists of a group of communicating agents which create and share data and an authorization authority which may audit agents. The creation of data, as well as the communication between agents, is assumed to leave some evidence and hence is observable from the perspective of the authorization authority (this is discussed in more detail in section 4). As we do not continuously monitor agents, the internal computations of agents are not considered to be observable. However, when auditing an agent, the data and policies currently stored by an agent become visible to the authorization authority. Thus, the model of an agent consists of storage, (unobservable) internal computation and (observable) actions such as communication.

EXAMPLE 1 *As a running example we consider a scenario with three agents, a content provider Alice (a), a reviewer/distributer Bob (b) and a user Charlie (c). In this setting Alice creates content data (d) and sends it to Bob for review with permission for Bob to read the data but not to retransmit it, in effect protecting the data with a non-disclosure agreement (NDA). After some time Alice lifts the NDA by giving Bob permission to resend the data to Charlie. Bob sends the data to Charlie with permission to read it. Charlie does not produce any observable actions but the policy allowing him to read the data is in his storage after Bob sends it.*

The following subsections introduce the logical language used to express policies and describe the system in more detail.

2.1 The syntax

For the formal model we will use a set of *agents* $\mathcal{G}$ ranged over by a, b and c and a set of *data objects* $\mathcal{D}$ ranged over by d. As the order of actions can be relevant we also introduce a notion of (global discrete) time described by using a well-founded totally ordered set $\mathcal{T}$, ranged over by t (in examples we will use the natural numbers for $\mathcal{T}$).

The *policy formulae*, expressing data usage policies, further require a set of *predicates* $\mathcal{C}$, ranged over by p, which express basic operations that can be performed on data. For example, read(a, d) and print(a, d) respectively indicate that user a may read and print data d. For readability we will restrict our definitions to binary predicates taking a single agent and a single data object.

DEFINITION 2 *The set of* policy *formulae* Φ, *ranged over by* ϕ *and* ψ, *is defined by the following grammar (with* $a, b \in \mathcal{G}$, $d \in \mathcal{D}$, $p \in \mathcal{C}$):

$$\phi \quad ::= \quad p(a, d) \mid a \text{ owns } d \mid a \text{ says } \phi \text{ to } b \mid \phi \wedge \phi \mid \phi \vee \phi \mid \phi \to \phi$$

First, a policy formula can be a simple predicate $p(a, d)$, such as read(a, d) mentioned above. Second, we have the a owns d formula. This formula indicates that a is the owner of data object d. As we will see below, an owner of data can create usage policies for that data. A third construction is a says ϕ to b which expresses the claim that agent a is allowed to give policy ϕ to agent b. The 'says' contains a target agent to which the statement is said instead of the broadcast interpretation used for a similar construct in e.g. [7, 1]. This allows us to provide a precise way of expressing policies to certain agents. Finally, the logic constructions *and, or* and *implication* have their usual meaning.

The *base data set* of a policy formula ϕ, denoted $dv(\phi)$, consists of the data objects the policy refers to. It is defined as one would expect:

$$dv(a \text{ owns } d) = dv(p(a, d)) \quad := \quad \{d\}$$
$$dv(a \text{ says } \phi \text{ to } b) \quad := \quad dv(\phi)$$
$$dv(\phi \wedge \psi) = dv(\phi \vee \psi) = dv(\phi \to \psi) \quad := \quad dv(\phi) \cup dv(\psi)$$

We denote a formula ϕ whose base data set is D, i.e. $dv(\phi) = D$, as $\phi[D]$. If D is a singleton set, i.e. $D = \{d\}$, we simply write $\phi[d]$. Note that the base data set of a formula is always non-empty.

EXAMPLE 3 *The policy which allows Bob to read the data d is expressed as* read(b, d). *Allowing agent Bob to send to data on to Charlie provided he already has permission to read it is expressed by* read$(b, d) \to b$ says read(c, d) to c.

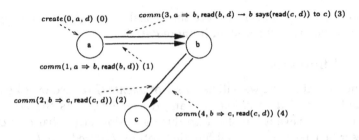

Figure 1.   The actions of Alice (a), Bob (b) and Charlie (c) in our example. Solid arrowed lines represent communications, dashed lines represent observable events.

Beside usage policies we also have the *observable actions* of agents. We will use *evidence formulae* to describe observable actions. As mentioned above, communication and creation of data are the observable actions possible in our system. For simplicity we will only consider these two types of observable actions though extension with other types of observable actions is possible.

DEFINITION 4 *The set of* evidence formulae *EV, ranged over by ev, is defined by the grammar (with $t \in \mathcal{T}$ $a, b \in \mathcal{G}$, $d \in \mathcal{D}$ and $\phi \in \Phi$):*

$$ev \quad ::= \quad creates(t, a, d) \mid comm(t, a \Rightarrow b, \phi)$$

First, we have the $creates(t, a, d)$ evidence formula which states that an agent a has created a piece of data d at time t. As we shall see later, this will automatically make a the owner of d. Secondly, we have a communication evidence formula $comm(t, a \Rightarrow b, \phi)$, which states that agent b has received a policy formula ϕ from agent a at time t. To refer to the time of an evidence formula we define the function $\text{time} : EV \rightarrow \mathcal{T}$ as $\text{time}(creates(t, a, d)) = \text{time}(comm(t, a \Rightarrow b, \phi)) := t$.

EXAMPLE 5 *The formula $creates(0, a, d)$ expresses that Alice created data d at time 0. The formula $comm(1, a \Rightarrow b, \text{read}(b, d))$ expresses that Alice sent the permission for Bob to read d to Bob at time 1.*

2.2   The model

The observable actions executed by agents (in a run of the system) are combined in the so called *evidence set* $\mathcal{E}$. We will simply use evidence formulae to describe these observable actions, i.e. $\mathcal{E} \subseteq EV$. We make the natural restriction that only finitely many actions can be executed at any given moment in time.

As mentioned before, agents may be audited by an authorization authority, say at time T. At this time each agent $a \in \mathcal{G}$ has a state $\mathcal{S}_a$, representing a's storage, which contains her present data policies. Note that we do not assume that the store retains all internal actions performed by the agent.

EXAMPLE 6 *Let assume the actions of the agents be the one in Figure 1. where Bob actually sends the read permission for the data to Charlie twice: the second time this is fine but the first time violates the NDA. This gives the following evidence set:*

$$\mathcal{E} \;=\; \{create(0, a, d), comm(1, a \Rightarrow b, \mathsf{read}(b, d)), comm(2, b \Rightarrow c, \mathsf{read}(c, d)),$$
$$comm(3, a \Rightarrow b, \mathsf{read}(b, d) \rightarrow b \; \mathsf{says}(\mathsf{read}(c, d)) \; to \; c), comm(4, b \Rightarrow c, \mathsf{read}(c, d))\}$$

When Charlie is audited at time 5 his storage S_c contains (among others) $\mathsf{read}(c, d)$. This is discovered e.g by the authority examining his storage. Apparently Charlie has done some (unobservable) internal computation to arrive at the conclusion that he may read d. The question now is, did Charlie correctly conclude that he was allowed to read d and has anything unauthorized happened to the data. We will address this issue in the next section.

3. Using usage policies: The proof system

This section describes the proof system used to derive the actions on data that are allowed by the policies that a user possesses. We first give the inference rules followed by the notion provable. Note that each agents locally reasons about policies therefore the rules include the *subject*, i.e. the agent doing the reasoning. Inference rules have the format *premises/conclusions* where a *premise* can be either a policy formula (in Φ) or an evidence formula (in EV), *conclusion* is a policy formula. Moreover we subscript each rule with a *subject* i.e., an agent in $\mathcal{G}$. The rules of our proof system are presented in two parts. The first, includes standard rules from the propositional logic:

$$\wedge\text{I} \; \frac{\phi \quad \psi}{\phi \wedge \psi} \; a \qquad \wedge\text{EL} \; \frac{\phi \wedge \psi}{\phi} \; a \qquad \wedge\text{ER} \; \frac{\phi \wedge \psi}{\psi} \; a \qquad \vee\text{IL} \; \frac{\phi}{\phi \vee \psi} \; a$$

$$\vee\text{IR} \; \frac{\phi}{\psi \vee \phi} \; a \qquad \vee\text{E} \; \frac{\phi \vee \phi' \quad \overset{[\phi]}{\psi} \quad \overset{[\phi']}{\psi}}{\psi} \; a \qquad \text{MP} \; \frac{\phi \rightarrow \psi \quad \phi}{\psi} \; a \qquad \rightarrow\text{I} \; \frac{\overset{[\psi]}{\phi}}{\psi \rightarrow \phi} \; a$$

We have the standard rules for respectively *and* introduction and elimination, *or* introduction and elimination and *implication* introduction and elimination (modus ponens). An overscript $[\phi]$ above ψ says that ϕ is required as *temporary assumption* in the proof of ψ. The second part of proof system consist of the following rules which deal with creation of policies and with the delegation of responsibility.

$$\text{COMM} \ \frac{\text{comm}(t, a \Rightarrow b, \phi)}{a \text{ says } \phi \text{ to } b} \ b \qquad\qquad \text{CREATES} \ \frac{\text{creates}(t, a, d)}{a \text{ owns } d} \ a$$

$$\text{SAY} \ \frac{a \text{ says } \phi \text{ to } b}{\phi} \ b \qquad\qquad \text{DERPOL} \ \frac{a \text{ owns } d_1 \ \dots \ a \text{ owns } d_n}{\phi[\{d_1, \dots, d_n\}]} \ a$$

Note that these rules do not take time or existence of evidence into account. This will be done in our notion of (authorization) proofs. Rule (COMM) states that if agent b has received message ϕ from an agent a at some time, then b may conclude the corresponding a says ϕ to b formula. Rule (CREATES) expresses that by creating a piece of data, the agent becomes the owner of that data. Rule (SAY) expresses delegation of responsibility. If agent a says ϕ to b then b can assume ϕ to hold. It is a's responsibility to show that it had permission to give ϕ to b. Note that in our current setup it would also have been possible to omit this rule and derive ϕ directly in rule (COMM). We expect, however, that with extension of our logic the separation of these two steps will become useful. Rule (DERPOL) allows the creation of policies. An agent a can create any usage policy for data that she owns.

3.1   Building Proofs

We are ready to introduce proofs built from our logic system. The first definition states what is in fact a proof for some agent x.

DEFINITION 7 *A proof $\mathcal{P}$ of ϕ for x is a finite derivation tree such that: (1) each rule of $\mathcal{P}$ has x as its subject; (2) each rule of $\mathcal{P}$ belongs to one of the above rules (3) the root of $\mathcal{P}$ is ϕ.*

Given a proof $\mathcal{P}$, we write $prem(\mathcal{P})$ for the set of premises in the initial rules of $\mathcal{P}$ which are *not* temporary assumptions (like in rules $\vee E$ and $\rightarrow I$). We also write $conc(\mathcal{P})$ to denote the conclusion of the last rule of $\mathcal{P}$, and $subject(\mathcal{P})$ to denote the subject.

For auditing purposes, we want to restrict to proofs that only have evidence formulae as premises and whose time of the evidences is bounded. We call such proofs *justification* proofs.

DEFINITION 8 *A proof $\mathcal{P}$ is called a* justification proof *(of ϕ for x) at time t if every formula in $prem(\mathcal{P})$ is an evidence formula ev satisfying $time(ev) < t$. We denote the set of all justification proofs with $\mathcal{J}$.*

Note that a justification proof at time t is just a proof which is potentially valid at time t. Any evidence formula can be used as a premise. To check whether the proof is indeed valid, a link has to be made with the actions observed, i.e. those in the set $\mathcal{E}$. This will be done in the next section. It is easy to see that justification proofs are *monotonic*, i.e. any proof that is a justification at time t is also a justification at time t' for any $t' > t$.

As an aside, our policy language is negation free and all proofs have a 'constructive' flavor. For extensions of the logic, it may be necessary to go to intuitionistic or linear logic altogether. The constructive nature of the proofs inherently means that the derivation system is not complete: For example, $\mathsf{read}(c, d) \to \mathsf{print}(c, d)$ can hold simply because $\mathsf{read}(c, d)$ does not. However, there is no constructive derivation for this (Also, as soon as read permission is obtained, the predicate may no longer hold.)

EXAMPLE 9 *In our running example agent Charlie can provide an justification proof for* $\mathsf{read}(c, d)$ *at time 5 as follows.*

$$\mathcal{P}_1 \left\{ \quad \mathrm{COMM} \dfrac{\mathsf{comm}(4, b \Rightarrow c, \mathsf{read}(c, d))}{\mathrm{SAY} \dfrac{b \ \mathsf{says} \ \mathsf{read}(c, d) \ \mathsf{to} \ c}{\mathsf{read}(c, d)} \ c} \ c \right.$$

Note that replacing the first premise by $\mathsf{comm}(0, b \Rightarrow c, \mathsf{read}(c, d))$ *also gives a justification proof for* $\mathsf{read}(c, d)$ *at time 5. This second proof should not be accepted by the authorization authority as Bob did not actually send anything to Charlie at time 0. The next section will treat what agents should prove and which proofs are accepted by the authority.*

4. Accountability

As noticed in the example in the previous section, agents can potentially provide different justification proofs. We model an agent *providing* a proof of ϕ at time t as a function $\mathtt{Pr} : \Phi \times \mathcal{G} \times \mathcal{T} \to \mathcal{J} \cup \{\bot\}$. Here the value $\bot$ represents that the agent cannot provide a proof.

We present two notions of accountability. The first notion, *agent accountability*, focuses on whether the actions of a given agent where authorized. The second notion, *data accountability*, expresses that a given piece of data was not misused.

Recall that in our system, an agent a can be audited at time T at which point $\mathcal{S}_a$, the storage of a, becomes visible to the authorization authority. The observable actions performed in the system are collected in $\mathcal{E}$. For both notions of accountability, it is important to link proofs to actual observable actions. To this end we introduce the notion of *authorization proof*, which is a justification proof that is backed by actual evidence.

DEFINITION 10 *We say that a justification proof* $\mathcal{P}$ *of* ϕ *for* a *at time* t *is* authorized, *written* $\mathtt{Aut}(\mathcal{P})$, *when* $\mathsf{prem}(\mathcal{P}) \subseteq \mathcal{E}$. *In this case we call* $\mathcal{P}$ *an* authorization proof *of* ϕ *for* a *at time* t.

An agent is accountable for the policies she possesses *and* for the usage policies she gives to others. Thus to pass the audit, the agent needs to authorize her storage and her communication.

DEFINITION 11 (ACCOUNTABILITY OF a) *We say that agent a is authorized to have ϕ at time t, denoted $\text{Aut}_\phi(a, t)$, if she provides an authorization proof, i.e. $\Pr(\phi, a, t) \neq \perp$ and $\text{Aut}(\Pr(\phi, a, t))$.*

We write $\text{Aut}(a)$ if a is authorized to have all usage policies in her storage at the time T of auditing, i.e. $\forall \phi \in S_a : \text{Aut}_\phi(a, T)$

We write $\text{ComAut}(a)$ if a was authorized to send all the policies that she did send, i.e. $\forall comm(t, a \Rightarrow b, \psi) \in \mathcal{E} : \text{Aut}_{a \text{ says } \psi \text{ to } b}(a, t)$.

Finally, we say that agent a passes the accountability test, written $\text{Acc}(a)$, if both $\text{Aut}(a)$ and $\text{ComAut}(a)$ hold.

EXAMPLE 12 *In our running example Charlie can show to be authorized for having read(c, d) by providing the proof from Example 9. Assuming he is also authorized for other policies in his storage we have $\text{Aut}(c)$ and also $\text{Acc}(c)$ as Charlie did not send any messages (so $\text{ComAut}(c)$ is emptily satisfied).*

Bob, on the other hand, cannot pass the accountability test as he cannot provide an authorization for b says read$(c, d) \to c$ at time 2.

Checking authorization, $\text{Aut}(c)$, is relatively easy: The agent has to provide the proof and it is in the agents interest to show that the communications used in the proof have indeed happened. Thus a setup with undeniable communications, e.g. through use of some non-repudiation scheme, will be sufficient. To check $\text{ComAut}(c)$, a setup with a much stronger authority is needed as the authority to find and check all communications of the agent looking e.g. at communication logs. (Note that the authority does not need to be able to decryption messages, the agent can be required to do this at the time of the audit.) Missing communications may cause an unauthorized communication of the agent to go unnoticed but will not cause the system to break down completely. Also, the unauthorized communication may still be discovered if the agent receiving the communication is audited.

Agent accountability is useful to check the behavior of a single agent. However, a data owner may be more interested in whether a specific piece of data (with corresponding usage policy) was obtained correctly. To describe this we introduce the notion of data accountability.

4.1   Data Accountability

Data accountability describes the authorization requirements for a single data usage policy. Unlike agent accountability, this may require authorizations from several different agents. We first introduce weak data accountability, which describes that a given usage policy *may* have been obtained correctly. We will then discuss some potential issues with this notion and introduce the notion of strong data accountability.

Weak data accountability expresses that an agent must provide a authorization proof and that all delegated responsibilities must also be accounted for, i.e. for any received policies used to derive the policy, there is data accountability for sending of that policy at the sending agent.

DEFINITION 13 (WEAK DATA ACCOUNTABILITY) *We say that ϕ at a passes the* weak data accountability *test at time t, written* $\text{Dac}(\phi, a, t)$ *if a is authorized to have ϕ at time t (i.e. a provides an authorization proof) and for all communications in the premise of the provided authorization proof, $comm(t', b \Rightarrow a, \psi) \in prem(\text{Pr}(\phi, a, t))$, we have $\text{Dac}(b \text{ says } \psi \text{ to } a, b, t')$.*

We write $\text{Dac}(\phi, a)$ for weak data accountability at the time T of the audit, i.e. for $\text{Dac}(\phi, a, T)$.

Note that this recursive definition is unproblematic, as time must decrease $(t' < t)$ by definition of authorization proof and time is well founded. Weak data accountability corresponds to either of the proofs depicted in solid or dashed lines (but not both) derivations in Figure 2-(C). Intuitively, after checking authorization of ϕ, we 'recurse' to the sending agents where data accountability is checked for the policy which allowed sending the communication.

If data accountability does not hold, then we can deduce that, at some point, some agent did not provide an authorization proof. Clearly this agent does not pass the agent accountability test. The proof of the following proposition is straightforward.

PROPOSITION 14 *If $\text{Dac}(\phi)$ does not hold, then $\exists a \in \mathcal{G}$ such that $\text{Acc}(a)$ does not hold.*

EXAMPLE 15 *Weak data accountability of $read(c, d)$ at c implies that Charlie needs to provide an authorization proof. If Charlie provides the proof given in example 9 then data accountability of b says $read(c, d)$ to c for Bob at time 4 will be required. Bob can indeed provide an authorization proof: $read(b, d) \rightarrow (b \text{ says } (read(c, d)) \text{ to } c)$.*

$$\text{MP} \dfrac{\mathcal{P}_2 \left\{ \text{COMM} \dfrac{comm(1, a \Rightarrow b, read(b, d))}{\text{SAY} \dfrac{a \text{ says } read(b, d) \text{ to } b}{read(b, d)} b} b \quad \mathcal{P}_3 \left\{ \text{COMM} \dfrac{comm(3, a \Rightarrow b, \psi)}{\text{SAY} \dfrac{a \text{ says } \psi \text{ to } b}{\psi} b} b \right.}{b \text{ says } read(c, d) \text{ to } c} b \quad (1)$$

Clearly Alice can provide authorization proofs for the two policies she sent as she, being the owner of the data, may create any policy. Thus we have Dac(*read*(*c, d*), *c*, 5). *We do not have* Dac(*read*(*c, d*), *c*, 3). *The only authorization proof Charlie can provide uses the fact that Bob sent read permission at time 2. As we have seen before, Bob cannot authorize sending this permission at time 2.*

The example above shows an issue with weak data accountability. The result of the data accountability check depends on the authorization proof that Charlie provides. Both the proof using Bobs read permission at time 2 and at time 4 could be used by Charlie. If Charlie and Bob are working together to try to hide that Bob did something wrong, the weak data accountability test of read(*c, d*) for Charlie at time 5 will not reveal that Bob violated the NDA.

To capture situations like this we introduce the notion of strong data accountability. As the internal computations of an agent are not visible, the authority cannot check if the provided proof is the proof an agent actually used to arrive at a policy. Or even if the agent created a correct proof at all before using the policy. The fact that there is no way to check this is an unpreventable limitation due to the unobservability of some of the agents actions. We can, however, check all correct proofs an agent could have used to obtain a policy. This will allow us to prevent situation as in the example above where Charlie behaves correctly but can still hide Bobs violation of the NDA. With *strong data accountability* we do not look at the authorization proof the agent provides but instead look at all (reasonable) proofs. In this way we force checking of all communication that may have been used to derive a policy.

A *minimal proof* $\mathcal{P}$ of ϕ is a proof of ϕ for which there are no unnecessary premises, i.e. there is no proof of ϕ using a strict subset of $prem(\mathcal{P})$ as premises.

DEFINITION 16 (STRONG DATA ACCOUNTABILITY) *We say that ϕ at a passes the* strong data accountability *test at time t, written* SDac(ϕ, a, t) *if a is authorized to have ϕ at time t and for all minimal authorization proofs $\mathcal{P}$ of ϕ for a at time t and all comm($t', b \Rightarrow a, \psi$) in prem($\mathcal{P}$), we have* SDac($b$ says ψ to a, b, t').

We write SDac(ϕ, a) *for strong data accountability at the time T of the audit, i.e. for* SDac(ϕ, a, T).

Strong data accountability corresponds to following both the solid or dashed lines in Figure 2-(C). If we assume that agents provide minimal proofs, strong data accountability is a stronger notion that weak data accountability. However, as with checking ComAut(c), a setup with a much stronger authority that is able to monitor communication is needed.

EXAMPLE 17 *We do not have strong data accountability of read(c, d) for Charlie at time 5. Although Charlie can provide authorization, checking all possible minimal proofs will also lead to checking the communication from Bob to Charlie at time 2 which Bob cannot authorize.*

5. Semantics

Even though the meaning of our logic operators is intuitive, in this section we shall make that more precise and define a semantic evaluation function $\models$ for policy formulae. Recall that the truth value of a policy formula depends on the time, the agent doing the reasoning and the observable actions in the system.

DEFINITION 18 (SEMANTIC EVALUATION OF POLICY $\phi \in \Phi$) *The semantic function* $\models: \mathcal{G} \times \mathcal{P}(EV) \times \mathcal{T} \times \Phi \rightarrow \{\text{true}, \text{false}\}$, *denoted* $\mathcal{E} \models_a^t \phi$, *is defined as the least function (*false $<$ true*) satisfying:*

$\mathcal{E} \ \models_a^t \ \phi$ *when ever* $\mathcal{E} \models_a^t b$ says ϕ *to* a *for some* $b \in \mathcal{G}$

$\mathcal{E} \ \models_a^t \ \phi[D]$ *when ever* $\mathcal{E} \models_a^t a$ owns d *for all* $d \in D$

$\mathcal{E} \ \models_a^t \ \phi \vee \psi$ *exactly when* $\mathcal{E} \models_a^t \phi$ *and* $\mathcal{E} \models_a^t \psi$

$\mathcal{E} \ \models_a^t \ \phi \wedge \psi$ *exactly when* $\mathcal{E} \models_a^t \phi$ *or* $\mathcal{E} \models_a^t \psi$

$\mathcal{E} \ \models_a^t \ \phi \rightarrow \psi$ *exactly when* $\mathcal{E} \models_a^t \phi$ *implies* $\mathcal{E} \models_a^t \psi$

$\mathcal{E} \ \models_a^t \ a$ owns d *when ever* $\text{creates}(t', a, d) \in \mathcal{E}$ *for some* $t' < t$

$\mathcal{E} \ \models_a^t \ b$ says ϕ *to* a *when ever* $(\text{comm}(t', b \Rightarrow a, \psi)) \in \mathcal{E}$ *for some* $t' < t$

One can construct $\models$ basically by building it starting from what follows directly from the evidence set (the last 2 rules) and then repeatedly adding formulae using the other rules. A complication with implication requires that this construction is done by induction on the number of implications in a formula. We omit further details of this construction. Note that agents "do not care" about communications and data of other agents; For instance, formula b says ϕ to c will not be valid for a other than b or c, *unless* somebody explicitly tells a about this (e.g., by c says (b says ϕ to c) to a. However, even in this case a is not able to use ϕ.)

We have that our logic is sound for this semantics.

THEOREM 19 (SOUNDNESS) *If* $\mathcal{P}$ *is a authorization proof of* a *for* ϕ *at time* t, *then* $\mathcal{E} \models_a^t \phi$.

Proof. By induction on the length of $\mathcal{P}$. $\square$

6. Related Work

Our discussion of related work is brief due to space constraints. A more complete discussion may be found in the extended version of this paper (http://www.ub.utwente.nl/webdocs/ctit/1/000000fe.pdf).

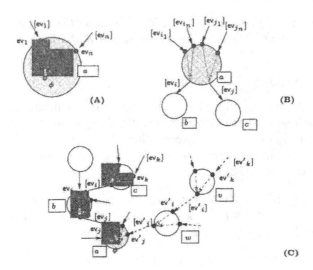

Figure 2. (A) An *authorization proof* of ϕ for a is a derivation tree whose leaves are evidence formulae e.g., $\mathsf{ev}_1 \ldots \mathsf{ev}_n$ which are supported by (global) evidences (here with [ev] we indicate that $\mathsf{ev} \in \mathcal{E}$); (B) *accountability* requires authorization for every communication for which there is evidence that a sent it; (C) *weak data accountability* of ϕ for a, requires a global proof which prove the authorization of ϕ back along all the communication events; There can be more than one path, as illustrated here in solid and dashed arrows. *Strong data accountability* requires that all paths are accountable.

[10] was extended by Samarati and De Capitani di Vimercati [11] to allow the transfer of object privileges when an associated copy flag was present. By contrast, we allow subjects to transfer privileges even if the subject does not have a right. Abadi presents in [1] a logic based method to represent the AM model where subjects can make statements or delegate part of their rights. This is somewhat similar to ours, differing in our formula a says ϕ to b, emphasizing the target agent. Appel and Felten [2] propose a distributed authentication framework based on proof-carrying proofs from a higher order logic. The agents are authenticated and authorized to access other users' resources, based on the proofs they construct (similarly to a centralized approach). On the other hand, our proposal is *decentralized*, with the data and usage policies flowing between the agents. Moreover, proofs of accountability are only required when a specialized authority inquires a proof, and not continuously. More similar to ours is the work of DeTreville [7], introducing the language Binder, designed to express statements in a distributed system. In that work, statements from any context can be exported from any other context. This implies a total network connectivity, which we do not require. Sandhu and Samarati [12] mention the importance of auditing and having a decentralized administration of authorizations. In a similar vein, Blaze et al. [5] study trust-management systems. These

systems support, like in our approach, delegation and policy specifications. The recent work of Chun and Bavier [6] presents an approach to continuously monitor the trust relations over time, and the use of accountability to check the behavior of users along a chain of trust. However, implementing this approach is expensive and sometimes infeasible. On the other hand, our lightweight approach can be easily deployed, thanks to the fact that we avoid the monitoring of agents. Our system can be used to protect private data, in the vein of Karjoth et al. [9] and Ashley et al. [3], which have also introduced the Enterprise Privacy Authorization Language(EPAL) [4]. However, EPAL is more suitable for a centralized approach, in which the users are forced to accept the policy of the company. This applies also to the work of Gunter, May and Stublebine [8], where agents are required to follow the privacy rights guarding its actions.

7. Conclusions and Future Work

We have presented a logic for data access and agent accountability in a distributed, heterogeneous setting in which data can be created, distributed and re-distributed. This framework can be used for distributing personal data as well as valuable digital assets. In our system, the owner of the data attaches a usage policy to the data, which contains a logical specification of what actions are allowed with the data, and under which conditions it can be (re-) distributed. This logic allows for different kind of accountability. We have also demonstrated the soundness of the logic.

We are working on extensions of our system, which can be explained as follows. Suppose Alice gives to BigBrother her personal data d together with a policy ϕ; ϕ might allow BigBrother to re-sell d to BigSister with a policy ϕ'. In our setting ϕ must incorporate ϕ' in some way. In other words, ϕ' must be determined by Alice (the owner of the content) in the first place. In a more realistic scenario, however, BigBrother might legitimately want to supply a ϕ' devised by himself, and what we should check is whether ϕ' complies with Alice's wishes (encoded in ϕ). For instance ϕ might say that each time that BigBrother resells d to someone, Alice should receive a dollar, so everything we should check about ϕ' is whether ϕ' has such a provision. The crucial feature of this extension is that of allowing non-owners to define policies on a content, provided that these policies are in accordance to the owner's wishes. In extend our logic with variables and quantifiers. The use of conditions should allow us to model policies such as the *chinese wall* security policy. The second extension will consist in adding *obligations* (e.g., the obligation to pay the creator a dollar for each used/resent/... / or to notify the creator/owner if the data is resent/ resold/, etc.). This will be done by extending the notion of observable action. Once conditions and obligations are in place, we can allow non-owners to define a policy; in the example above, the crucial condition we need to check is that ϕ' is not more liberal than ϕ; e.g., that each time that ϕ' allows for an action under certain conditions and obligations, then (a derivative of) ϕ allows the same action under the same conditions and obligations.

Notes

1. This work is partly funded by the EU under project nr. IST-1-507894-IP, by IOP GenCom under project nr. IGC03001 and by Telematica Institute under project nr. 10190

2. This work is partly funded by the EU under project nr. IST-1-507894-IP, by IOP GenCom under project nr. IGC03001 and by Telematica Institute under project nr. 10190

3. This work is partly funded by the EU under project nr. IST-1-507894-IP, by IOP GenCom under project nr. IGC03001 and by Telematica Institute under project nr. 10190

4. This work is partly funded by the EU under project nr. IST-1-507894-IP, by IOP GenCom under project nr. IGC03001 and by Telematica Institute under project nr. 10190

5. This work is partly funded by the EU under project nr. IST-1-507894-IP, by IOP GenCom under project nr. IGC03001 and by Telematica Institute under project nr. 10190

6. This work is partly funded by the EU under project nr. IST-1-507894-IP, by IOP GenCom under project nr. IGC03001 and by Telematica Institute under project nr. 10190

References

[1] M. Abadi. Logic in access control. *18th IEEE Symposium on Logic in Computer Science*, June 2003.

[2] A. W. Appel and E. W. Felten. Proof-carrying authentication. *Proceedings of the 6th ACM Conference on Computer and Communications Security*, pages 52–62, November 1999.

[3] P. Ashley, S. Hada, G. Karjoth, and M. Schunter. E-p3p privacy policies and privacy authorization. *Proceeding of the ACM workshop on Privacy in the Electronic Society*, 2002.

[4] P. Ashley, S. Hada, C. Powers, and M. Schunter. Enterprise privacy authorization language (EPAL). *Research Report 3485, IBM Research*, 2003.

[5] M. Blaze, J. Feigenbaum, and A. D. Keromytis. The role of trust management in distributed systems security. *Secure Internet Programming, Security Issues for Mobile and Distributed Objects*, pages 185–210, 1999.

[6] B. N. Chun and A. C. Bavier. Decentralized trust management and accountability in federated systems. *37th Hawaii International Conference on System Sciences*, January 2004.

[7] J. DeTreville. Binder, a logic-based security language. *IEEE Symposium on Security and Privacy*, pages 105–113, May 2002.

[8] C. A. Gunter, M. J. May, and S. G. Stubblebine. A formal privacy system and its application to location based services. In *Proc. of the 4th Workshop on*

Privacy Enhancing Technologies (PET 2004), LNCS, Toronto, Canada, 26-28 May 2004. Springer-Verlag.

[9] G. Karjoth, M. Schunter, and M. Waidner. Platform for enterprise privacy practices: Privacy-enabled management of customer data. *Privacy Enhancing Technologies*, 2002.

[10] B. W. Lampson. Protection. *In Proc. Fifth Princeton Symposium on Information Sciences and Systems*, pages 437–443, March 1971. Reprinted in Operating Systems Review, 8,1, January 1974, pp. 18-24.

[11] P. Samarati and S. De Capitani di Vimercati. Access control: policies, models, and mechanisms. *Foundations of Security Analysis and Design, LNCS*, 2171:137–196, 2001.

[12] R. S. Sandhu and P. Samarati. Authentication, access control, and intrusion detection. *The Computer Science and Engineering Handbook*, pages 1929–1948, 1997.

A FORMAL APPROACH TO SPECIFY AND DEPLOY A NETWORK SECURITY POLICY

F. Cuppens[1], N. Cuppens-Boulahia[1], T. Sans[1], A. Miège[1,2]

[1]*GET/ENST Bretagne, 2 rue de la Châtaigneraie, 35512 Cesson Sévigné Cedex, France*
[2]*GET/ENST, 46 rue Barrault, 75634 Paris Cedex 13, France*

Abstract

Current firewall configuration languages have no well founded semantics. Each firewall implements its own algorithm that parses specific proprietary languages. The main consequence is that network access control policies are difficult to manage and most firewalls are actually wrongly configured. In this paper, we present an access control language based on XML syntax whose semantics is interpreted in the access control model Or-BAC (Organization Based Access Control). We show how to use this language to specify high-level network access control policies and then to automatically derive concrete access control rules to configure specific firewalls through a translation process. Our approach provides clear semantics to network security policy specification, makes management of such policy easier for the administrator and guarantees portability between firewalls.

1. Introduction

It is well known in the computer security community that specifying and managing access control rules is a hard task whatever the level of abstraction considered. These access control rules are actually part of a more global set of rules called an organizational policy. We argue that this organizational policy has to be unfolded to obtain packages of access control rules. Each rule package is handled by a security component. For instance, environmental security package, physical security package, operating system security package, staff package and network security package. Firewalls are those components that deal with network security packages. They are used to block to some extent any suspicious communication from Internet to the private local area network (LAN) and to deny the members of the private LAN access the all harmful Internet temptations. One of the problems encountered with firewalls is the difficulty the administrators have to well configure them. There is really a lack of methodology and corresponding supporting tools to help them in setting the network security policy part, and generating and deploying the rules derived from this policy. There is actually no intermediary levels between the policy requirement formulated as an English sentence and its equivalent set of firewall rules, say the code.

Even if the firewall administrator is proficient in many configuration languages and tools, this expertise does not avoid from making mistakes. Without a clear methodology and some corresponding supporting tools, this may lead to the generation of configuration rules that are not consistent with the intended network security policy. We claim that the use of a high level language to specify a network security policy will avoid such mistakes and will help to consistently modify the firewall rules when necessary. Moreover, this high level language must allow administrators to specify security requirements and have to be expressive enough to specify any network security policy.

We also notice that there is not a global security policy specification so that an underlying hypothesis is always done: a single security component is used, say a single firewall. Now, it is sometimes more convenient to deploy security rules on several security components. In particular, access security rules can be separated into relevant packages and enforced by more than one firewall on the same LAN.

Furthermore, in most of firewalls, administrators use dual security policy. That is they specify both permission and prohibition rules. In this case, the selection by the firewall of the appropriate rule is based on a first matching or a last matching procedure. In both cases, the decision depends on how the security rules are sorted. Hence, administrators have to find out the correct and efficient order of the rules, order that is dependent on the filtering procedure. This is a complex task to manage especially when the security policy has to be updated. Moreover, in some cases, it is even not always possible to sort the rules. So, a closed access control policy that only includes permissions may be an alternative.

In this paper, we present an access control language based on XML syntax. This language is supported by the access control model Or-BAC [Kalam et al., 2003] to specify access control meta-rules. The concepts introduced by Or-BAC are used all top-down specification long to properly generate firewall configuration rules. There are other attempts to suggest such a top-down approach. For instance, [Hassan and Hudec, 2003] applies the RBAC model [Sandhu et al., 1996] but fails to fit the model semantics to low level implementation. The reason is largely due to the fact that RBAC is less expressive than Or-BAC and hence network level security rules are not naturally derived (see section 5).

To handle a network security policy, some topology of the organization's local area network must be enforced. Hence, the LAN is parcelled out into *zones*. The access control consists in securely managing communications between these *zones*. We show in this paper that view and role definitions of Or-

BAC allow a fine grained specification of zones. The hierarchy frameworks of extended Or-BAC [Cuppens et al., 2004a] avoid the use of artifices like *open* and *closed* groups – a specialization of zones – as suggested in [Bartal et al., 1999] (see section 5). In this connection, we also investigate if it is possible to specify a network security policy by making use of permissions only. The great contribution of this closed policy is to avoid having to sort firewall rules that are derived to enforce this policy. Sorting the rules is actually complex to manage and is a major source of errors. It is one of the main drawbacks of many firewall configuration languages.

There are some tools that help administrators to build their security policy and to translate it to the actual configuration language (for instance Cisco PIX [Degu and Bastien, 2003], Ipfilter [Russell, 2002], ...) but these tools, for example firewall builder [Kurland, 2003], are bottom-up approaches. That is, they deal with the particular problem of producing the code in the configuration language of the target firewall. The reasoning process on the access control policy is not considered. Hence, there is a lack of accurate semantics that allows the security administrator to avoid firewall mis-configuration (see section 5). We also investigate the automatic generation of the target firewall rules *from the formal specification of a network security policy.*

The remainder of this paper is organized as follows. Section 2 presents the main concepts of Or-BAC using an XML syntax [W3C, 2004] in expectation of its translation into a given target platform. We explain in section 3 how to specify a network security policy in Or-BAC and its counterpart in XML. Section 4 presents the compilation process of the abstract policy into concrete firewall rules through a real application. A comparison with other similar works is done in section 5 and finally section 6 concludes this paper.

2. Modelling Or-BAC in XML

2.1 Basic model

The Or-BAC model was first presented in [Kalam et al., 2003] using first order logic formalization. In this paper, we present an interpretation of Or-BAC in XML. The complete XML schema corresponding to the basic Or-BAC model is available in [Cuppens et al., 2004b].

The Or-BAC model enables organizations to define their access control policy. An organization corresponds to any entity in charge of managing a set of security rules. In the basic Or-BAC model, security rules are restricted to permissions, but they may be extended to also include prohibitions and obligations (see section 2.2 below). For instance, a given hospital is an organization. A concrete security component, such as a firewall, may be also viewed as an organization since it manages a set of security rules. In the organization, subjects will request to perform actions on objects and the final objective of an access control policy is to decide if these requests are permitted or not. However, permissions in Or-BAC model do not directly apply to subject, action and object. Instead, subject, action and object are respectively abstracted into role, activity and view.

Thus, subjects obtain permission based on the role they play in the organization. We use a similar approach for actions and objects. An action is permitted based on the role this action plays in the organization. In Or-BAC, an action role is called an *activity*. For instance, a given organization may specify that *consult* is an activity and that a possible role of action *acroread* is to *consult* medical record. Similarly, permissions to have an access to an object are based on the role this object plays in the organization. In Or-BAC, an object role is called a *view*. For instance, a given organization may specify that *medical record* is a view and that a possible role of object *fich27.pdf* is to be used as a *medical record*.

Each organization respectively specifies the roles, activities and views that are relevant in this organization.

For each relevant role, the organization specifies the subjects that are assigned to this role using the XML element empower. Similarly, for each relevant activity, actions are assigned to this activity using the XML element consider and, for each relevant view, objects are assigned to this view using the XML element use.

The XML schema is interpreted by the set of predicates suggested in [Cuppens et al., 2004a] to define a logical model for Or-BAC: (1) Predicate $relevant\_role(org, r)$ where org is an organization and r a role to define roles that are relevant in a given organization, (2) Predicate $relevant\_activity(org, a)$ where org is an organization and a an activity to define activities that are relevant in a given organization, (3) Predicate $relevant\_view(org, v)$ where org is an organization and v a view to define views that are relevant in a given organization, (4) Predicate $empower(org, s, r)$ where org is an organization, s a subject and r a role to define subjects that are empowered in a given role in a given organization, (5) Predicate $consider(org, \alpha, a)$ where org is an organization, α an action and a an activity to define actions that implement a given activity in a given organization, (6) Predicate $use(org, o, v)$ where org is an organization, o an object and v a view to define objects that are used in a given view in a given organization, (7) Predicate $permission(org, r, a, v)$ where org is an organization, r a role, a an activity and v a view to define that in a given organization, some roles are permitted to perform some activities over some views.

The Or-BAC model also provides means to automatically derive concrete permissions between subjects, actions and objects. For this purpose, the following predicate (not represented in the XML schema) is used:

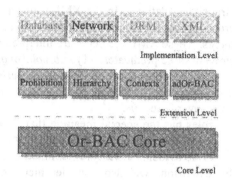

Figure 1. Or-BAC architecture

$Is\_permitted(s, \alpha, o)$ where s is a subject, α an action and o an object to define that some subjects are permitted to perform some actions on some objects.

In Or-BAC, triples that are instances of the predicate $Is\_permitted$ are derived from permissions granted to roles, views and activities by the predicate *permission* using a logical general rule to specify that: if an organization *org* grants role r permission to perform activity a on view v, and if *org* empowers subject s in role r, and if *org* uses object o in view v, and if *org* considers that action α implements activity a then s is permitted to perform α on o.

2.2 Or-BAC extensions

There are several possible extensions to the basic model presented in the previous section (called Or-BAC core in figure 1). In particular, security rules may include prohibitions and obligations in addition to permissions. Considering both permissions, prohibitions and obligations may lead to conflicts. Managing conflicts in Or-BAC is discussed in [Cuppens and Miège, 2003a]. It is also possible to consider contextual security rules. This problem is further addressed in [Cuppens and Miège, 2003b] where we show how to manage various types of context, such as temporal, spatial, prerequisite, user-declared and provisional contexts (see [Cuppens and Miège, 2003a] for further details). Another possible extension consists in activating AdOr-BAC, the administration model of Or-BAC [Cuppens and Miège, 2004].

However, in the following, we shall suggest defining a network security policy using only non contextual permissions so that the context, prohibition and obligation extensions are not activated. The only extension we shall actually consider is the hierarchy extension.

In Or-BAC, it is possible to consider role, activity, view and organization hierarchies (see [Cuppens et al., 2004a] for a more complete presentation and formalization in first order logic). All these hierarchies are partial order relations, i.e. reflexive and transitive relations. In the XML schema, role, activity and view hierarchies are respectively specified using the subRole, subActivity and subView elements. These XML elements are interpreted in a logical formalism by the following three predicates: (1) $sub\_role(org, r_1, r_2)$: in organization org, role r_1 is a sub-role of role r_2, (2) $sub\_activity(org, a_1, a_2)$: in org, activity a_1 is a sub-activity of activity a_2, (3) $sub\_view(org, v_1, v_2)$: in org, view v_1 is a sub-view of view v_2.

The hierarchy on roles has the special meaning that, in organization org, role r_1 inherits from r_2 all the permissions associated with r_2. The hierarchy on activities and views are associated with similar inheritance mechanisms.

In the hierarchy extension, we also consider hierarchies on organization that may be specified using the subOrganization element in the XML schema. This is interpreted by the following logical predicate: $sub\_organization(org_1, org_2)$ meaning that organization org_1 is a sub-organization of organization org_2.

For those roles of org_2 that are relevant in org_1, we consider that the role, activity and view hierarchies defined in org_2 also applies in org_1. We also accept a similar principle for inheritance of permissions through the organization hierarchy provided that the role, activity and view in the scope of the permission are relevant in the sub-organization.

3. Using Or-BAC to specify a network security policy

3.1 Principles

In this section, we show how to use Or-BAC in the context of network security. Our final objective will be to derive security rules to configure specific firewalls (see section 4).

A firewall may be viewed as a security component that filters IP packets with respect to a given security policy. How can we interpret the concepts of subject, action and object in this case? Our proposal is the following. A subject is any host machine. A host machine is modelled by two elements: IP address and network mask. An action is any implementation of a network service such as http, snmp or ping. In our model, a service has three elements: a protocol, a source port and a destination port. Finally, an object is a message sent to another host machine. A message is represented by two elements: a content and a receiver (a host machine).

Thus, triples ⟨subject, action, object⟩ are interpreted as host machines that use services to send messages to other host machines. Notice that messages have content so that we can define security rules to make filtering decision based on the IP packet content. However, this possibility is not used in the remainder of this section but is further discussed in the conclusion.

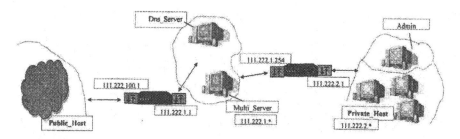

Figure 2. Application example

We shall now give interpretation to the Or-BAC notions of organization, role, activity and view. To illustrate our approach, we reuse the example used in Firmato [Bartal et al., 1999]. The objective is to model the access control policy of a corporate network used in an organization H. H has a two-firewall network configuration, as shown in figure 2. As presented in [Bartal et al., 1999], the external firewall guards the corporation's Internet connection. Behind is the DMZ, which contains the corporation's externally visible servers. In our case these servers provide HTTP/HTTPS (web), FTP, SMTP (e-mail), and DNS services. The corporation actually only uses two hosts to provide these services, one for dns and the other (called Multi_server) for all the other services. Behind the DMZ is the internal firewall which guards the corporation's intranet. This firewall actually has two interfaces: one for the DMZ and another one for the private network zone. Within the private network zone, there is one distinguished host, *Admin*, which provides the administration for the servers in the DMZ and firewalls.

3.2   Organization

In Or-BAC, a security policy will be generally modelled using several organizations. Of course, the organization H which is defining its access control policy is an organization for Or-BAC. The network security policy of H will be managed by a sub-organization of H. Let us call H_LAN this sub-organization. A first objective in this section is to show how to use Or-BAC to define the network security policy of H_LAN.

Since the network security policy is actually managed by two firewalls, we shall consider that H_LAN has two sub-organizations denoted H_fwi and H_fwe that respectively correspond to the internal and external firewalls. Another objective of our approach is to show how to derive specifications of policies managed by H_fwi and H_fwe from the one defined for H_LAN using inheritance rules presented in section 2.2.

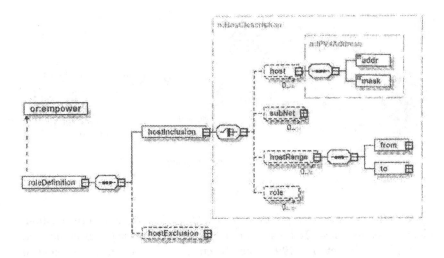

Figure 3.   Role Definition

3.3   Role

As mentioned in section 3.1, subjects correspond to host machines. So, we consider roles that may be assigned to hosts. Examples of such roles may be *dns_server* or *firewall*. Using the Or-BAC core model, the only way to assign roles to hosts is by using the empower element. This means that the security administrator must enumerate every host assigned to each role. This would never be practical nor efficient since security configuration rules of firewalls would be derived for each host.

This is why we suggest using roleDefinition to define assignment conditions of hosts to roles (see figure 3). Role definition has two parts: hostInclusion that corresponds to the positive condition a given host must satisfy to be assigned to the role and hostExclusion that corresponds to the negative condition the host must not satisfy. Each of these two conditions has four sub-parts: host to enumerate hosts, subnet to specify network zones identified by their mask, hostRange to specify intervals of IP addresses and role to refer to other roles.

Role definition of a role R in a given organization *org* can be interpreted by a logical rule as follows:

- $\forall s, (host(s) \wedge host\_inclusion(s) \wedge \neg host\_exclusion(s))$
  $\rightarrow empower(org, s, R)$

where $host\_inclusion(s)$ and $host\_exclusion(s)$ respectively represents the disjunction of conditions specified by elements host, subnet, hostRange or role. If the hostInclusion element is actually empty, then we assume that *host_inclusion(s)* is equivalent to true (meaning that any host is included); If the hostExclusion element is empty, then *host_exclusion(s)* is equivalent to false (meaning that no host is excluded).

For instance, the following XML structure [W3C, 2004] represents the Private role definition:

```
<relevantRole name="Private">
  <n:roleDefinition>
    <n:hostInclusion>
      <n:subNet>
        <n:addr>111.222.2.0</n:addr>
        <n:mask>24</n:mask>
      </n:subNet>
    </n:hostInclusion>
    <n:hostExclusion>
      <n:role roleName="FW_intern"/>
      <n:role roleName="Admin"/>
    </n:hostExclusion>
  </n:roleDefinition>
</relevantRole>
```

This structure says that a given host is empowered in the Private role if it belongs to the subnet 111.222.2.0/24 (host inclusion condition) and if it is not empowered in role FW_intern or in role Admin (host exclusion condition).

3.4   Activities

Activities are abstractions of network services. Our approach is similar to the one suggested for role definition. Instead of enumerating actions assigned to activities, we suggest using activityDefinition (see figure 4).

To specify an activity definition corresponding to network services, one has first to choose a protocol tcp, udp or icmp. If the protocol is TCP, two elements can be used to specify the activity: scrPort and destPort to respectively express conditions on source and destination port numbers. Both elements have similar structure. It is then possible to use the portRange element to specify an interval of port numbers or singlePort to enumerate a set of port numbers.

The structure is similar to define activities corresponding to UDP protocols. For ICMP protocol, the structure is different. It must be defined using two elements: type and code.

For instance, the following XML structure represents the activity Web_HTTP:

```
<relevantActivity name="Web_HTTP">
  <n:activityDefinition>
    <n:tcp>
      <n:destPort>
        <n:singlePort>80</n:singlePort>
      </n:destPort>
```

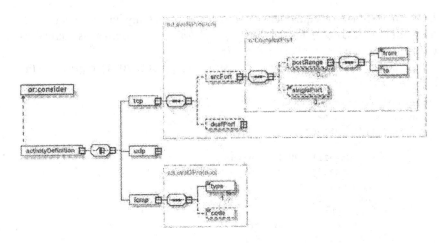

Figure 4.   Activity Definition

```
    </n:tcp>
  </n:activityDefinition>
</relevantActivity>
```

This structure says that a given action corresponds to activity Web_HTTP if protocol is equal to TCP and destination port number is equal to 80. Notice that the srcPort element is not used. In this case, we assume that any source port number are acceptable.

3.5   Views

Views are abstraction of messages sent to destination hosts. A view definition can be defined by using the element toTarget that must be assigned to a role name. A view definition of a given view V defined by organization org and having toTarget element equal to role R may be interpreted by the following logical rule:

- $\forall m, (message(m) \wedge dest(m, h) \wedge empower(org, h, R))$
  $\rightarrow use(org, m, V)$

This rule says that a message m is used in a given view V if the destination host h of this message is empowered in the role R specified in the view definition.

For instance, the following XML structure defines a view corresponding to the messages whose destination hosts are empowered in the Internet role:

```
<relevantView name="To_Internet">
  <n:viewDefinition>
    <n:toTarget roleName="Internet"/>
  </n:viewDefinition>
```

```
</relevantView>
```

In the following, we shall call such a view "target role" for short. Notice that, since we do not consider filtering rules based on the message content in the following, the view definition does not include possibility to specify condition on the message content attribute. However, we plan to provide this extension in the near future.

3.6   Permission

To specify the access control policy using our approach, we have simply to express permissions between role, activity and view. For instance, the following XML structure specifies that role Private is permitted to perform activity Web_HTTP on view To_Internet:

```
<permission roleName="Private"
            activityName="Web_HTTP" viewName="To_Internet"/>
```

Notice that our approach enables the administrator to precisely specify which hosts are empowered in a given role. This is why it is not necessary to include prohibitions in the network security policy specification. Our methodology is based on a closed policy that only includes permissions, even though deny rules may be generated from these permissions to configure a given target firewall. This point is addressed in the following section.

4.   Derivation of concrete firewall rules

We aim at deriving network components configuration from a network security policy. This policy is expressed in the XML syntax based on the Or-BAC semantics. In this section, we illustrate with the help of the running example introduced in section 4, how our approach is used to derive firewall rules. There are two steps in this derivation process. In the first step, we generate, from the Or-BAC policy, rules expressed in an intermediary multi-target[1] firewall language that also uses an XML syntax (see section 4.1 below). In the second step, we derive, from this intermediary language, concrete configuration rules expressed in the specific target firewall language. In the next two sub-sections, we give details about these two-steps derivation process.

4.1   From abstract policy to generic firewall rules

The aim of this first XSL transformation is to derive generic firewall rules from the abstract network security policy expressed with the Or-BAC formalism. This process uses hierarchy mechanisms to derive concrete rules relevant for each firewall involved in the security architecture. For this purpose, once

---

[1] That is to say a language that is independent from the the target firewall.

the network security policy of a given organization is specified (organization H_LAN in our example), we have simply to specify which entities (roles, activities and views) are relevant in the sub-organizations (firewalls H_fwi and H_fwe in our example).

The derivation process is then able to automatically distribute every permission that each firewall has to manage. More precisely, if there exists a permission that bounds a role R_1 and a "target role" view corresponding to role R_2, and if both roles R_1 and R_2 are relevant in a sub-organization, it means that this permission will be managed by this sub-organization. For example, the permission that bounds the role Private and a target role To_DNS_server is relevant for the internal firewall H_fwi because both roles Private and DNS_Server are relevant in this sub-organization. When a role is relevant in a sub-organization and the target role is relevant in another organization, we cannot distribute the permission on only one organization. So, in this case we conclude that this rule must be managed by both firewalls. For instance, with this mechanism the permission that bounds Private and To_Internet presented in section 3.6 is relevant to the two firewalls and must be duplicated on both of them.

Notice that the derivation process must check that there is no loops in role definitions. That is we construct a graph between roles where an edge from role R_1 to role R_2 means that role R_2 appears in the inclusionRole or exclusionRole elements of R_1 role definition. Then, we have to check that this graph is free of loops else the security policy is rejected by the derivation process.

To generate the security rules in the multi-target firewall language, the derivation process parses abstract security rules specified in the Or-BAC model to unfold role definition, activity definition and view definition.

4.2   From generic rules to specific firewall rules

In order to validate our approach, we have chosen to derive concrete rules for NetFilter[2]. So we have designed XSL transformations to derive NetFilter rules from the multi-target firewall language. Using the same example of permission, the following configuration script for NetFilter shows the rules we obtain when applying the specific XSL transformations for NetFilter:

```
iptables -N Intranet-Web_HTTP-To_Internet
iptables -A FORWARD -s 111.222.2.0/24 -p tcp --dport 80
        -j Intranet-Web_HTTP-To_Internet
iptables -A Intranet-Web_HTTP-To_Internet -s \$Admin -j RETURN
iptables -A Intranet-Web_HTTP-To_Internet -s 111.222.2.1/32 -j RETURN
iptables -A Intranet-Web_HTTP-To_Internet -s 111.222.1.254/32 -j RETURN
```

---

[2]NetFilter is embedded in all Linux kernels upper than 2.4 version.

```
iptables -A Intranet-Web_HTTP-To_Internet -d 111.222.0.0/16 -j RETURN
iptables -A Intranet-Web_HTTP-To_Internet -j ACCEPT
```

The first rule creates a chain called *Intranet-Web_HTTP-To_Internet*. The second rule corresponds to the positive inclusion condition. When a given packet matches this rule, the decision is to jump to the chain *Intranet-Web_HTTP-To_Internet* to check the negative exclusion conditions. If this packet matches a condition in the sub chain, then the decision is to return to the main chain and the next rule in this chain will be checked. Else, if all exclusion conditions expressed in the chain do not match, the packet is accepted. In our example, the first exclusion condition corresponds to the Admin that is excluded from the Private role. The next two conditions exclude the two internal firewall interfaces. The third condition excludes every destination address that does not belong to the H_LAN network. Notice that it is possible to optimize the rule generation to remove the condition on the firewall interface with address 111.222.1.254 because this firewall interface (corresponding to the DMZ interface) is not included in the subnet 111.222.2.0/24.

Notice also that the order of the generated rules does not matter, as for the abstract security rules, except for the last rule in our example (the rule that takes the decision to accept the packet) that must be at the end of the chain. Thanks to the chain mechanism of NetFilter, we can derive rules without ordering exclusion conditions. But for firewall languages that do not provide such mechanism, exclusion conditions will correspond to *deny* rules. These *deny* rules have to be interleaved with *accept* rules to obtain the same result as with NetFilter chains. Ordering the rules has to be done by the XSL transformation process.

5. Comparison with related works

Most of firewall products are supplied with configuration tools with friendly user interfaces. But these tools discard the main problem of managing security. They do not give a way to think and specify an access control policy before deriving firewall configuration rules that enforce this policy. When the security administrator chooses a particular firewall, may be a commercial product like Cisco PIX [Degu and Bastien, 2003] or Checkpoint Firewall-1 [Checkpoint, 2004] or an open source product like FireHOL [Tsaousis, 2004] or Firewall builder [Kurland, 2003], it is quite easy to set filtering rules using the configuration tool included in the offering. There is however a snag: These rules can be inconsistent with each other or/and with the global security policy leading to security holes. Our approach avoids the administrator pondering on access security using filtering rules. The specification of the access control policy is done at a more abstract level and problems like inconsistency are solved before generating the concrete filtering rules [Cuppens and Miège, 2003a].

There are some works coming under the same topic as ours, that is: (1) specifying a network security policy which is not topology-dependent but rather inspire it, (2) specifying a network security policy which is independent from a particular firewall product and (3) generating automatically the configuration rules from the high level network security policy. Hence, firewall management toolkit Firmato [Bartal et al., 1999] uses an entity-relationship model to specify both the access security policy and the network topology and makes use of the concept of *roles* to define network capabilities. In this approach there is some mixing between the net topology – a particular concrete level – and the access security policy to be enforced so that the role concept becomes ambiguous. Indeed, the authors are bounded to introduce the *"group"* concept with an unclear semantics ; sometimes *group* is used to design a set of hosts and sometimes it stands for a role. This can lead to some difficulties to assign network entities to the model entities. In this connection, Firmato's authors use privileges inheritance through hierarchy of groups to derive automatically permissions. They also make use of artifices to avoid permission leakage. Hence, they introduce notions of *"open group"* to authorize inheritance of permissions and *"closed group"* to prohibit it. The reason is the fact that concept of group is not well defined and we claim that this concept is not needed at the access control policy specification level.

Another work whose motivations are close to ours is the RBNS model [Hassan and Hudec, 2003]. Although authors claim that their work is based on the RBAC model [Sandhu et al., 1996], it seems that they keep from this model only the concept of *role*. Indeed, the specification of network entities and role and permission assignments are not rigorous and does not fit any reality. In particular, (1) all RBNS relations are binary even though an access control security goal and its equivalent filtering rule are always a triple (source, service, target). This leads to a loss of information: *permissions* are missing in RBNS model although authors consider the assignment of a service to an IP address as a permission which is semantically weak. (2) Hosts are of two kinds, *client* or *server* and roles are assigned to hosts thanks to the pre-declared type of hosts. This is a wrong assignment as at the abstract level role of a given host is service-dependent. (3) the approach makes an excessive use of the concept of *role*, hence this leads authors to introduce a role-to-role assignments which is a *"limping"* use of a role based access control model as it means assigning a permission package to another permission package.

Using Or-BAC to model network security policy allows security administrator to make a clear separation between network entities and abstract model entities like roles, services, groups of hosts having the same role, hosts concerned by the source host query, and so on. Indeed, Or-BAC gives an accurate semantics to permissions assigned to hosts (roles), services (activities) and hosts targeted by the client host queries (views). Hence, some one is never surprised when he/she checks or analyzes configuration rules of the LAN firewalls as they are derived from well specified access control policy. If a security problem occurs, it is due to a wrong security policy.

6.   Conclusion

We have presented a formal approach to specify network security policies based on the semantics of the Or-BAC model. We suggest an XML syntax to specify an abstract level network security policy independently from the implementation of this policy in a given firewall. Our proposal uses high level concepts such as inheritance hierarchies between organizations, roles, activities and views. We show how to use these inheritance hierarchies to distribute the abstract level network policy specification over several security components. We illustrate this approach by an example of security architecture based on two firewalls. We then design a translation process in XSLT to generate filtering configuration rules of specific firewalls. This approach has been implemented for the NetFilter firewall.

The originality of our proposal is that it provides a clear semantics link between an abstract access control model, namely Or-BAC, and its implementation into specific security components, namely firewalls. Our approach provides a high level of abstraction compared to the final security rules used to configure a firewall. This should simplify management of such security rules and guarantee portability between firewalls.

There are several perspectives to this work. First, we plan to apply our approach to derive security configuration rules of other network security components, in particular other firewall configuration languages (Cisco PIX, CheckPoint Firewall-1, ...) but also Network Intrusion Detection System (for instance Snort). In this later case, we plan to use the content element associated with the message structure suggested in section 3.1 to specify high level IDS signatures. A similar approach may also apply to configure other security components such as access control modules of operating systems or database management systems. Our final objective would be to actually use Or-BAC to specify the global security policy of a given organization, and then using a decomposition mechanism, derive configuration rules of various security components involved in a given security architecture.

Finally, in the case of already configured security components, another application of our approach would be to specify an abstract security policy and then develop mechanisms to check if the concrete security rules are consistent with this abstract security policy. Some proposals for such an approach are already suggested in [Mayer et al., 2000].

Acknowledgement

The work presented in this paper is supported by the ACI DESIRS of the French ministry of Research.

References

Bartal, Y., Mayer, A., Nissim, K., and Wool, A. (1999). Firmato: A novel firewall management toolkit. In *20th IEEE Symposium on Security and Privacy*, pages 17–31, Oakland, California.

Checkpoint (2004). Firewall-1. In http://www.checkpoint.com/.

Cuppens, F., Cuppens-Boulahia, N., and Miège, A. (2004a). Inheritance hierarchies in the Or-BAC Model and application in a network environment. In *Second Foundations of Computer Security Workshop (FCS'04)*, Turku, Finland.

Cuppens, F., Cuppens-Boulahia, N., Sans, T., and Miège, A. (2004b). A Formal Approach to Specify and Deploy a Network Security Policy. In http://www.rennes.enst-bretagne.fr/ fcuppens/articles/fast2004.pdf (full version of the paper presented at FAST 2004).

Cuppens, F. and Miège, A. (2003a). Conflict management in the Or-BAC model.

Cuppens, F. and Miège, A. (2003b). Modelling contexts in the Or-BAC model. In *19th Annual Computer Security Applications Conference*, Las Vegas.

Cuppens, F. and Miège, A. (2004). Administration Model for Or-BAC. *Journal of Computer Systems Science and Engineering (CSSE)*. To appear.

Degu, C. and Bastien, G. (2003). CCP Cisco Secure PIX firewall Advanced Exam Certification Guide.

Hassan, A. and Hudec, L. (2003). Role Based Network Security Model: A Forward Step towards Firewall Management. In *Workshop On Security of Information Technologies*, Algiers.

Kalam, A. A. E., Baida, R. E., Balbiani, P., Benferhat, S., Cuppens, F., Deswarte, Y., Miège, A., Saurel, C., and Trouessin, G. (2003). Organization Based Access Control. In *Proceedings of IEEE 4th International Workshop on Policies for Distributed Systems and Networks (POLICY 2003)*, Lake Come, Italy.

Kurland, V. (2003). Firewall Builder. *White paper*.

Mayer, A., Wool, A., and Ziskind, E. (2000). Fang: A Firewall Analysis Engine. In *21th IEEE Symposium on Security and Privacy*, pages 177–187, Oakland, California.

Russell,   R.   (2002).   Linux   2.4   Packet   Filtering.   In http://www.netfilter.org/documentation/HOWTO//packet-filtering-HOWTO.html.

Sandhu, R., Coyne, E. J., Feinstein, H. L., and Youman, C. E. (1996). Role-Based Access Control Models. *IEEE Computer*, 29(2):38Ű47.

Tsaousis, C. (2004). FireHOL, R5 V1.159. In http://firehol.sourceforge.net/.

W3C (2004). Extensible Markup Language (XML) 1.0 (Third Edition). In http://www.w3.org/TR/REC-xml/.

DISCRETIONARY OVERRIDING OF ACCESS CONTROL IN THE PRIVILEGE CALCULUS

Erik Rissanen
SICS
Box 1263
164 29 KISTA
SWEDEN
mirty@sics.se

Babak Sadighi Firozabadi
SICS
Box 1263
164 29 KISTA
SWEDEN
babak@sics.se

Marek Sergot
Department of Computing
Imperial College London
180 Queen's Gate
London SW7 2BZ
UK
mjs@doc.ic.ac.uk

Abstract   We extend a particular access control framework, the Privilege Calculus, with a possibility to override denied access for increased flexibility in hard to define or unanticipated situations. We require the overrides to be audited and approved by appropriate managers. In order to automatically find the authorities who are able to approve an override, we present an algorithm for authority resolution. We are able to calculate from the access control policy who can approve an override without the need for any additional information.

1.   Introduction

Traditional access control models either permit access or deny it completely. There is an implicit assumption that all access needs are known in advance and that the conditions of those needs can be expressed in machine readable form. There are many reasons why it is difficult to specify the policy completely in advance, and therefore the policy will be incomplete. That will cause a conflict between needs for legitimate access and needs to protect against unauthorised access. We have in a previous position paper Rissanen et al., 2004 categorised access needs as follows:

1 *Anticipated, allowed and machine encodable*: Access situations for which we can say ahead of time that access should be allowed and for which we can express the conditions in machine readable form. Ex. "All employees can read the company newsletter."

2 *Anticipated, denied and machine encodable*: Access situations for which we can say ahead of time that access should be denied and for which we can express the conditions in machine readable form. Ex. "Non-medical personnel may not read patient records."

3 *Anticipated, allowed and not machine encodable*: Access situations for which we can say ahead of time that access should be permitted but we cannot express the conditions in machine readable form. Ex. "In case of an emergency, any doctor may read the patient's records." (We cannot formally define "an emergency".)

4 *Anticipated, denied and not machine encodable*: Access situations for which we can say ahead of time that access should be denied but we cannot express the conditions in machine readable form.

5 *Unanticipated*: Situations that we have forgotten to consider or cannot predict.

What is needed is some kind of flexibility, which will allow for granting of access rights retroactively. We suggest as a solution to distinguish between what a principal *can* do, what it is *permitted* to do, and what it is *forbidden* to do. The intersection of *can* and *not permitted* is what we refer to as *possibility-with-override* or (sometimes) *ability to override*. In our framework which we present here, the presence of a permission for an access means that the access may be performed. The presence of an possibility-with-override, but no permission for an access means the access may not be performed, but can be performed if the user explicitly overrides the denial. If there is neither a permission or a possibility-with-override, the access is not permitted and cannot be done.

In addition to the possibility to override we introduce the notion of authority resolution, which is an automatic procedure that will, given information about an override and an access control policy, find who is in a position to audit and approve the override.

1.1   Related Work

The idea of being able to override denied access is by no means new. Lee Badger Badger, 1990 describes a formalism for integrity constraints that can be recovered after an override. Many commercial applications, for instance for health care, have emergency override in them. There is also more recent work, which is presented below.

Povey, 2000; Povey, 1999 focus is on guaranteeing system integrity by means of transactions that can be rolled back.

Gunnar Stevens and Volker Wolf Stevens and Wulf, 2002 have performed a case study at a steel mill and found practices to grant access rights either before, during or after an access is performed, which is in line with our ideas.

Jaeger et. al. Jaeger et al., 2002 introduce a concept called *access control spaces*. This concept is used primarily for analysing conflicts in access control policy or to analyse whether a set of assigned permissions and constraints on possible assignments completely cover all possible assignments. The relation to our work is that access control spaces, which present a partition of permissions similar to which we use, can be used to eliminate any 'forgotten' access possibilities. However, there is nothing access control spaces can do for those cases where the desired policy cannot be expressed in the given policy language. Jaeger et. al. in fact suggest the use of access override and audit in some cases.

Provisional access control Kudo and Hada, 2000, which is included in XACML OASIS, 2004 in the form of the obligation concept, can be used for instance to specify different access levels and that an access should be logged.

Our main contribution in this paper is the concept of automatic authority resolution, which we have not been able to find any previous work on.

2.   Extending the Privilege Calculus

Here we present a framework for decentralised management of authorisations. It is a modified version of the framework presented in Bandmann et al., 2002; Firozabadi et al., 2001, extended to include possibility-with-override. We have chosen this particular framework since it provides information about the source of authorisations.

We want possibility-with-override to be a part of the access control policy, in contrast to a mechanism outside the policy, since for efficiency of implementation and administration it should be manageable in similar ways as regular permissions.

The goals of the original Privilege Calculus were to decentralise access control management and to differentiate between administrative and access level authorisations. All authorisations are expressed in the form of delegation certificates and removals are done by revoking certificates. Administrative rights contained in the certificates dictate which other certificates are considered valid, as explained below.

The Privilege Calculus is based on the concept of "constrained delegation", which means that an administrative right contains constraints on what it applies to and how it may be delegated further. With these constraints it is possible to divide up the management of access control at a central level in the organisation, without the need to micromanage the details. When we developed the override mechanism, our goal was to use this existing division in the access control policy to automatically send notifications of overrides to the right people in the organisation without the need of any central planning specifically for handling of the override audits.

The following presents the semantics of the calculus in a very brief manner. Due to space constraints, for a more thorough understanding, we refer to the original papers.

2.1　Semantics of the Privilege Calculus

Definition 1..　Let $PRIN$ be the set of principals in the system. Further let $\preceq$ denote a *subsumes* relation over $PRIN$ as follows:

- $p \preceq p$ if p is an atomic principal and $p \in PRIN$.

- $p \prec P$ if $p \in P$ and $P \subseteq PRIN$;

- $P_1 \preceq P_2$ if $P_2 \subseteq PRIN$, and $P_1 \subseteq P_2$.

Informally the relation $\preceq$ is used for comparing group membership of principals. We assume the existence of the relation, but leave its definition and management outside the scope of this paper. We have chosen to not include groups of objects and actions in order to be brief.

Definition 2..　Let I denote a time interval of type $[t_1, t_2]$, where $t_1, t_2 \in \mathbf{R}$. We define a *subsumes* relation between two time intervals as follows:

- $t_i \preceq [t_1, t_2]$ if $t_1 \leq t_i$ and $t_i \leq t_2$;

- $[t_1, t_2] \preceq [t_3, t_4]$ if $t_3 \leq t_1$ and $t_2 \leq t_4$.

Definition 3..　Let $PRIN$, ACT, and OBJ be (disjoint, non-empty) sets of agents, actions, and objects, respectively. We define the set of privileges Φ inductively as follows:

- $perm(s, a, o) : I \in \Phi$, if $s \preceq PRIN$, $a \in ACT$, and $o \in OBJ$;

- $can(s, a, o) : I \in \Phi$, if $s \preceq PRIN$, $a \in ACT$, and $o \in OBJ$;

- $auth(s, \phi) : I \in \Phi$, if $s \preceq PRIN$, and $\phi \in \Phi$;

- $auth^*(s, \phi) : I \in \Phi$, if $s \preceq PRIN$, and $\phi \in \Phi$.

I represents the time interval for which a privilege is valid. Privileges of the form $perm(s, a, o) : I$ denote access-level permissions. Privileges of the form $can(s, a, o) : I$ denote access-level possibilities-with-override. Privileges of the form $auth(s, \phi) : I$ and $auth^*(s, \phi) : I$ denote management-level authorities, that is, the right to create the privilege ϕ. The difference between $auth$ and $auth^*$ is explained below.

We call s in the above expressions the *subject* of the privilege.

Please note that the privilege expressions themselves do not grant any access rights. Instead they are placed inside authorisation certificates and the validity of the certificates are calculated based on what management-level authorisations are present. Thus, the semantics of these expressions are defined by the following definitions in combination.

Definition 4.. We define the set of declaration certificates Σ^+ and the set of revocation certificates Σ^- as:

- $declares(s, \phi, t, id) \in \Sigma^+$, if $s \in PRIN$, $\phi \in \Phi$, $t \in \mathbf{R}$, and $id \in \mathbf{N}$, where $\mathbf{R}$ denotes the real numbers, and $\mathbf{N}$ denotes the natural numbers;

- $revokes(s, id, t) \in \Sigma^-$, if $s \in PRIN$, $id \in \mathbf{N}$, and $t \in \mathbf{R}$.

Note that declarations and revocations can only be performed by atomic principals and not by groups of principals.

Informally an element $declares(s, \phi, t, id) \in \Sigma^+$ means that s claims at time t that ϕ is true. The definitions below define when such a declaration is considered to be valid.

Definition 5.. We define a comparison relation denoted by $\sqsubseteq$ between two privileges as follows:

$\phi \sqsubseteq \psi$ if:

1   $\phi = perm(s_1, a, o) : I_1$, $\psi = perm(s_2, a, o) : I_2$, $s_1 \preceq s_2$ and $I_1 \preceq I_2$;

2   $\phi = can(s_1, a, o) : I_1$, $\psi = perm(s_2, a, o) : I_2$, $s_1 \preceq s_2$ and $I_1 \preceq I_2$;

3   $\phi = can(s_1, a, o) : I_1$, $\psi = can(s_2, a, o) : I_2$, $s_1 \preceq s_2$ and $I_1 \preceq I_2$;

4   $\phi = auth(s_1, \alpha) : I_1$, $\psi = auth(s_2, \beta) : I_2$, $\alpha \sqsubseteq \beta$, $s_1 \preceq s_2$ and $I_1 \preceq I_2$;

5   $\phi = auth(s_1, \alpha) : I_1$, $\psi = auth^*(s_2, \beta) : I_2$, $\alpha \sqsubseteq \beta$, $s_1 \preceq s_2$ and $I_1 \preceq I_2$;

6 $\phi = auth^*(s_1, \alpha) : I_1$, $\psi = auth^*(s_2, \beta) : I_2$, $\alpha \sqsubseteq \beta$, $s_1 \preceq s_2$ and $I_1 \preceq I_2$;

7 $\psi = auth^*(s_1, \beta) : I_2$, $\phi \sqsubseteq \beta$

8 $\phi = auth(s_1, \alpha) : I_1$, $\psi = auth^*(s_2, \beta) : I_2$ if $s_1 \preceq s_2$, $\alpha \sqsubseteq auth^*(s_2, \beta) : I_2$, and $I_1 \preceq I_2$;

9 $\phi = auth^*(s_1, \alpha) : I_1$, $\psi = auth^*(s_2, \beta) : I_2$, if $s_1 \preceq s_2$, $\alpha \sqsubseteq auth^*(s_2, \beta) : I_2$, and $I_1 \preceq I_2$.

These comparisons are used below to make sure that administrators do not exceed their authorisations when delegating. We can see in 2 that a permission implies a possibility-with-override, that is, if an administrator can create a permission, he will also be able to create the weaker privilege of possibility-with-override for the same object and action.

The $auth^*()$ construct needs some explanation. It is used to give flexibility for administrators. The authorisation
$auth(p, auth(G, perm(G, o, a) : I_1) : I_2) : I_3$ means that we permit p to appoint an administrator from within the group G, who then in turn can create access permissions for object o and action a for principals within group G. Let us call this administrator g. p will be limited in that he must appoint an administrator from G and will not be able to issue the access level permission himself. Also, p cannot create more than one immediate administrator, that is p will hand the right to g, who in turn will create the permission to access o. If we instead create the authorisation $auth(p, auth^*(G, perm(G, o, a) : I_1) : I_2) : I_3$, we will give additional possibilities to p. p will be able to create the access level permission directly if he chooses to do so, as given by rule 7. He can appoint an administrator g as previously, as given by rule 8. He can also permit g to delegate the authority in several steps by appointing intermediary managers chosen from G. This allows p to let subordinates organise their own sub-organisations within G. For instance we could have p delegate to g who will delegate to g' who will in turn create the access level permission. The use of the $auth^*()$ construct is explained in more detail in Bandmann et al., 2002.

Definition 6.. We define a certificate database to be a tuple $\mathcal{D} = (\mathbf{SoA}, \mathbf{D}^+, \mathbf{D}^-)$, where $\mathbf{SoA} \subset \Phi$ is a finite set of *Source of Authority* privileges, $\mathbf{D}^+ \subset \Sigma^+$ is a finite set of declaration certificates and $\mathbf{D}^- \subset \Sigma^-$ is a finite set of revocation certificates. It is the combined contents of this certificate database that will decide which accesses are permitted.

We adopt the following constraints on a certificate database.

1 If $declares(s_1, \phi_1, t_1, id) \in \mathbf{D}^+$, and $declares(s_2, \phi_2, t_2, id) \in \mathbf{D}^+$, then $s_1 = s_2$, $\phi_1 = \phi_2$, and $t_1 = t_2$. This says that $\mathbf{D}^+$ cannot contain two different certificates with the same id.

2 If $declares(s_1, \phi, t_1, id) \in \mathbf{D}^+$ and $revokes(s_2, id, t_2) \in \mathbf{D}^-$, then $s_1 = s_2$ and $t_1 \leq t_2$. This says that a certificate can be revoked only by its issuer and not before it is declared. In fact, the first restriction can be relaxed but this introduces the need for extra components which are omitted here for simplicity.

3 If $revokes(s_1, id, t_1) \in \mathbf{D}^-$ and $revokes(s_2, id, t_2) \in \mathbf{D}^-$, then $s_1 = s_2$ and $t_1 = t_2$. This says that there cannot be two revocations of the same declaration certificate in the same database. We adopt this restriction to simplify the database in order to streamline the theory.

Definition 7.. Let $\vdash$ be the *validates relation* between a privilege and a declaration certificate, where

- $auth(s_2, \phi_2) : I \vdash declares(s_1, \phi_1, t, id)$, if $s_1 \preceq s_2$, $\phi_1 \sqsubseteq \phi_2$ and $t \preceq I$;

and,

- $\Gamma \vdash d$, if $\Gamma \subseteq \Phi$, and $\exists q \in \Gamma$ such that $q \vdash d$.

Informally this defines the semantics of the administrative permission $auth()$, that is, it makes us consider certain declarations to be valid. Also notice that the $auth^*()$ form does not validate a declaration. $auth^*()$ is only used inside an $auth()$ expression. We will use the validates relation below to recursively define which permissions are valid.

Definition 8.. We define the set of *effective* declaration certificates $\mathbf{E}_\mathcal{D}(t) \subseteq \mathbf{D}^+$ of a database $\mathcal{D}$ at a certain time t, as:

$$\mathbf{E}_\mathcal{D}(t) = \{declares(s, p : I, t_1, id) \in \mathbf{D}^+ \mid t \preceq I \wedge$$
$$revokes(s, id, t_2) \in \mathbf{D}^- \rightarrow t_2 > t\}.$$

Informally, we define that the interval I defines when the authorisation is usable.

Definition 9.. Let $d_1, d_2 \in \mathbf{D}^+$, where $d_1 = declares(s_1, \phi_1, t_1, id_1)$ and $d_2 = declares(s_2, \phi_2, t_2, id_2)$. We define the *supports* relation $S_\mathcal{D}$ as follows:

$$d_1 \ S_\mathcal{D} \ d_2 \text{ if } d_1 \in \mathbf{E}_\mathcal{D}(t_2), \ \phi_1 \vdash d_2 \text{ and } t_1 < t_2.$$

Informally, we define that a declaration depends on another previous declaration to be valid.

We have modified this definition compared with the presentation in Firoz-abadi et al., 2001 in that we have added the condition $t_1 < t_2$ to prevent cycles in the support relation. Cycles are not possible in Firozabadi et al., 2001, but together with the *auth** form from Bandmann et al., 2002 cycles become possible unless prevented with this extra constraint. Although cycles are not a problem in principle, the authority resolution algorithm later on becomes more complicated to explain for a cyclic graph, so we make this simplification.

Definition 10.. The set of certificate chains C_D in a certificate database D is the transitive closure of S_D.

Definition 11.. We define the set of true privilege statements at a time-point t, in our calculus, by defining function $h_D : \mathbf{R} \to 2^{\Phi}$ as:

$$h_D(t) = \{p \mid p\!:\!I \in \Phi \wedge$$
$$(p\!:\!I \in \mathbf{SoA} \vee$$
$$(d_1, declares(s, p\!:\!I, t_2, id)) \in \mathbf{C}_D \wedge declares(s, p\!:\!I, t_2, id) \in \mathbf{E}_D(t) \wedge$$
$$\mathbf{SoA} \vdash d_1)\}.$$

We also say that a privilege p *holds* at time-point t when $p \in h_D(t)$.

Informally, this means that although anybody can make a privilege statement in the form of a declaration certificate, we will not accept the statements as true unless they can be traced back to the SoA.

2.2 Access Requests

When we receive an access request, which is a tuple in the form of (u, o, a, t), where u is a principal, o an object, a an action and t is the time of access, we search among $h_D(t)$ for a $perm(s, o, a)\!:\!I$ such that $u \preceq s$ and $t \preceq I$. If there is such a permission, then the response is "yes". In case there is no permission, we search for a $can(s, o, a)\!:\!I$ such that $u \preceq s$ and $t \preceq I$. If there is such an ability then the response is 'requires override'. In that case the user would be presented with the option to override the denied access and the application will log the access if the users chooses to override. If there is neither a matching permission nor a possibility-with-override, the response is 'access denied'.

3. Approval mechanism and authority resolution

When a user performs an override to make an access, the override is logged, and a message is sent to an appropriate authority for approval. In a large organisation it may not be possible to have a single person or unit which is able to comprehend or have authority over the whole organisation. We therefore need to decentralise the responsibility of audit and approval of overrides. We call the search for an appropriate authority for a given override *authority resolution*.

3.1   Approval Mechanism Properties

In our earlier paper we identified two properties for an authority resolution mechanism. The mechanism should be:

- *Safe:* Only legitimate authorities should be notified.

- *Unobtrusive:* Among the legitimate authorities, we should notify those who are most likely to understand the override and least likely to be bothered unnecessarily.

The first property is critical, but it is easily defined, as we will show below. The second property is not critical if we define the approval mechanism appropriately and all legitimate authorities are potentially consulted. In that case the ordering is thus somewhat arbitrary.

Since an approval of an override is in effect a retroactive granting of a permission, the authorities who should be able to approve an override are precisely those who can create a permission for the access that was overridden. In this framework they correspond to the subjects of effective certificates who have a valid support chain from the SoA such that their certificates support the creation of a permission for the access at the time of the override. So, for an access override (u, o, a, t) that is approved at time t', they are all authorisations from $h_D(t') \cap E_D(t')$ of the form $auth(s_1, perm(s_2, o, a) : I_2) : I_1)$ such that $u \preceq s_2$, $t \preceq I_2$ and $t' \preceq I_1$. In this case s_1 would be a legitimate authority.

Since it is possible that there are multiple legitimate authorities for approving a given override, we would like to contact them in such an order that we are least likely to bother many authorities.

We note that the access control framework we are using does not contain negative permissions. We do not wish to introduce negative permissions just because of the override approval mechanism. Since we view an approval as a retroactive granting of a permission, in case some authorities approve and some disapprove, the approvals should have precedence. If all of them disapprove (or do not care), we view the override as disapproved. With these semantics we can define an approval mechanism in which the order of authorities notified does not affect the result.

For ordering the authorities we note that the person who created the possibility-with-override that made an override possible is a prime candidate to be notified first, as long as he is a legitimate authority. The rationale is that whoever made the override possible is best placed to judge whether to approve the override. The source of authority of a resource is always a legitimate authority, but we want to keep him last in the notification list since he is the highest authority. For authorities between the SoA and the lowest level administrators, we can use the order of their appearance in the chain as a heuristic. In case of parallel chains we can use an arbitrary ordering or notification in parallel.

3.2   An Algorithm for Authority Resolution

Here we present a simple algorithm that is based on the above discussion. Input to the algorithm is a performed override and a certificate database.

The algorithm consists of two parts. In the first part we create a reduced graph from the delegation database. Let G_d be the graph that describes the delegation database by letting there be a node in G_d for each certificate and an edge between nodes that correspond to certificates between which there is a direct support relation. G_d is directed and acyclic. It is acyclic because of the condition on the time stamps in definition 9 of the access control framework.

Now form the reduced graph G_r by letting there be a node in G_r for each certificate from $h_D(t) \cap E_D(t)$ which authorises approval of the given override (as explained earlier). Let there be an edge in G_r between two nodes if there is a path between the corresponding nodes in G_d. The motivation behind this is that we want to remove all certificates that do not empower approval (to satisfy the safety property of the authority resolution), but still keep as much of the structure of decentralisation as possible (to be able to satisfy the unobtrusiveness property).

G_r can be calculated by performing a depth first search on G_d starting only from the nodes that will be in G_r. When doing the search we need to keep in each node, n, a lists of nodes, which will be filled with a list of all nodes of G_r which can be reached from n. Once the search is complete, these lists will give the edges of G_r.

In the second part of the algorithm we order the authorities by means of a modified breadth first search on G_r from the bottom going up.

```
1     R ← empty list of sets of principal names
2     for each node n of G_r
3         n.counter ← number of children of n
4     S ← the set nodes for which counter = 0
5     do while S is not empty
6         add the set of subjects of all nodes in S to R
7         Q ← S
8         S ← ∅
9         for each q in Q
10            for each parent p of q
11                reduce p.counter with one
12                if p.counter is zero
13                    add p to S
```

Table 1 lists some sample certificates. Figure 1 shows the support relations among those certificates and illustrates the first part of the algorithm.

Id	Issuer	Authorisation
1	r	$auth(b, auth^*(G, perm(G, o, a)))$
2	b	$auth(c, auth(G, perm(G, o, a)))$
3	c	$auth(d, perm(G, o, a))$
4	d	$can(e, o, a)$
5	b	$auth(f, auth^*(G, perm(G, o, a)))$
6	f	$auth(g, auth^*(G, perm(G, o, a)))$
7	g	$auth(h, auth^*(G, perm(G, o, a)))$
8	f	$auth(h, auth^*(G, perm(G, o, a)))$
9	h	$auth(i, perm(G, o, a))$
10	i	$can(e, o, a)$

Table 1 Example delegation certificates. For brevity we have not included the time intervals. The validity intervals of all the authorisations are [1,100] and all of the certificates are issued at the time point equal to the id of the certificate.

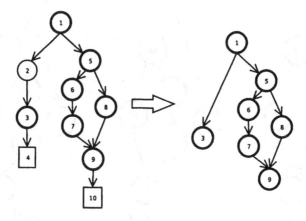

Figure 1.   Example of the graph reduction step in the authority resolution algorithm. The graph on the left shows the support relations between the certificates in table 1. Circles represent certificates that grant administrative authorisations. The rectangles represent certificates that grant abilities. Thick circles are certificates that grant authority to issue a permission. The graph to the right shows the reduced graph. Certificate 2 does not support direct granting of access rights. Certificates 4 and 10 do not represent administrative permissions. The remaining certificates all permit the granting of access permissions, thus approval.

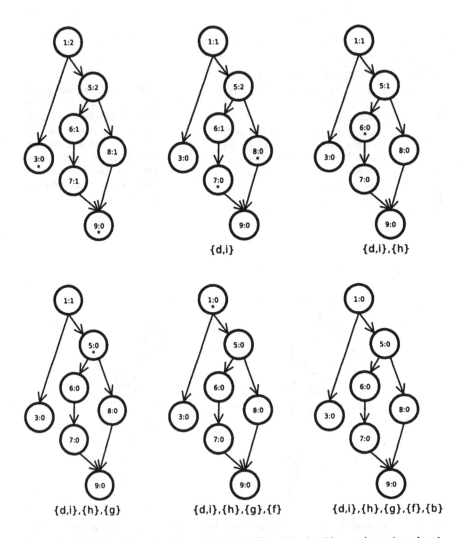

Figure 2. Example of the authority resolution algorithm. The algorithm works on the reduced graph from figure 2. Each figure presents the state of the algorithm at each iteration of line 5. The asterisks represent the set S. The numbers after the colons inside the nodes are the counters. The lists below the graphs are the accumulated result lists of the algorithm. The final list is the output of the algorithm. In this case we should notify the users d and i first, and if neither approve, notify h, g, f, and b in that order. If none of them approves, the override is considered unauthorised.

Figure 2 illustrates the second part of the algorithm.

The result is an ordered list of sets of authorities to notify. We would send the notification to all authorities in the first set. As a special case we could divide this set into those who have issued a relevant possibility-with-override, and notify them before the others.

In case someone approves the override we do not notify anyone else and the override is considered to be approved. In case all notified authorities either disapprove or take no action, we would notify the next set of authorities from the list, and so on. If anyone approves, the override is considered to be approved. If in the end no one has approved the override, we view the override as disapproved, and the relevant authorities can take some kind of sanctioning action. We leave the coordination of the sanctioning outside the scope of this paper. We can see that the order in which authorities are notified does not affect the end result.

Properties of the Algorithm.   To see that the algorithm terminates, we note that because a counter is reduced just before it is tested at line 12, a node can be included in S only once. Because of line 8, S will be cleared in every iteration of the loop. Since the number of nodes is finite, eventually there will be no more nodes which can be included in S at line 13, and the loop at line 5 will terminate.

Define the *upper height* of a node N as the length of the longest path originating from N. We can prove by induction on the upper height that every node of the graph will be included in S.

Theorem:.   A node with upper length n will be included in S.

Proof: Any node with upper height 0 will be included in S in lines 1-4. Thus the theorem is true for $n = 0$.

Now, assume that the theorem is true for $n = k$. If a node N has upper height $k + 1$, then all its children must have upper height k or less. By our assumption, all those children will be included in S before the algorithm terminates. Then, because of lines 9-13, the counter of N will reach zero and N will be included as well. Thus we have proved that a node with upper height $k + 1$ will be included in S, and by induction it follows that any node with upper height of 0 or more will be included in S. ∎

Since every subject of the nodes of the graph will be included in the result, all possible authorities will be included in the result.

We choose to not formalise the order in which the notifications are generated, but just note that since we start from the bottom, lower level managers will be notified before higher level managers.

4. Conclusion and Further Work

In many cases it is not possible to define the security policy completely in a machine readable form and we may not anticipate all needs. The incompleteness of the policy will lead to a conflict between need to protect against unauthorised access and the need for legitimate access. In case availability is important, a solution may be to allow users to override access denials and then have managers audit the override. Authority resolution is a mechanism for improving the efficiency of this audit. We have shown that it is possible to use only existing information in the Privilege Calculus framework to implement authority resolution.

What we present is early work and many issues remain. Of main interest is to perform a study of the usefulness of the approach.

Another area is to improve on the work-flow of the mechanism, which right now is not as good as we wish in the case of disapproval of override. By using an access control framework with negative permissions or additional information, different mechanisms for propagation of notifications may be possible.

We are also interested in applying our ideas to other access control frameworks such as XACML.

References

Badger, Lee (1990). Providing a flexible security override for trusted systems. In *Computer Security Foundations Workshop III, 1990. Proceedings*, pages 115–121.

Bandmann, Olav, Dam, Mads, and Firozabadi, B. Sadighi (2002). Constrained Delegations. In *proceedings of 2002 IEEE Symposium on Security and Privacy*.

Firozabadi, B. Sadighi, Sergot, M., and Bandmann, O. (2001). Using Authority Certificates to Create Management Structures. In *Proceedings of Security Protocols, 9th International Workshop, Cambridge, UK*, pages 134–145. Springer Verlag.

Jaeger, Trent, Edwards, Antony, and Zhang, Xiaolan (2002). Managing access control policies using access control spaces. In *Proceedings of the seventh ACM symposium on Access control models and technologies*, pages 3–12. ACM Press.

Kudo, Michiharu and Hada, Satoshi (2000). Xml document security based on provisional authorization. In *Proceedings of the 7th ACM conference on Computer and communications security*, pages 87–96. ACM Press.

OASIS (2004). http://www.oasis-open.org/committees/tc_home.php?wg_abbrev=xacml.

Povey, Dean (1999). Enforcing well-formed and partially formed transactions for UNIX. In *Proceedings of the 8th USENIX Security Symposium*, pages 47–62.

Povey, Dean (2000). Optimistic security: a new access control paradigm. In *Proceedings of the 1999 workshop on New security paradigms*, pages 40–45. ACM Press.

Rissanen, Erik, Firozabadi, Babak Sadighi, and Sergot, Marek (2004). Towards a mechanism for discretionary overriding of access control, position paper. Presented at Security Protocols, 12th International Workshop, Cambridge, UK.

Stevens, Gunnar and Wulf, Volker (2002). A new dimension in access control: studying maintenance engineering across organizational boundaries. In *Proceedings of the 2002 ACM conference on Computer supported cooperative work*, pages 196–205. ACM Press.

A FORMAL MODEL FOR PARAMETERIZED ROLE-BASED ACCESS CONTROL

Ali E. Abdallah and Etienne J. Khayat
Research Institute for Computing,
London South Bank University,
103 Borough Road,
London SE1 0AA, U.K.
{ A.Abdallah@lsbu.ac.uk, E.Khayat@lsbu.ac.uk }

Abstract   Role-Based Access Control (RBAC) usually enables a higher level view of authorization. In this model, access permissions are assigned to roles and, in turn, roles are allocated to subjects. The usefulness of the RBAC model is well documented. It includes simplicity, consistency, scalability and ease of manageability. In practice, however, only limited versions of RBAC seem to have been successfully implemented, notably in applications such as databases and operating systems. The problem stems from the fact that most applications require a finer degree of authorization than what core RBAC models are able to provide. In theory, current RBAC models can be adapted to capture fine grained authorizations by dramatically increasing the number of distinct roles in these models. However, this solution comes at an unacceptably high cost of allocating low level privileges which eliminates the major benefits gained from having a high level RBAC model.

This paper presents a methodology for refining abstract RBAC models into new Parameterized RBAC models which provide finer grain of authorizations. The semantics of the Parameterized RBAC model is given as a state-based core RBAC model expressed in the formal specification notation Z. By systematically applying this methodology the scope of applications of RBAC is substantially extended and the major benefits of having the core model are maintained.

1.   Introduction

RBAC is an access control mechanism based on the rationale that access rights are assigned to roles, rather than to the subjects that perform these roles [1–5]. This approach is attractive for concisely describing authorization, particularly within organizations, because responsibilities are often assigned to employees (subjects) based on their duties (roles). RBAC is also very useful when it is adapted to fit the organizational structure of an institution because it bridges the gap between its functional requirements and the technical authorization aspects of its security policy. Hence, offering a high level view of authorization and its operational management. However, few examples can be found where only limited versions of RBAC are applied, namely in databases and in operating systems such as Solaris [7, 8]. The reason for this is that the direct application of abstract RBAC requires significant expressive power to cater for access requirements in large organizations. For instance, the way permissions are currently described in RBAC suggest that every role has a unique set of permissions, which are assigned to its associated subjects or principals. With this, two different subjects, occupying exactly the same role, will have identical permissions. This might not be desirable because every subject exercises its permissions in the context of its own duties [9]. This type of definition makes a successful direct application of RBAC requiring large amount of work to express access rights. Its success might be more related to the advanced techniques provided by the implemented application, such as the "views" in databases [6], rather than the features of the adopted RBAC. To clearly illustrate the lack of expressiveness in a direct application of RBAC, consider the case of online banking. In this case, the clients are the *subjects* and the bank accounts are the *objects*, and the role to describe the clients who have bank accounts is referred to as *Account_Holder*. Although this role applies to all bank clients, which can reach hundreds of thousands, the access permissions associated with every client (subject) occupying this role should be different. When using the online banking service, every client can only access its own account details, and not those of other clients occupying the role *Account_Holder*. It is possible to express the permissions for such clients by directly applying RBAC, but only at a considerable cost:

Firstly, although roles such as *Account_Holder* are defined as a single role, their implementation suggests their instantiation into a large number of roles to cater for every client, which presents a huge burden on the intellectual manageability of access rights.

Secondly, the direct implementation of RBAC reduces the scalability of the mechanism in large organisations because instances of role have to be treated as different roles instead of being grouped under a single definition.

Thirdly, the consistency of the distribution of access rights is affected because similar roles will have to be treated differently and managed separately.

These advantages, generally associated with RBAC models, can be maintained if this case study is modelled as a parameterized RBAC. In this model, core RBAC components, such as roles, would depend on values of a parameter. To extend RBAC into a parameterized model, data about the values of the parameters should be provided. New permissions that might be created due to the parameterization should also be identified. Hence, the construction of the

Parameterised RBAC (*PRBAC*) results from the combination of the new components as follows:

$$RBAC + Parameters\ Data + New\ Parameterized\ Permissions \implies PRBAC \quad (1)$$

When the direct implementation of the core RBAC results in many drawbacks, the Parameterised RBAC achieves the same effect and avoids these drawbacks. Reconsidering the online banking example, the role *Account_Holder* can be generalised to a parameterized role (*Account_Holder, m*), where *m* is an account number. This role can later be instantiated to each account to give the appropriate instances of the permissions. Following this, there will be a single general parameterized definition for a role. This parameterization can be repeated to support further levels of granularity by including additional parameters such as bank branch. In this case, a role would be defined as ((*Account_Holder, m*), m_1), where m_1 is the bank branch number. This series of "nested" parameters can be related in a hierarchy that depends on the type of the used parameters and the way the parameterization is performed. This hierarchy is not to be confused with the role hierarchy such as job positions in organisation.

In this paper, we present a rigorous formal model for a parameterized RBAC [4], in the Z notation [12–14]. We refer to it as *PFRBAC* because it is derived from an extension of *FRBAC*, a flat RBAC presented in a previous work by the authors of this paper [5]. Being formal, *PFRBAC* presents a clear and mathematically concise way for the implementation of *FRBAC*. It is detailed in its modelling of the components and features of a Parameterised RBAC and complete in its presentation of the necessary semantics. With its type of a general parameterized definition of RBAC components, this model enables a good and comprehensive intellectual manageability of access rights and provides a consistency in their distribution. The support of a hierarchy of parameters helps to achieve an extremely fine granularity in access control, which is difficult to achieve in a non-parameterized RBAC.

The remainder of this paper is structured as follows. Section 2 provides a brief overview of related work on Parameterised RBAC. The parameterized model is constructed in Section 3. This section details the derivation of the parameterized concepts from the core ones. It presents the formal state based description of the model in Z and shows the process of building a nested parameterized model from an hierarchy of parameters. Section 4 presents a discussion of the effect of the choice of the parameterized concepts on the expressiveness of the model and Section 5 concludes the paper.

2.   Related Work

There has been few attempts to model the Parameterised RBAC in the contexts of many works [9, 11, 15]. One of these attempts included a very useful definition of the parameterized role [11]. This definition was general and very expressive, however, the rest of this work did not reflect its usefulness because it was restricted in terms of the presented semantics and did not expand in a way that enables a useful way of implementing the Parameterised RBAC. This attempt did not also present full formal semantics of a parameterized RBAC which treat all its features and concepts, such as the parameterized roles, permissions and objects. The relation between the RBAC concepts in this attempt and the ones in the widely known RBAC models such as [1–5] is not explicit.

Another parameterization of the definition of *role* was presented in [15]. This work aimed to suit the problem of controlling access to the contents of objects in RBAC and focused on databases as its area of application. Although this might be useful in the mentioned applications (databases), it drifts from the concepts of RBAC models such as the RBAC standard [4], *RBAC96* [1] and *FRBAC* [5] which consider the object as the primitive unit that can be assigned access rights and do not model its content. The focus of the parameterized RBAC to solve a particular problem has undermined the generality of the approach because of its limited applicability to cases outside the presented scope. Another definition of *role* as *a series of policy statement and constraints* has been proposed when constructing another solution-specific version of a parameterized RBAC [9]. The data type definition for roles has been substituted for role classes in order to be instantiated. Because of these changes in the concepts, it was difficult see how the commonly known RBAC models, such as the ones in [1, 4, 5], would fit in this work.

All these attempts did not present a methodology to guide into the parameterization of RBAC. The parameterized RBAC concepts have been defined without specifically mentioning their original RBAC definitions. This makes it difficult for implementers to derive a Parameterised RBAC from an existing RBAC model because the parameterization would need a significant amount of work. It also undermines the advantages of scalability, consistency and ease of manageability that a Parameterised RBAC offers.

3.   Model for the Parameterized RBAC

The parameterized RBAC model presented in this paper is based on an extension of *FRBAC* [5]. It supports the commonly known RBAC adopted concepts and definitions [1–5], and the results of this paper equally apply to the core model in the RBAC standard [4]. This section presents the methodology to construct a parameterized RBAC from *FRBAC* and a supply of data about parameters and of newly created permissions (according to (1)). One important property of this approach is that the parameterization can be done several times and successively in order to obtain very fine grained access control. It turns out that this property of nesting is directly associated with the hierarchy of data representing the parameters.

3.1 The Flat RBAC

The components of a flat RBAC model are derived from the following entities: ROLE, OBJECT, SUBJECT, PRINCIPAL, OPERATION, TASK, PERMISSION, which are respectively the sets (or data types) for all roles, objects, subjects, principals, operations, tasks and permissions. The sets of components of an implemented RBAC model are referred to as: *Roles, Objects, Subjects, Principals, Operations, Tasks* and *Permissions*. For instance, *Roles* is the set of roles that are defined in the organisation implementing RBAC. The same analogy applies to the other components. *FRBAC* is summarised in the following schema [5].

Referring back to the online banking example. *Subjects* would be the clients and the employees of the bank, and *Principals* would the set of their associated usernames. We consider four roles in this example:
Account_Holder, Manager, Clerk, System_Administrator. To illustrate the initialisation of an RBAC model for the case of the online banking application, we use this following toy example. We assume that the sets of all accounts and pin numbers are referred to respectively as *Accounts*, and *Pins*. The " $'$ " sign is a convention for the initialisation of the components in the Z notation [14].

$$
\begin{array}{l}
\underline{\quad FRBAC \quad} \\
\quad Roles : \mathbb{P}\, ROLE \\
\quad Principals : \mathbb{P}\, PRINCIPAL \\
\quad RoleAllocation : PRINCIPAL \rightarrow \mathbb{P}\, ROLE \\
\quad Subjects : \mathbb{P}\, SUBJECT \\
\quad SubjectAssociation : SUBJECT \rightarrow \mathbb{P}\, PRINCIPAL \\
\quad SubjectRole : SUBJECT \rightarrow \mathbb{P}\, ROLE \\
\quad Objects : \mathbb{P}\, OBJECT \\
\quad Operations : \mathbb{P}\, OPERATION \\
\quad Tasks : \mathbb{P}(OPERATION \times \mathbb{P}\, OBJECT) \\
\quad Permissions : ROLE \rightarrow \mathbb{P}\, TASK \\
\hline
\quad \mathrm{dom}\, RoleAllocation = Principals \\
\quad \mathrm{ran}\, RoleAllocation \subseteq Roles \\
\quad \mathrm{dom}\, SubjectAssociation = Subjects \\
\quad \mathrm{ran}\, SubjectAssociation \subseteq Principals \\
\quad \mathrm{dom}\, SubjectRole = Subjects \\
\quad \mathrm{ran}\, SubjectRole \subseteq Roles \\
\quad \mathrm{dom}\, Permissions = Roles \\
\quad \bigcup \mathrm{ran}\, Permissions \subseteq Tasks
\end{array}
$$

Initialisation of an Example State:

Roles' =	{Account_Holder, Manager, Clerk, System_Administrator}
Principals' =	{c_1, c_2, c_3, c_4, john_1, ema_1, ema_2, denise_1}
RoleAllocation' =	{(c_1, {Account_Holder}), (c_2, {Account_Holder}), (c_3, {Account_Holder}),
	(c_4, {Account_Holder}), (john_1, {Clerk}), (ema_1, {Manager}),
	(ema_2, {Manager, Clerk}), (denise_1, {System_Administrator}) }
Subjects' =	{Anne Roling, Mike Lowe, John Brown, Ema Thomas, Denise Logan}
SubjectAssociation' =	{(Anne Roling, {c_1}),(Mike Lowe, {c_2}),(John Brown,{john_1, c_3}),
	(Ema Thomas, {ema_1, ema_2}), (Denise Logan, {denise_1, c_4})}
SubjectRole' =	{(Anne Roling, {Account_Holder}), (John Brown, {Clerk, Account_Holder}),
	(Ema Thomas, {Manager, Clerk}),(Mike Lowe, {Account_Holder}),
	(Denise Logan, {System_Administrator, Account_Holder})}
Objects' =	{ Accountnumbers: P(N), Accounts: N $\rightarrow$ Account, Pins: N $\rightarrow$ Pin }
Operations' =	{ Create, Deposit, Withdraw, View, Transfer, Assign, Backup}
Tasks' =	{ (Create(n:N, a: Account, p:Pin), {Accountnumbers, Accounts, Pins}),
	(Deposit(k:N, n:N),{Accounts}, (Withdraw(k:N, n:N), {Accounts}),
	(View(n:N),{Accounts}), (Transfer(k:N, n_1, n_2:N), {Accounts}),
	(Assign(n:N), {Pins}), (Backup, {Accountnumbers, Accounts, Pins}) }
Permissions' =	{(Manager, {Create, Deposit, Withdraw, View, Transfer, Assign}),
	(Clerk, {View, Deposit, Withdraw}), (Account_Holder, {}),
	(System_Administrator, {Backup}) }

3.2   Construction of the Parameterized Model

Parameterizations.   By associating privileges with roles instead of principals, RBAC offers a scalable means for expressing access control. The size of the privilege table grows proportionally to the number of roles (which is usually small) as opposed to the number of principals (which can be very large indeed). However, in practice, most real applications require a finer grain of access control. As we have seen in the previous example of a pure RBAC model of a Bank , we were able to fully specify access control for some roles such as Manager and Clerk but not for other roles such as Account_Holder. The privileges of two different customers holding the Account_Holder role are not identical. Hence, new information needs to be added to the model to correctly capture the appropriate privileges for this role. To overcome this limitation, we propose parameterizations of the RBAC model. The effect of parameterizations is usually to enlarge the size of one of the components of the pure RBAC model, that is *roles, objects,* or *tasks*. This aim is achieved by the addition of parameters to values in one of the RBAC components or their attributes, i.e. *roles*. Hence, in the refined parameterized RBAC model of a Bank, the Account_Holder role will no longer exist! It will be replaced by several instances of Account_Holder(m) where m is a parameter (variable) drawn from an appropriate set of values.

Choice of Parameters.   The choice of parameter and the set of values from which it can be instantiated is application dependent. The overriding objective is to be able to adequately and fully capture the privileges of each role in the refined model. In theory, the values from which a parameter can be instantiated is just a set of abstract labels and does't have to have any meaning! The purpose is to refine a single entity (such as a role name) into a set of labelled (or "colored") alternatives. In practice, however, the parameter may correspond to the focus of access control (object or subject), may reflect an underlying concept such as ownership (files and accounts) or the primary key in a relational database, or may reflect a level in the organizational hierarchical structure for managing the application (faculty, department, course or module). Let *PARAMETER* be the type of the required parameter, say a variable m, and let M be the set values from which it can be drawn in the application. We have:

$$m : PARAMETER; \quad M : \mathbb{P}(PARAMETER); \quad m \in M \qquad (2)$$

In the banking example, since objects are parameterized by the account numbers currently allocated to clients, the set *accountnumbers*, it will be useful to use the same values to parameterize the Account_Holder role. Hence, the new role Account_Holder(m) denotes the role of holding a specific account, namely that whose number is m.

$$M = \{n\_1, n\_2, n\_3, n\_4\} \qquad (3)$$

Generating refined Roles for Parameterised RBAC.   Having chosen an adequate parameter and identified the range of its possible values, the next step is to identify what RBAC components, such as objects and roles, to parameterize. The most useful candidate for parameterizations is usually the *Roles* component. The objective is to fully define the privileges for each role in the model. Those roles for which access control is fully defined in the core RBAC model, however, parameterizations may not be appropriate and will not bring any benefits. Therefore, not all the values in a core RBAC component can be parameterized. Hence, our approach is to split the content of each core RBAC component into two parts: those which will be replaced by the refined parameterized versions (*ParamComponent*) and those which will be left unchanged (*Component − ParamComponent*). The process of generating the *Roles* component in the Parameterised RBAC model is illustrated in Figure 1. The set of roles, *PRoles*, in the new model is derived as:

$$PRoles = (Roles - ParamRoles) \cup (ParamRoles \times M) \qquad (4)$$

The type for a role in the parameterized RBAC model can be inferred as:

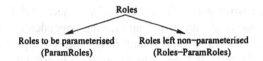

Figure 1.   Division of *Roles* for parameterization.

$$PROLE = ROLE \uplus (ROLE \times PARAMETER) \qquad (5)$$

For ease of readability, we adopt the following syntactic convention:

$$(c, m) \equiv c(m) \qquad (6)$$

where m is a parameter and c is an RBAC component such as a role or an object. In the Banking application, for instance, only the role of *Account_Holder* is to be parameterized; hence, *ParamRoles* = {*Account_Holder*}. All the other roles, (*Roles* − *ParamRoles*), will migrate unchanged into the parameterized model. The set *PRoles* can be calculated as follows:

$$PRoles = \{Account\_Holder(m) \mid m \in \{n\_1, n\_2, n\_3, n\_4\}) \\ \cup \{Manager, Clerk, System\_Administrator\} \qquad (7)$$

Please note that *Account_Holder* is no longer a role in the new model.

Generating Subjects and Principals for Parameterised RBAC.

Subjects refer in general to human users [4, 5] and may not be useful for parameterizations. Because parameterizations only addresses the issue of fully capturing access control, it would seem odd to allow the underlying set of human users to change from the core model. Therefore, we have taken the view that the *Subjects* component should remain unchanged after parameterizations.

The same reasoning may not necessarily apply to the generation of the set *Principles*, that consists of usernames and public keys acting on behalf of users. Parameterizations of principles may lead to a classification of usernames upon which aspects of access control could be determined. Therefore, by analogy with the role parameterizations, (Figure 1), the *PPrincipals* component of the parameterized model can be calculated as follows.

$$PPrincipals = (Principals - ParamPrincipals) \cup (ParamPrincipals \times M) \quad (8)$$

The data type of principals in the Parameterised RBAC can be inferred as:

$$PPRINCIPAL = PRINCIPAL \uplus (PRINCIPAL \times PARAMETER) \qquad (9)$$

In the banking example, the set of principles remains the same as in the core model. That is, *ParamPrincipals* = {}.

$$PPrincipals = \{c\_1, c\_2, c\_3, c\_4, john\_1, ema\_1, ema\_2, denise\_1\} \qquad (10)$$

Generating refined Objects for the Parameterised RBAC. the *PObjects* component of the parameterized model can be calculated as follows.

$$PObjects = (Objects - ParamObjects) \cup (ParamObjects \times M) \qquad (11)$$

The data type of objects in the Parameterised RBAC can be inferred as:

$$POBJECT = OBJECT \uplus (OBJECT \times PARAMETER) \qquad (12)$$

In the banking example, the set of objects remains unchanged. That is, *ParamObjects* = {}.

$$PObjects = Objects \qquad (13)$$

Generating Permissions for Parameterised RBAC. First the tasks component in the parameterized model should take into consideration the changes in the object component. If the object component remains unchanged then the tasks component will also remain unchanged. Hence, in the banking example, we have:

$$PTasks = \{(Assign, p : Pins), (Create, a : Accounts), (Deposit, a : Accounts),$$
$$(Withdraw, a : Account), (Transfer, [a_1 : Account, a_2 : Accounts]),$$
$$(View, a : Accounts)\}$$
$$(14)$$

What would only change in this case is the association of these tasks to new roles (the parameterized ones), which are the permissions. A parameterized permission relates a parameterized role to its authorized tasks. In a Parameterised RBAC, the permissions include 3 types:
Firstly, *ParamPermissions*, the permissions of RBAC parameterized as a result of the instantiation of the roles that *would be parameterized*, associated with the authorized tasks, and defined as:

$$ParamPermissions = \{(r(m), p) \bullet$$
$$(r, p) \in Permissions \wedge r \in ParamRoles \wedge m \in M\} \qquad (15)$$

In the online banking example, these permissions are:

$$ParamPermissions = \{(Account\_Holder(m), (View, Accounts(m))),$$
$$(Account\_Holder(m), (Withdraw, Accounts(m))), \qquad (16)$$
$$(Account\_Holder(m), (Transfer, \{Account(m), a_2 : Account\}))\}$$

Secondly, the permissions of the RBAC model that need not be parameterized, i.e. the permissions of RBAC whose domain of application is restricted to

Roles—ParamRoles. These permissions are defined as: $(Roles - ParamRoles?) \lhd$
Permissions. In the online banking case, they are listed as:

$$PPermissions = Permission \cup ParamPermissions \qquad (17)$$

Thirdly, new permissions that result due to the required private accesses for some parameterized components such as roles. Again, the data type of parameterized parameters can be deduced as:

$$PPERMISSION = PROLE \times TASK \qquad (18)$$

Generating the Parameterised RBAC Model:.   As shown in the previous example, a non-parameterized RBAC cannot capture permissions such as the one that authorise a bank client to view his own account $(Account\_Holder, (View, a : Accounts))$, because it cannot guarantee that a is exactly the account of the client requesting to view it. In this case, a parameterization of RBAC is needed. To be accomplished, this procedure requires the following entities to be provided:

1 The non-parameterized RBAC model, containing all the declarations and concepts of RBAC shown in $\langle 1 \rangle$ in the schema called *Parameterize_RBAC*. Note the Z convention to postfix the symbol "?" after a variable's name to denote an input, and to postfix the symbol "!" after a variable's name to denote an output.

2 The list of parameters M, shown in $\langle 2 \rangle$.

3 The list of components to be parameterized, namely *ParamProles*, *ParamPrincipals* and *ParamObjects* respectively defined in $\langle 3 \rangle$, $\langle 4 \rangle$ and $\langle 5 \rangle$. These are derived from the components of the RBAC model that need to be parameterized.

4 The newly induced private permissions, referred to as *New_Permissions* in $\langle 7 \rangle$, which are particular to the instances of the components.

The output Parameterised RBAC (*PFRBAC* in $\langle 8 \rangle$) would be induced from the extension of *FRBAC* using the schema *Parameterize_RBAC*. The components of this model would be named in conformity with RBAC, with the convention that they would be prefixed by the capital letter P. As demonstrated earlier on, the set of parameterized roles in the Parameterised RBAC (*Proles* in $\langle 9 \rangle$) would contain both the parameterized roles of *FRBAC* (*ParamRoles* $\times$ M), and the remaining roles of *FRBAC* that have not been parameterized (*Roles* — *ParamRoles*). The same reasoning applies to the derivation of principals (*PPrincipals* in $\langle 12 \rangle$) and derivation of objects (*Pobjects* in $\langle 17 \rangle$) of the parameterized model.

$\lceil$ _Parameterize_RBAC_ _____

⟨1⟩ $\Delta FRBAC?$

⟨2⟩ $M? : \mathbb{P} PARAMETER$

⟨3⟩ $ParamRoles? : \mathbb{P} ROLE$

⟨4⟩ $ParamPrincipals? : \mathbb{P} PRINCIPAL$

⟨5⟩ $ParamObjects? : \mathbb{P} OBJECT$

⟨7⟩ $New\_Permissions? : \mathbb{P} PPERMISSION$

⟨8⟩ $PFRBAC!$

⟨9⟩ $PRoles! = (Roles - ParamRoles?) \cup (ParamRoles? \times M)$

⟨10⟩ $\mathrm{dom}\, PRoleAllocation = PPrincipals$

⟨11⟩ $\mathrm{ran}\, PRoleAllocation = PRoles$

⟨12⟩ $PPrincipals! = (Principals - ParamPrincipals?) \cup$
$(ParamPrincipals? \times M)$

⟨13⟩ $\mathrm{dom}\, PSubjectAssociation = PSubjects$

⟨14⟩ $\mathrm{ran}\, PSubjectAssociation = PPrincipals$

⟨15⟩ $\mathrm{dom}\, PSubjectRole = PSubjects$

⟨16⟩ $\mathrm{ran}\, PSubjectRole = PRoles$

⟨17⟩ $PObjects! = (Objects - ParamObjects?) \cup (ParamObjects? \times M)$

⟨18⟩ $POperations! = Operations$

⟨19⟩ $PTasks! = Tasks$

⟨20⟩ $PPermissions! = ((Roles - ParamRoles?) \lhd Permissions) \cup$
$ParamPermissions \cup New\_Permissions?$

⟨21⟩ $ParamPermissions = \{(r(m),p) \bullet (r,p) \in Permissions \wedge$
$r \in ParamRoles \wedge m \in M\}$

⟨22⟩ $\mathrm{dom}\, New\_Permissions \subseteq (ParamRoles \times M)$

3.3 The Nesting Property of the Parameterised RBAC Model

This work presents a methodology for parameterizing RBAC components in order to deduce a Parameterised RBAC model. The resulting model, which is also an RBAC model, can be further parameterized in order to achieve an additional level of granularity. The components of the new model would now depend on two parameters as shown in Figure 2. This figure depicts a hierarchy of parameters data. In it, we use the tree notation whereby a filled square denotes a leaf and a circle denotes a node with children. This parameterization can be repeated successively, and in a nested way, as long as required to achieve the required access control granularity. In this way, new parameterized RBAC model would be devised following the parameters' hierarchy, as shown in Figure 2. However, there can be another way of nesting parameters; which is by using the cross product of the set of parameters M and the RBAC com-

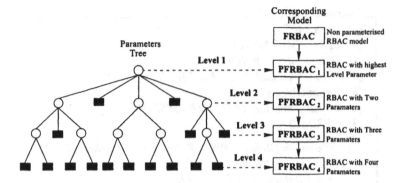

Figure 2.   The nesting of the parameterized models following the level of the appropriate parameters.

ponents at every level. This means that we would parameterize all components at every level. In this type of nesting parameterization the order of parameters is not important. For instance, if in the online banking example both roles *Account_Holder(branch(account₁))* and *Account_Holder(account₁(branch))* are considered the same. The nesting by cross product results in a number of redundant parameterized RBAC components at every level, which might not be necessarily needed. This is prevented when using our methodology of parameterization because it enables the choice of parameters at every level of the parameters' tree. Also, it enables to parameterize only the required components such as roles, objects and principals. This reduces the number of parameterized components at every level and eases the manageability of the access rights.

4.   Discussion

Two of the main advantages of RBAC are the simplification of access rights management and the presentation of a high level view of security in an organisation. However, in its current form, RBAC does not seem to have enough power to express a wide range of security requirements and capture fine access control granularity when put into application. These features can be accounted for by extending RBAC to the Parameterised RBAC, in order to support parameters, as shown earlier on in this work. The Parameterised RBAC provides finer granularity by creating instances of RBAC components according to the contexts of their use. With this, it can cater for special security requirements such as the support of private access rights for each of the instances of the same role, and the differentiation between the access rights of subjects associated with the same role. Providing very fine granularity can however complicate the access control list (ACL) because it involves handling access rights for a significantly higher number of roles, which is due to the instantiation of the RBAC roles. This undermines the advantage of the simplicity of access rights management, for which RBAC is known. It seems there is a tradeoff between simplifying the management of access rights and providing fine granularity; and between providing a higher view of security, and parameterizing RBAC concepts to increase the expressive power of the Parameterised RBAC. Providing a balance between these advantages in a Parameterised RBAC model is greatly affected by the way the parameterization is performed. More specifically, this balance depends on two factors:

- The choice of the parameterized RBAC concepts: this involves deciding which RBAC concepts, such as *roles*, *objects* and *principals*, are to be parameterized.

- The type of parameters: the parameters according to which the parameterization would be performed are often related to the environment or context where the Parameterised RBAC is applied. As seen earlier on, parameters can be faculty names and unit names in a university, or a department name in a commercial organisation.

5. Conclusion

This paper has the proposed a rigorous formal model for the Parameterized RBAC (*PFRBAC*). One strength of this model lies in the methodology that is used to migrate from the direct implementation of an RBAC model, which suffers the drawbacks of inconsistency of access rights distribution, difficulty of intellectual manageability and the weak scalability of the model, into a parameterized RBAC which achieves the same results without bearing these drawbacks. This parameterized implementation of RBAC is very important for realistic applications because it achieves extremely fine grained access control granularity. Another strength of *PFRBAC* is its completeness in terms of investigating all the concepts and semantics of a Parameterised RBAC and supporting all the definitions and features of the well-known RBAC models in [1, 2, 4, 5]. The formalisation of *PFRBAC* in the Z notation makes it clear to understand and eliminates ambiguities at the application phase.

References

[1] R. Sandhu, E. Coyne, H. Feinstein, and C. Youman, "Role-Based Access Control Models," *IEEE Computer*, vol. 29, no. 2, pp. 38–47, Nov. 1996.

[2] R. Sandhu, D. Ferraiolo, and R. Kuhn, "The NIST Model for Role-Based Access Control: Towards A Unified Standard," in *Proc. of the 5th ACM workshop on Role-Based Access Control*. Technical University of Berlin, Berlin, Germany: ACM Press, June 2000, pp. 47–63.

[3] D. Ferraiolo, R. Sandhu, S. Gavrila, R. Kuhn, and R. Chandramouli, "Proposed NIST Standard for Role-Based Access Control," *ACM Transactions on Information and System Security (TISSEC)*, vol. 4, no. 3, pp. 224–274, 2001.

[4] American National Standard for Information Technology, "*Role Based Access Control,*" Draft BSR INCITS 359, Apr. 2003. Online: http://csrc.nist.gov/rbac/rbac-std-ncits.pdf.

[5] E. Khayat and A. Abdallah, "A Formal Model for Flat Role-Based Access Control," in *Proc. of the ACS/IEEE International Conference on Computer Systems and Applications.* Tunis, Tunisia: IEEE Press, July 2003.

[6] R. Elmasri and S. Navathe. *Fundamentals of Database Systems.* Addison-Wesley, 2003.

[7] Sun Microsystems. *RBAC in the Solaris Operating Systems.* White Paper, April 2001. http://wwws.sun.com/software/whitepapers/wp-rbac/wp-rbac.pdf.

[8] T. Chalfant.   *Role Based Access Control and Secure Shell–A Closer Look At Two Solaris^{TM} Operating Environment Security Features,* June 2003. http://www.sun.com/solutions/blueprints/0603/817-3062.pdf.

[9] E. Lupu and M. Sloman, "Reconciling Role Based Management and Role Based Access Control," in *Proceedings of the 2nd ACM workshop on Role-based Access Control.* Fairfax, Virginia, USA: ACM Press, Nov. 1997, pp. 135–141.

[10] D. Gollmann, *Computer Security.* John Wiley & Sons, 1999.

[11] T. Jaeger, T. Michailidis, and R. Rada, "Access Control in a Virtual University," in *Proc. of the 8th International IEEE Workshops on Enabling Technologies: Infrastructure for Collaborative Enterprises,* California , USA, June 1999, pp. 135–140.

[12] L. Bottaci and J. Jones, *Formal Specification Using Z: A Modeling Approach.* International Thomson Computer Press, 1995.

[13] J. Bowen, *Formal Specification & Documentation Using Z: A Case Study Approach.* International Thomson Computer Press, 1996.

[14] I. Toyn (Ed.), "*Information Technology-Z Formal Specification Notation-Syntax, Type System and Semantics,*" Consensus Working Draft 2.7, Oct. 2001.

[15] L. Giuri and P. Iglio, "Role Templates for Content-Based Access Control," in *Proc. of the 2nd ACM Workshop on Role-Based Access Control.* Fairfax, Virginia, USA: ACM Press, Nov. 1997, pp. 153–159.

[16] Jean Bacon, Ken Moody and Walt Yao. A model of OASIS role-based access control and its support for active security. *ACM Trans. Inf. Syst. Security.* 5(4): 492-540 (2002)

[17] Andras Belokosztolszki, David M. Eyers and Ken Moody. Policy Contexts: Controlling Information Flow in Parameterized RBAC. *POLICY 2003*: 99-110.